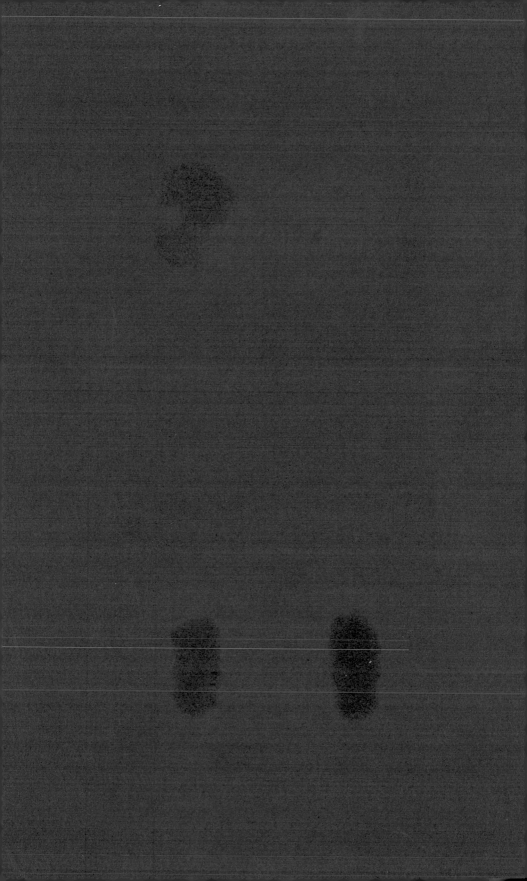

The CRAFT of RALPH ELLISON

The CRAFT of

RALPH ELLISON

Robert G. O'Meally

HARVARD UNIVERSITY PRESS

Cambridge, Massachusetts
London, England
1980

Copyright © 1980 by the President and Fellows of Harvard College

Printed in the United States of America

Publication of this book has been aided by a grant from
the Andrew W. Mellon Foundation

Library of Congress Cataloging in Publication Data

O'Meally, Robert G   1948-
    The craft of Ralph Ellison.

    Bibliography: p.
    Includes index.
    1.   Ellison, Ralph — Criticism and interpretation.
I.   Title.
PS3555.L625Z8   818'.5409   80-12680
ISBN 0-674-17548-4

FOR MY PARENTS
George and Ethel Browne O'Meally

Acknowledgments

My ideas for this book began to take shape during graduate study at Harvard University. Many fine scholars and friends there encouraged me and provided incisive advice on research methods, approaches to literature, and clarity of expression. I am especially indebted to Daniel Aaron, Joel Porte, and Monroe Engel.

I profited greatly from my discussions with Sterling A. Brown, who gave me many insights into the meaning of black folklore and literature, especially the experience of blacks on the Federal Writers Project.

I also wish to thank Bess Walcott, Frank Meade, Louis A. Rabb, Edward and Woodia Pryce, Laly Washington, Vivian Chandler, and Charles Davidson, friends of Ellison's, who gave generously of their knowledge and time. To Jimmy Stewart, who sent me materials about Oklahoma and who talked at length about the young Ellison, I am deeply indebted. I am also most grateful to Albert Murray, James L. Randolph, and William L. Dawson, who provided me with many insights and much information. Hollie West permitted me to hear tapes of his interviews with Ellison and led me to other pertinent materials.

I profited enormously from discussions with colleagues and friends: Arthur P. Davis, Geneva Smitherman, C. Edwin Baker, William J. Harris, Ernest J. Wilson III, Bernard Osterdorf, Vattel Rose, Jennifer Jordon, Robert B. Stepto, Robert E. Hemenway, Henry L. Gates, Jr., Henry H. Kennedy, Jr., and Randall Kennedy.

To Howard University, which twice supported this project with Faculty Research Grants, I am very grateful.

Random House, Inc., has kindly granted me permission to quote from the following copyrighted works of Ralph Ellison: *Shadow and Act* and *Invisible Man.*

Special thanks must go to Ralph Ellison, whose encouragement was inspiring.

Finally, it is really impossible to express the depth of gratitude I feel toward my family, who endured my absorption in these pages with understanding and love. Vital faith and help came always from the beautiful Jacqueline Malone O'Meally, who read this book in many forms, first to last.

Contents

The CRAFT of RALPH ELLISON

Introduction

With the publication of *Invisible Man* in 1952, Ralph Ellison moved, suddenly, into the front ranks of American writers. Before that startling moment of public success, however, he had published ten short stories (two later used in the novel) and thirty-seven essays on literature and politics. Ellison has published no second novel, and instead has seemed to be taking on the role of an invisible underground man in his own right. Still he has published twelve stories since *Invisible Man*, along with dozens of essays and interviews, some of which were collected in *Shadow and Act* (1964).

We see in this work the evolution of a central theme: the more conscious a person is of his personal, cultural, and national history, the freer he becomes. As a young writer, Ellison quickly became dissatisfied with the typical naturalistic scenarios in which characters, struggling to survive the merciless American environment, are eventually overcome by impersonal forces. To Ellison, this documentary fiction was dull—and it failed to capture the richness and variety of black American life. Influenced by a broad range of writers, including Richard Wright, André Malraux, and Ernest Hemingway, Ellison began to focus on the man or woman who, by force of character and will, manages to *endure*.

Accordingly, we also see in Ellison's work a shift in style from social realism to surrealism. His efforts to devise a language to express the mad and variegated world as seen by his self-aware characters led him to experiment with symbolic forms generally unused by the writer of hard-fact

1

realism. "Flying Home," "King of the Bingo Game," *Invisible Man*, and several of the Hickman stories (appearing after *Invisible Man*) employ modernist techniques—surrealism, multiple perspectives, stream of conscious ness—to reveal a world tempestuous and out of focus. But what makes these works distinctively Ellisonian is the infusion of black American folklore.

Folklore, an index to the Afro-American and thus to the general American past, is a key to Ellison's fictional world. Under the spell of the modern poets—particularly T. S. Eliot—Ellison introduced more and more folklore into his stories, giving them not only great accessibility (folklore being at once particular and universal), but a dimension beyond that of realism. In Ellison's fiction, folklore, stylized and transformed by modernist techniques, gives special resonance and power to his language as it frees his characters to fly toward the moon, dive unmarked into the briarpatch, or become invisible and sail through the air unseen. Here the vernacular and the symbolist traditions in American literature converge. The folklore itself is heavily metaphorical. And Ellison links the central question of identity to that of history and folklore. The protagonists of several short stories and of *Invisible Man* are freed of their self-alienation and blindness with the unlocking of the past. The key is folklore.

Folklore is not considered here as a body of quaint, "folksy" items for a catalogue of oddments. Nor is folklore associated with a particular level of society or with a particular historical era. Folklore is a dynamic, current process of speaking and singing in certain circumstances. Afro-American folklore—sermons, tales, games, jokes, boasts, toasts, dozens, blues, spirituals—is a rich source for the writer. Here the values, styles, and character types of black American life and culture are preserved and reflected in highly energized, often very eloquent language.

Ellison has argued that folk art accounts, to a large extent, for the black American's self-awareness and endurance. Indeed, for blacks, folklore—more than written literature—has served art's classic functions: it not only delights, but it teaches. Refusing to subscribe totally to the white Americans' ethos and world view, blacks created in folklore their own ways of expressing themselves: "another instance," observes Ellison, "of man's triumph over chaos." In folklore, experiences of the past are refined, evaluated, celebrated, and remembered. Black folk art projects "symbols which express the group's will to survive . . . values by which the group lives and dies . . . the group's attempt to humanize the world." As he has said, "In the folklore we tell what Negro experience really is . . . with a complexity of vision that seldom gets into our writing . . . We back away from the chaos of experience and from ourselves, and we depict the humor as well as the horror of our lives." During slavery, folk art was "what we had in place of freedom." Echoing Constance Rourke, whose *American Humor* Ellison studied closely in the thirties, he says, "Great literature is erected upon this humble base of folk forms."

Ellison is by no means the first writer to inlay his work with the silver and gold of Afro-American folklore. Mark Twain, Charles Chesnutt, James Weldon Johnson, William Faulkner, Zora Neale Hurston, Sterling A. Brown, and Langston Hughes used it before Ellison, often with supreme skill. But Ellison's case is special, because of the sheer virtuousity of *Invisible Man*, which, replete with its "inside" use of black folklore, is also very modern in its technique. In this contemporary novel, the vital transformation from folk item to written literature seems wonderfully complete. The language is consistently astir with actual Afro-American speech, as well as with the tales, songs, and games of folklore. What Ellington and Wagner achieved in music is here achieved in fiction: the transmutation of folk materials into a fully orchestrated masterpiece.

Not, of course, that folklore is Ellison's or any writer's *only* source. One does not learn to structure a novel by merely "counting the dozens" or copying jump-rope games and rhymes. As Ellison has said, "For the novelist, of any cultural or racial identity, his form is his greatest freedom and his insights are where he finds them." And for Ellison, a particularly circumspect writer, insights are to be found in classical and commonplace literature, in fairy tales as well as barbershop jive. A novelist learns his craft—including the process of introducing folklore into fiction—by studying novels.

During the thirties and forties, Ellison was immersed in radical politics. He saw clearly the writer's responsibility to create works encompassing the great social issues of the times, and wrote several hotly radical essays, reviews, and short stories. By the early forties, however, he was refusing to tailor his conceptions of black culture and character to conform to political theory. Gradually he came to feel that an accurate and well-crafted picture of black life is by definition revolutionary; reduce the artistic visions to meet the specifics of politics and the art's true life, including its most earthy radicalism, pales and shrivels. As the forties wore on, it became clear to Ellison that lasting art transcended political argumentation after argumentation:

> The ideology changes, but the human experience, the joy and the pain, the anger and the exultation which should go into art remains . . . It isn't yours; it's a group thing which you share in and which you communicate . . . If you *do* that, then it seems to me a far more

important thing than being ideologically committed. The novel is a form which attempts to deal with the contradictions of life and ambivalence and ambiguities of values. It isn't easy for ideologues to deal with it. They don't trust it because the form itself insists upon a certain kind of truth, a certain kind of objectivity.[1]

Such views made radicals of the forties and fifties uneasy about Ellison's politics. Even his friend Wright worried that his talented protégé would unwittingly sell him out. And during the sixties, when Black Arts Movement artists and critics were calling for ever more radical poems and stories, Ellison was regarded with particular suspicion. On speaking tours at college campuses, he often was met by black students' indifference and sometimes even contempt. In his own way, however, Ellison has kept the faith, bearing his allegiance not to current "ideologues" but to his artistic form and to his own sense of rightness.

Ellison's artistic vision is always ironical, complex, ambiguous. And easy answers prove troubling. He points out, for instance, that paradoxical as it may seem, blacks are in certain ways the freest of Americans. Living at the bottom of the American social hierarchy, blacks have been left alone to experiment with new styles of expression. Echoing James Weldon Johnson, Ellison has observed that much that the world knows as uniquely American (particularly with regard to language, music, and dance) was created by black slaves and their offspring.

Were Ellison consistently sanguine concerning the black experience, he would be in less trouble with his politically oriented critics. But Ellison is the first to point out that, just as there could be no American experience as we know it without the input of blacks, black American culture is also a product of cultural blending. Blacks are *not*, Ellison has said, an African people but an American people of varied bloodlines and cultural traditions. Nor are blacks a people whose sense of who they are depends on lower- or working-class styles. More characteristic than any blue-collar identification is black identification with *elegance* in clothing, food, music, dance, speech, and mode of transportation. "Black Americans," says Ellison, "expect elegance even from prizefighters and basketball players and much of the appeal of Jack Johnson and Joe Louis sprang from the fact that each was as elegant as the finest of ballet dancers." Are not blacks, whether unemployed or not, in a sense as much *upper*-class as lower-class in their values?

Such questions slice against the grain of black and white nationalism, of Marxism, and of social science as it traditionally has been conceived in America. They spring, though, from the writer's discipline and from his ironical perspective. "The novel," says Ellison, "is a complex agency for the symbolic depiction of experience, and it demands that the writer be willing to look at both sides of character and issues—at least while he's working. You might say that the form of the novel imposes its morality upon the novelist by demanding a complexity of vision and an openness to the variety and depth of experience."[2]

It is ironic that James Weldon Johnson's fictional character, the Ex-Colored Man, retreats from the black world into the white one, but nonetheless narrates one of the most affirmative novels about black life. It is odd that the Invisible Man, who ends by escaping into a dark hole, tells a tale full of hope. In Ellison's fiction, especially from the forties on, the portraits of such strong black characters as Jefferson, Mary Rambo, Trueblood, and Hickman have been diverse and affirming. Characters are cheated, tricked, left for dead, beaten, and even lynched. But certain powerful figures, aware of roots in a sustaining tradition, manage to persevere with heroism and high style. The insistence on the heroic impulse in black life has contributed to Ellison's influence.

He has had a lasting impact on many younger writers, notably Al Young, Ishmael Reed, Leon Forrest, Toni Morrison, Alice Walker, and James Alan McPherson. His special contribution to the new wave of black writing is his unceasing insistence upon connections between the contemporary writer, and not only the American realistic tradition, but the symbolist tradition that nourished Melville and Faulkner, and the vernacular tradition, rooted in American language and lore.

My critical study of Ellison's work from 1937 to 1979 is structured, for the most part, chronologically. The first two biographical chapters seek to identify forces that shaped his particular sensibilities and values as a musician, then as a writer. The later chapters chart Ellison's maturity as a prose stylist, his development of certain themes, and the uses of folklore in his fiction. Above all, my purpose is to direct as much light as possible on Ellison's characters (many of whom, like Faulkner's, appear in story after story and are seen from several narrative angles) and on the fictional world through which they struggle: a world of uncertain glories, shadows, and, to be sure, much trouble.

1

Beginnings

Ralph Waldo Ellison was born in Oklahoma City in 1914, seven years after the Territories were granted statehood. He grew up among people who were optimistic, tough, and aggressive.[1] His parents, Lewis Ellison from Abbeyville, South Carolina, and Ida Milsap Ellison from White Oak, Georgia, had left Chattanooga, Tennessee, to test the proclaimed greater freedom of the western state. At least Oklahoma had no long-standing tradition of slavery or segregation. As it turned out, segregation laws eventually were imported from neighboring Texas and Arkansas; but, even so, the blacks who had trekked and wagon-trained west to escape southern oppression fought hard for their political rights. Ellison recalls that Oklahoma blacks felt that "no matter what their lives had been, their children's lives would be lives of possibility." This sense of possibility, the fighting spirit of the people, and the vast expanses of undeveloped land gave Oklahoma a frontierlike aspect. Despite its frontier edges, however, Oklahoma City was an established place. The capital city, recalls Ellison, "seemed fully articulated with its streetcars and its tall buildings. It appeared to be in the same class with say Kansas City or St. Louis or Chicago — only it was much smaller and very much better."[2]

Especially after the death in 1917 of Lewis Ellison (who had worked as a construction company foreman and then as an independent businessman, selling ice and coal), the Ellisons were poor — at times extremely poor.[3] Still, Ralph and his younger brother Herbert were made to feel that the worlds of the rich and the white were approachable. This early confidence started off with Lewis Ellison, the avid reader who named his son after Emerson. It was reinforced by Ida Ellison, a determined woman, a stewardess in her church who valued action in *this* world. She brought home records, magazines, and books discarded in the white homes where she worked as a maid. And Mrs. Ellison saw to it that her sons had electric and chemistry sets, a roll-top desk and chair, and a toy typewriter. Her activism extended to politics. "If you young Negroes don't do something about things," she would tell Ralph and Herbert, "I don't know what's going to happen to this race."[4] For her part, she was an ardent supporter of Eugene Debs's Socialist Party and canvassed for the party's gubernatorial candidate of 1914. In 1934, after Ralph had gone off to Tuskegee Institute, she was often jailed for attempting to rent buildings that Jim Crow laws had declared off limits to blacks.[5]

Breaks in the pattern of segregation contributed to the relatively free atmosphere of Oklahoma. Indians and blacks had lived side by side for generations. "There were Negroes who were part Indian," observes Ellison, "and who lived on reservations, and Indians who had children who lived in towns as Negroes."[6] The Ellisons had many white friends, and black-white integration on a cultural level, at least, was widespread. Downtown theaters were not segregated until the 1920s. And after blacks were barred from the white theaters, black actors like Richard B. Harrison continued to perform regularly in Oklahoma City's black section; Harrison included in his repertory renditions of Shakespearean soliloquies.[7] A woman named Miss Clark, the maid of the English actress Emma Bunting, used to stay with the Ellisons when the British company came to Oklahoma City, and she brought experiences from professional theaters and from England into the household.

As teenagers Ellison and his comrades dreamed of being latter-day "Renaissance Men"; they snatched up desired symbols along with attitudes and values from blacks, Indians, and whites. Ralph wanted to walk like the haberdasher he admired, Milton Lewisohn; to read everything he could get his hands on at the Paul Lawrence Dunbar Library; to play expert "sheenee" (a kind of street hockey game of sticks and tin cans) and varsity football; to imitate the styles of certain "vague and constantly shifting figures"—from the community, from lore and literature, from the movies—figures who were "somehow comic but always versatile, picaresque and self-effacingly heroic." He identified with persons he met on odd jobs around town: in private clubs where he waited tables, at buildings where he ran the elevator, on downtown streets where he shined shoes and hawked newspapers. He identified, too, with the tellers as well as the characters of tales he heard in J. L. Randolph's pharmacy where he also worked. On rainy or snowy days, local men would pack the store and trade yarns, some of which had been told best, he was informed, years before by his father.[8]

In a town that was music-centered, the heroes most revered were the musicians. Ellison heard church performers (including his father, who sometimes sat in on drums), marching bandsmen, and those who amused themselves by playing yukes, kazoos, and C-melody saxophones. Ellison himself wanted to become a musician who could read music as well as improvise. Thanks to Zelia N. Breaux, supervisor of music instruction for Oklahoma City's black schools, Ellison learned music theory at Douglass High School, and he picked up a working knowledge of several brass instruments as well as the soprano saxophone. But trumpet was his instrument. As first-chair trumpeter in the Douglass school band, and then as the group's student conductor, Ellison played light classics and marches at church recitals, graduation exercises, football games, parades, and social functions of lodges and fraternities. Ludwig Hebestreit, conductor of the Oklahoma City Orchestra, also gave Ellison private music lessons and, in return, the youngster cut his lawn.

Most of all, Ellison admired the elegant styles, the artistic discipline, and the seemingly endless capacity for self-expression that were the hallmarks of jazz musicians. These men and women, some of whom played by ear, some of whom were conservatory-trained, stood out as the exemplary heroes and role models of Deep Second (the blacks' nickname for the sunken streets at the center of Oklahoma's black neighborhood).[9] At the Aldridge Theater and at Slaughter's Hall, Ellison heard King Oliver and Ida Cox as well as the Old Blue Devils Band, with Walter Page, Oran "Hot Lips" Page, Eddie Durham, and Jimmy Rushing. As a high school student, Ellison also played occasional dance jobs in pickup combos and even sat in on rehearsals of the Blue Devils. And he also learned the jazz idiom at that other "academy" of jazz: the jam session. In Halley Richardson's Shoe Shine Parlor, a gathering place for jazz players, Ellison heard Lester Young playing with and against other tenor saxmen, "his head thrown back, his horn even then outthrust, his feet working the footrests."

By 1933, when he left Oklahoma City, Ellison had spent twelve years studying music, sacred and secular, classical and jazz. At nineteen he went to Tuskegee Institute as a scholarship student, wanting to write a symphony that might encompass his varied experiences: as a poor black boy who never felt inferior to anyone because of race or class; as a "frontier" boy with a certain city slickness; as a classically trained musician who was steeped in the blues and who wanted to capture their explosive power in classical forms.

At Tuskegee, Ellison majored in music and music theory and worked toward composing his symphony. Financial problems forced him to leave after three years there, but these were crucial years for his development as an artist. Eventually he left the Deep South, but it never left him; the conscious study and practice of the art of writing he began there became his life. His concern with history and race and their effects on individual character marks him as a distinctively southern black American writer.

The old slave quarters, the slower pace of life, the accents, and the more formal manners in Alabama all were new and fascinating to Ellison. In addition to the many people—students, teachers, local folk—who contributed to his growth as a thinker and an artist, there were constraints to cope with in the Deep South. Both white and black Alabamians attempted to force him to play roles he found distasteful. Nonetheless, the heated pressures and injustices he encountered at Tuskegee and in Macon County forged Ellison's artistic consciousness. He converted the essence of his Tuskegee experience into the symbolic action of *Invisible Man*, which illuminates certain aspects of his college years in Alabama.

Segregation was far more deeply entrenched in Alabama than in Oklahoma and required, as Ellison soon discovered, greater exercises in personal restraint. He already knew that it was not necessary "to meet every challenge some peckerwood came along with."[10] And in time he found it relatively easy to

> outmaneuver those who interpreted my silence as submission, my efforts at self-control as fear, my contempt as awe before superior status, my dreams of faraway places and room at the top of the heap as defeat before the barriers of their stifling, provincial world. And my struggle became a desperate battle which was usually fought, though not always, in silence.[11]

Taking aim at liberal preconceptions about the black southern world, Ellison has written that the color line did not obliterate the meaning of his life in Alabama any more than it had in Oklahoma. Blacks had their own way of life and, again, interracial exchange occurred on a cultural level despite racism. Ellison attended certain theaters in the town of Tuskegee which he says actually were "separate and equal":

> in a double movie house in the town of Tuskegee . . . Negroes and whites were accommodated in parallel theaters, entering from the

same street level through separate entrances and with the Negro side viewing the same pictures shortly after the showing for whites had begun. It was a product of social absurdity and, of course, no real relief from our resentment over the restriction of our freedom, but the movies were just as enjoyable or boring . . . I went to the movies to see pictures, not to be with whites.[12]

Even when Jim Crow policies were at their rigid worst, Ellison found that he was able to "escape the reduction" imposed on him: he was secure in himself and in the knowledge that he was the target of stupid cruelty. Confronted by segregated facilities, he would

move to the back of a Southern bus, or climb to the peanut gallery of a movie house—matters about which I could do nothing except walk, read, hunt, dance, sculpt, cultivate ideals, or seek other uses for my time . . . thus was I disciplined to endure the absurdities of both conscious and unconscious prejudice, to resist racial provocation and, before the ready violence of brutal policemen, railroad "bulls," and casual white citizens, to hold my peace and bide my time.[13]

At least in Alabama Ellison knew "where I could go and where I could not go. The contempt which was held for me by whites was obvious in the most casual interracial contacts."[14]

Alabama's blacks also exerted a certain amount of pressure on Ellison to keep his place. Nine years after leaving Tuskegee, Ellison presented some of his thoughts about this southern pressure in a review of Richard Wright's autobiography, *Black Boy*. In that critical essay, partly inspired by his wish to refute certain romanticized notions about the South, Ellison characterized the black southerner as oppressively community-minded. Behind the glow of black southern hospitality, wrote Ellison, burns a defensive intolerance. The "personal warmth" of black southerners

is accompanied by an equally personal coldness, kindliness by cruelty, regard by malice . . . This personal quality, shaped by outer violence and inner fear, is ambivalent . . . The pre-individualistic black community discourages individuality out of self-defense. Having learned through experience that the whole group is punished for the actions of the single member, it has worked out efficient techniques of behavior control . . . The member who breaks away . . . becomes a stranger even to his relatives.[15]

Although five percent of his entering class at Tuskegee also came from Oklahoma, Ellison felt himself an outsider. Proud, curious, artistically and intellectually inclined, Ellison was held suspect by some Alabaman blacks who feared that his swagger could bring trouble to the whole community.

With its new emphasis on liberal arts (which had begun in the twenties), Tuskegee was changing fast.[16] Nonetheless, old-line Tuskegans cherished Booker T. Washington's vision of progress through education and industry. The "ideal" Tuskegee student was eager to advance himself and felt that his performance could either sustain or injure his people.

Some of Ellison's own reactions to Tuskegee Institute can be seen in his novel's portrayal of the Invisible Man's college days. The protagonist of *Invisible Man* is a student at the "beautiful college," where he listens with reverential awe to Reverend Homer A. Barbee's account of the college founder's life. Very much like Booker T. Washington, *Invisible Man's* "Founder" conquered legendary hardships on his way to Negro leadership. Guest speaker Barbee's name, his actual blindness, and his outrageously inflated, mock-heroic rhetoric warn against his version of the Founder's exemplary career. Speaking in the college chapel (which strongly resembles Tuskegee's old chapel), Barbee's words are humorously reminiscent of Founder's Day speeches delivered at Tuskegee (and at every college's ceremonial gatherings) each spring.[17] Barbee says: "into this land came a humble prophet, lowly like the humble carpenter of Nazareth . . . I'm sure you have heard of his precarious infancy, his precious life almost destroyed by an insane cousin who splashed the babe with lye and shriveled his seed and how, a mere babe, he lay nine days in a deathlike coma and then suddenly and miraculously recovered."[18]

Missing the ironic suggestion that this "Father symbol" had his seed shriveled, the protagonist contemplates the fabulous tradition of the college. He laments his foolishness in endangering the great dream of the "humble prophet" and wishes that somehow he could have exhibited the Founder's enthusiasm for personal progress and dedication to The Race. If only, like Dr. Julian Bledsoe, the Founder's successor, he could have "walked to the school or pushed a wheelbarrow or performed some other act of determination and sacrifice to attest to his eagerness for knowledge."[19]

But the young hero of the novel *did* exhibit extreme eagerness. He did not sleep under the wooden planks of an old-fashioned street (as did Washington on his way to Hampton Institute) or survive being splashed with lye as a baby, but he endured the degradation of the battle royal: a fight to the finish broadly similar to the mass boxing tournaments involving many young blacks desperate for cash during the Depression.[20] The battle royal in the novel differs, however, from most actual ones in that the protagonist had not prearranged the act with his fellow participants. Thus, in this greenhorn's initiation into a crazy and prejudiced society, the Invisible Man's heroic efforts were turned to farce as he had to contend with the mocks and taunts of the white audience along with the scorn (and the heavy blows) of the other fighters who were angry at him for cutting into their night's pay. Before being given a scholarship to the beautiful college, the Invisible Man was blindfolded, kicked, boxed, hooted, and tricked by phony coins into leaping wet with perspiration onto an electrified carpet.

Tuskegee was originally chartered as a normal school, designed to train black teachers. A core curriculum in mathematics, science, language, and literature was always offered. As early as 1900, Tuskegee had a music department, and by the thirties the music school had been established to prepare both music teachers and concert performers. Still, Booker T. Washington was determined to promote Tuskegee as a trade school modeled after his beloved alma mater, Hampton Institute. He advocated education of the "head, heart and hand," as the school's motto announced. Washington was always suspicious of programs for Afro-Americans which were exclusively academic, and he tended to deprecate them in his writings and speeches. He wanted his students to have knowledge of "actual things instead of mere books alone."[21]

Some of the women in Washington's first class at Tuskegee, who had "the merest smattering" of "high-sounding" subjects, increased his determination to begin teaching "the trades." He discovered that these women "could locate the Desert of Sahara or the capital of China on an artificial globe," but "could not locate the proper places for the knives and forks on an actual dinner table, or the places on which the bread should be set."[22] Many students were not only unprepared for domestic service and other trades but also needed to learn the more fundamental "gospel of the toothbrush": they lacked a sense of personal hygiene. Washington depicts one such young man who "had attended some high school, sitting down in a one room cabin, with grease on his clothing, filth all around him, and weeds in the yard and garden, engaged in studying French grammar."[23] In an 1896 chapel address, he told students that "we are not a college, and if there are any of you here who expect to get a college training you will be disappointed."[24] In one Tuskegee teacher's words, "Mr. Washington thinks, with Miss Alcott's Professor, that 'Latin, Greek, and mathematics are all very well,' but that 'self-knowledge, self-help, and self-control are more important.' The Latin and Greek, Tuskegee does not include in her curriculum since her province is the promotion of progress among the many, not the special culture of the few."[25]

If blacks could master the trades, wrote Washington, whites would truly *need* their services, and together the races could build for the future. He felt that blacks had to sacrifice social and political advancement—as well as superfluous academic exercising—and concentrate on the industrial arts; black economic, and then political, power would come in time. The progress of black Americans, he said, could only be impeded by "fantastic" social and political ambitions; their real task was to work their way up "from the bottom." In his Atlanta Exposition speech, which the Invisible Man quotes at the battle royal, Washington told blacks neither to despair nor to seek relief beyond the South: "Cast down your buckets where you are. Cast down in agriculture, mechanics, in commerce, in domestic service, and in the professions." Whites, he advised, should "cast down among the eight millions of Negroes."[26] Perhaps the principal reason for Washington's enormous popularity among southern whites was his apparent willingness to acquiesce to segregation and to confirm the old southern ideal of paternalism.

Washington's determination to maintain white southern support through his powerful emphasis on industrial education for blacks led not only to conservatism at the institute but to anti-intellectualism.[27] Because it seemed senseless and possibly distasteful to the school's white patrons, many old-liners never quite accepted the institute's shift in emphasis from industrial to liberal arts.

And the ideal Tuskegee student was expected to obey the unspoken rule to be ever conscious of how the school impressed its "good white friends." W. E. B. Du Bois described Washington, a masterful fundraiser and diplomat, as "a wary and silent man" who "never expressed himself frankly or clearly until he knew exactly to whom he was talking."[28] Washington knew how to wear a broad smile in the company of powerful whites when it was appropriate.

Nowhere in Washington's autobiographical writings do we learn much about his private life. Instead, his autobiographies serve as polite public relations documents. He reports, for example, "In all my contact with the white people of the South I have never received a single personal insult."[29] He refers to the long gone "Ku Klux period," observing that "there are no such organizations in the South now . . . That such ever existed is almost forgotten by both races. There are few places in the South now where public sentiment would permit such organizations to exist."[30]

Washington's optimism is inflated to put whites at ease. Certainly he knew there was a Klan organization in Macon County. In July 1923, eight years after his death, hundreds of Klansmen marched on Tuskegee's campus to protest black staffing of the proposed black Veterans' Administration hospital.

Tuskegee's many northern and southern white patrons are extensively thanked and congratulated in Washington's autobiographies. These benefactors are "high," "dignified," and "Christlike in their charity." In fact, he writes, Tuskegee's philanthropists are absolutely "the best people in the world!"[31] The ideal Tuskegee student was supposed to know how to indulge in such flattery and posing for the good of the school. With no apparent ironic intention, one colleague of Washington eulogized him as a magnificent "showman."[32]

In *Invisible Man*, Bledsoe is the master showman, deft at pleasing rich white philanthropists like Mr. Norton (Mr. "Northern"). This fictionalized Washington figure (who is also based on other figures from history, literature, and myth) knows precisely how to "approach white visitors . . . with his hat in hand, bowing humbly and respectfully . . . he refused to eat in the dining hall with white guests of the school, entering only after they had finished and then refusing to sit down, but remaining standing, his hat in his hand, while he addressed them eloquently, then leaving with a humble bow."[33] During Barbee's chapel address before the students and white guests, Bledsoe conducts himself "with the decorum of a portly head waiter. Like some of the guests, he wore striped trousers and a swallowtail coat with black-braided lapels topped by a rich ascot tie. It was his regular dress for such occasions, yet for all its elegance, he managed to make himself look humble."[34] Accenting his modest image, Bledsoe's "trousers inevitably bagged at the knees and [his] coat slouched in the shoulders."

Behind Bledsoe's sagging exterior hides a cynical, powerful grandee. In his office he bellows at the Invisible Man for not knowing "the difference between the way things are and the way they're supposed to be." Bledsoe (who "bleeds his people so") says:

> Negroes don't control this school or much of anything else . . . nor any white folk either. True they *support* it, but I control it. I's big and black I say "Yes, suh" as loudly as any burr-head when it's convenient, but I'm still the king down here. I don't care how much it appears otherwise. It's a nasty deal and I always like it myself . . . I didn't make it, and I know that I can't change it . . . But I've made my place in it and I'll have every Negro in the coun-

try hanging on tree limbs by morning if it means staying where I am.[35]

Earlier Bledsoe shocked the Invisible Man with his ability to conceal his anger in the presence of Mr. Norton. Before entering the white man's room, Bledsoe, who had been ablaze with anger at the protagonist a moment before, "stopped and composed his angry face like a sculptor, making it a bland mask, leaving only the sparkle of his eyes to betray [his] emotion."[36]

Behind the boyish, willing-to-please mask, Tuskegee's founder worked as a ruthless wheeler-dealer, known by intimates as "The Wizard."[37] Washington vigorously (and secretly) fought his critics and rivals while he aided certain blacks in ways he never wanted the "good white friends of the school" to realize. Using an enormous number of controlled journalistic, educational, religious, fraternal, business, and political organizations (the aggregate of which formed what critics called "The Tuskegee Machine"), Washington was constantly jockeying for personal power. Furthermore, he privately sponsored many court suits against peonage, lynching, and black disenfranchisement while publicly he hedged or remained silent on such issues.[38]

It should not be overlooked that through personal charisma and toughness and through "a certain amount of sorcery," as historian Louis Harlan puts it, Washington built Tuskegee into the capital of black America and a mecca for blacks desiring to learn.[39] If he compromised to expediency, he also erected a model school with the best programs of their kind that money could afford. When it came to running the Institute, Washington placed his faith not in equality and democracy but in leadership and discipline; his results in terms of the school's physical plant and in its capacity to train black youth were remarkable.

Hand-picked by Washington to succeed him to the presidency was Major Robert Russa Moton, who took over in 1915, serving until October 1935 when, upon his retirement, he was succeeded by Tuskegee's third president, Frederick Douglas Patterson. In November 1933, when Ellison had been on campus only a few weeks, Moton delivered a chapel address in which he recalled his last interview with Washington. Much as the Founder in *Invisible Man* dramatically transfers the great responsibility of leadership to his colleague ("Now you must take on the burden," says the Founder to Bledsoe. "Lead them the rest of the way."), Washington called Moton to his deathbed. According to Moton, the dying Washington looked up and quietly said, "Major, don't forget Tuskegee."[40] By 1933, Moton had proved his resolute dedication to the principles of Washington.

His polemic *What the Negro Thinks* (1929) makes clear that Moton (another model for Ellison's Bledsoe) was a conservative and cautious spokesman for "the race." Even his racial pride was an extension of Washingtonism: with it came not only the ideal of bland respectability, but the willingness to denigrate blacks who were not on the social and economic "advance."[41] Sounding Bledsoe-like, Moton wrote that considering the shabby behavior of certain blacks on the public carriers, "it was no surprise when segregation came on the railroads and the argument for it could hardly be gainsaid."[42]

Despite Tuskegee's identity as a place to study agriculture and business, it was also one of the major centers for musical studies in the South.[43] The strong musical tradition, Ellison remembers, "bathed each and every thing that was done at Tuskegee . . . Underneath the desire for education, underneath the desire for possession of more technology, underneath the desire for intellectual competency is that other thing— that which can only be expressed through art."[44] In the thirties great musicians and orchestras who journeyed to Alabama for recitals or study came not to white schools like the University of Alabama but to Tuskegee Institute.

As early as the 1890s, Tuskegee's choir was known for its renditions of black folk music. The singing of spirituals and work songs had a great impact on visitors to the school. Not only because Booker T. Washington enjoyed hearing what he called "plantation songs," but because he saw their value in public relations, he insisted that these songs be presented by the choir. Indeed he fought for years against the attempts of Tuskegee's music teachers to introduce other music.[45]

Tuskegee's uniformed band was trained by Major Walter Loving and James Reese Europe. Its early orchestras gave concerts every Sunday at the Institute, and by 1900 Tuskegee was offering a major course of study in music.[46]

When Ellison came there, William L. Dawson, the composer, was director of Tuskegee's School of Music, which he had organized in 1931. Under Dawson's leadership and with Moton's blessing, the new school prospered. Dawson wished to build upon the institute's rich music tradition by inviting "the best people in our race" to teach in the music school. The department heads included Andrew Rosemund, Abbie Mitchell, and Hazel Harrison. Dawson himself taught composition and instrumentation. The 1933-34 *Tuskegee Institute Bulletin* announced that the School of Music was designed to meet the great demand for "well-trained music teachers . . . church organists, choir directors, as well as for concert performers."[47] Students could elect to prepare themselves as teachers or as concert artists. The 1933-34 *Bulletin* also boasted a choir of one hundred members, two glee clubs, an orchestra, and a concert band.[48] These groups performed works of European and American composers and had a very large repertory. The orchestra traveled widely around the nation. Student director Ellison recalls, in particular, a concert tour to Chicago during which he attended his first opera.[49]

The course of study for music majors was a rigorous one. Aside from English and physical education, in the freshman year there were required classes in a major instrument (three hours of practice daily), a minor instrument (one hour of practice daily), solfeggio (ear-training and sight-singing), harmony, and conducting. Sophomores continued these classes, replacing conducting with music appreciation, while juniors and seniors took counterpoint, composition and instrumentation, modern language, and psychology. Juniors and seniors were also required to play in the school's orchestra and other ensemble groups. Ellison brought to Dawson's program over ten years of musical experience, his own trumpet, his own ideas about musical taste and technique.

Ellison also brought to Tuskegee a conviction about the "New Negro." He had read Alain Locke's *The New Negro* in high school and believed that "the Sociologist, the Philanthropist, the Raceleader are not unaware of the new Negro, but they are at a loss to account for him. He cannot be swathed in their formulae. For the younger generation is vibrant with a new psychology; the new spirit is awake in the masses, and under the very eyes of the professional observers is transforming what has been a perennial problem into the progressive phases of contemporary Negro life."[50] Although in years to come he would be very harsh in his criticism of the New Negro Movement, at Tuskegee Ellison wanted to participate in the progressive leadership he associated with the "Renaissance."[51]

Ellison was impressed by the commitment to artistic and scholarly excellence advanced in *The New Negro*, and he was inspired by Locke's willingness to attach universal value to black American art forms, including jazz and blues. Locke later wrote that it was not until the thirties that the New Negro Movement came into its own.[52] Perhaps he was correct. Ellison and certain other young black intellectuals and artists of the thirties were intent upon extending the definition of black American life beyond the scope of the New Negroes of the twenties.

Under the impetus of the New Negro Movement (as well as his own "Renaissance Man" ideal) Ellison dabbled in several arts at Tuskegee. Music was his first love. During his third year, when he was experimenting for the first time with writing poetry, he began to test his powers in painting and photography. And between regular classes in 1935, he went to an art class to learn some of the techniques of water color. The instructor, Eva Hamlin, was occupied with other students at the moment and could not show Ellison how to use the water colors, but she gave him some clay and a cast catalogue containing some ideas for sculpture. Ellison discovered he had a knack for working in the three-dimensional form and made several clay heads of student friends in the weeks that followed.[53]

Faculties at black "cow colleges" (as some people considered Tuskegee) are often discounted as incompetent; however, there were instructors who were both talented and dedicated. Some were truly inspired by Washington's vision; others were caught up in the broadest streams of the New Negro Movement or the "*Newer* Negro Movement," as Locke and certain others had come to say.[54] At virtually every black college "there were scholars bringing to bear on Negro experience an academic technology that was of the highest order," says the writer Albert Murray, a Tuskegee alumnus of the thirties.[55]

Morteza Drexel Sprague, head of Tuskegee's English department, was part of the school's intellectual avant-garde.[56] This instructor, who taught a very popular course on the English novel, was pleased by Ellison's eagerness to learn and often directed him to many works beyond the class's regular syllabus. "Young Mister Sprague" (as some students called him) was a campus hero. Murray recalls that on his way across the school lawn, dressed in bright ivy-league suits and wing-tip shoes, walking erect as a soldier and "almost always with a clutch of new books and magazines," Sprague seemed to unleash "literary fallout that evoked the whole world of arts and letters." Continuing his description in mythic terms, Murray says that "the post-Booker T. Washington Liberal Arts Emphasis . . . was the very self and voice of Morteza Drexel Sprague."[57]

Dawson, too, was, in a sense, a New Negro. He grappled with a question that was crucial to the New Negro artist: What is the relation of folk art to "high" art? Certainly Dawson's use of black folk music in his symphony made Ellison more conscious of this folk-high relation. According to the 1933-34 Tuskegee catalogue, in his course on composition and instrumentation "Negro idioms" were emphasized.[58]

Dawson helped with the music for Tuskegee's 1934 Negro History week production of Willis Richardson's "Compromise," a play contained in Locke's *The New Negro*.[59] In this "folk play," so called because of its "realistic" portrayal of southern black life, Ellison was cast as Alec, a vengeful, hot-headed black boy who is disgusted with his parents' compromises with destructive neighboring whites. Learning that a white boy has impregnated his sister, Alec attacks the boy. The play closes with Alec disavowing all compromises and fleeing town.

Hazel Harrison, professor of music at Tuskegee, was a special inspiration to young Ellison.[60] He frequently mentions her in essays and lectures as a "dedicated individual" who added greatly to his understanding of music and to his notion of life's possibilities. Harrison was a concert pianist who had been one of Ferrucio Busoni's prize pupils in Berlin and who had known Egon Petri Sergei, Prokofiev, Percy Grainger, and other leading musicians of her time. She encouraged her students to study technique and to use the greatest range of sources available to them. Nor did she look down on jazz. One afternoon she gathered students in her studio to meet her personal friend, Alain Locke, long-time champion of black music of all kinds. Locke, an intellectual stimulus to Ellison for several years, had just returned from Paris, and at Tuskegee he talked informally about artistic and intellectual trends in Europe. Both Harrison and Locke, like Dawson, were role models for Ellison; they provided vital links to the world of artistic and intellectual pursuits of the highest order. They were tapping the deepest and broadest streams in black American culture, as well as those from different lands and eras.

Although during his second year at Tuskegee Ellison still considered music his primary field of artistic self-expression, that year, 1935, also marked an important touchstone toward his transition to writing. His first published prose was two years off, but in 1935 he began to study the sources and techniques of modern fiction and poetry.

The work that most deeply engaged him that year was T. S. Eliot's "The Waste Land," of which he wrote: "I was intrigued by its power to move me while eluding my understanding." It was compellingly jazzlike in its rhythms and "range of allusion," and Ellison wondered why he had read no literature of equal intensity by a black writer. By comparison, Ellison later said, works like Countee Cullen's "Heritage" seemed artificial and alien, even though they purported to describe black experience. As with the blues, the total meaning of "The Waste Land" was evasive: "Its changes of pace and its hidden system of organization . . . escaped me. There was nothing to do," he says "but look up the references in the footnotes to the poem."[61]

His determination to unlock the poem led Ellison to classical and popular mythology, to folklore, and to the plethora of subjects touched upon by Eliot. Now Ellison began a startling reevaluation of his own experience, for the more he read, the more the details of his life became transformed. In literature, he "heard undertones in remembered conversations which had escaped [him] before, and local customs took on a more universal meaning, values which [he] hadn't understood were revealed." If some of the people he had known "were diminished . . . others were elevated in stature." Furthermore, he began to see his "own possibilities with more objective, and in some ways, more hopeful eyes." Through his careful study of literature's sources, Ellison was confronted with the vast importance of myth and folk art. He realized that he "had been involved in folklore back in Oklahoma" and that many of his ideas about life were shaped by folk rhymes, stories, dances, ritual, and music.[62]

Eliot had written that, for the artist, knowledge of tradition is "nearly indispensable."[63] Writers lean on what has gone before. They must either "take T. S. Eliot's advice and become conscious as to where they link in with the past or . . . they lose the benefit of all those years of artistic discovery which have helped to give the language its radiance and to give human beings some sense of their greatest possibilities."[64]

Eliot's influence pervades *Invisible Man*. The novel's heavy symbolism and its imagery of death and rebirth, blindness and light, are reminiscent of Eliot and of Eliot's own primary sources, the Bible and classical mythology. One of the most wonderfully Eliotic passages in *Invisible Man* occurs when the protagonist describes the "beautiful college." After recalling the bright wisteria and the spirituals ringing plaintively at dusk, the narrator pauses to wonder

> what was real, what solid, what more than a pleasant, time-killing dream? For how could it have been real if now I am invisible? If real, why is it that I can recall in all that island of greenness no fountain but one that was broken, corroded and dry? And why does no rain fall through my recollections, sound through my memories, soak through the hard dry crust of the still so recent past? Why do I recall, instead of the odor of seed bursting in springtime, only the yellow contents of the cistern spread over the lawn's dead grass? Why? And how? How and why? . . . I'm convinced it was the product of a subtle magic, the alchemy of moonlight; the school a flower-studded wasteland, the rocks sunken, the dry winds hidden, the lost crickets chirping to yellow butterflies.
> And oh, oh, oh, those multimillionaires.[65]

The hard-crusted imagery here recalls not only "The Wasteland," but "Four Quartets" and "The Hollow Men." Like Eliot, searching for signs of life in a devastated land, the protagonist in *Invisible Man* looks back upon his experience with a degree of horror. Ellison himself, in reviewing his Tuskegee years, had to wonder, "What was real?" Like Eliot and the narrator of his novel, he observed much calamity, exhaustion, and death. He also sensed the hope for redemption through self-awareness.

During his third year at Tuskegee, Ellison tried his hand at writing poetry. He had become "curious about writing by way of seeking to understand the aesthetic nature of literary power, the devices through which literature could command [his] mind and [his] emotions." At first, however, writing was "far from a serious matter" but a result of his incessant reading which proved "a source of pleasure, escape and instruction." He had been told since high school that he handled prose well, although his grammar and punctuation were sometimes shaky. His first attempts at writing poetry turned out to be "an amusing investigation of what seemed at best a secondary talent . . . like dabbling in sculpture."⁶⁶ With practice, though, Ellison felt he was beginning to capture some of the force that Eliot unleashed in his poems. More and more time was spent playing with words and images and trying to incorporate sounds, accents, ideas, and feelings into his verse. "Almost imperceptively," he says, his main interests shifted from music to literature, its techniques and sources.

As one who on the dark side of his mind was becoming a writer, Ellison began to seek accurate descriptions of black American life. His Oklahoma upbringing, his desire to master many skills, and his identification with certain aspects of the New Negro Movement caused him to seek definitions that were broadly affirmative of black life. To his chagrin, Ellison was discovering that very few writers, black or white, had captured in poetry or fiction the variety, wonder, tragedy, humor, or even the basic forms of black American life as he knew it. Virtually no one expressed the black American condition with the color and exuberant spirit of the speakers and musicians Ellison had listened to in Randolph's drugstore, in churches, and in the shoeshine parlors of Oklahoma City. Most of his favorite writers did not deal at all with black American life. Even New Negro poets and novelists, Ellison found, presented too exhausted or romanticized a view of black life to suit his taste. The findings of white social scientists seemed even less satisfactory to him. Most of them overlooked blacks entirely or, when they did analyze black life, their conceptions were often divorced from reality as blacks knew it.

In 1935, just a few months before going to New York, Ellison took an introductory sociology class at Tuskegee. In that class he underwent "the humiliation of being taught . . . that Negroes represented the 'lady of the races.' This contention the Negro instructor passed blandly on to us without even bothering to wash his hands, much less his teeth."⁶⁷ The white sociologists Robert Park and Ernest W. Burgess, authors of *Introduction to the Science of Sociology*, the Tuskegee textbook, defined blacks in these austere terms:

> The Negro is, by natural disposition, neither an intellectual nor an idealist, like the Jew; nor a brooding introspective, like the East In-

dian; nor a pioneer and frontiersman, like the Anglo Saxon. He is primarily an artist, loving life for its own sake. His metier is expression rather than action. He is, so to speak, the lady among the races.[68]

Burgess and Park, cofounder of the influential University of Chicago School of Sociology, thus described the typical black American as a ridiculous reduction of the Washingtonian "ideal Tuskegee student": merrily expressive, mindless, and cloaked in frills.

In his angry 1944 review of Gunner Myrdal's *An American Dilemma*, Ellison links the rise of social studies, with its "graphs, charts, and other paraphernalia to prove the Negro's inferiority," and the post-Reconstruction decline of American justice for blacks. Ellison writes:

> In order to deal with this problem [of emancipated blacks] the North did four things: it promoted Negro education in the South; it controlled his economic and political destiny, or allowed the South to do so; it built Booker T. Washington into a national spokesman of Negroes with Tuskegee Institute as his seat of power; and it organized social science as an instrument to sanction its methods.[69]

Robert Park seems to stand at the center of this insidious circle. His metaphor, lady of the races, is "so pregnant with mixed motives as to birth a thousand compromises and indecisions."[70] Ellison terms Park, whom Booker T. Washington employed to research and ghost-write certain articles and letters, the "power behind Washington's throne."[71] Park was one of several writers who worked on Washington's *Up from Slavery*. Ellison implies a conspiracy here: behind the scenes lurked a sociologist hell-bent on retarding Afro-American development.

Social scientists have been the target of a fast and steady stream of Ellison's criticism since early in his career. Their "objective" findings, he discovered, were often based on preconceptions as sterile and grotesque as those of Burgess and Park, especially when they operated from the "double-distance of racial alienation and inexperience." Often, like "plantation school" novelists and poets, they seemed to fall back upon the stereotypes of the American minstrel show.

Sometimes, as Ellison was to discover in New York, even when artists and social scientists seemed sympathetic to black political causes, they presented portraits of blacks as the irremediably ravaged products of political and social prejudice. This vision of the deprived black, he observes, is merely a modern sociologist's counter-stereotype, which misses the wealth and variety of black American culture. Too often, says Ellison, liberal scholars who discuss black life "assume that as long as their hearts are in the right place, they can be as arbitrary as they wish in their formulations." Often their theories reveal more about their own lives than about the lives of blacks. Many white liberals

> seem to feel they can air with impunity their most private Freudian fantasies as long as they are given the slightest camouflage of intellectuality and projected as "Negro." They have made of the no-man's land created by segregation a territory for infantile self-expression and intellectual anarchy. They write as though Negro life exists only in the light of their belated regard, and they publish interpretations of Negro experience which would not hold true for their own or for any other form of humanity.[72]

Ellison's encounter at Tuskegee with *Introduction to the Science of Sociology* created an accelerated sense of urgency to learn about black American culture and to convert his knowledge into artistic forms. Who, after all, would tell *his* story? Even, as we shall see, in his writings of the 1930s, Ellison's primary criticism of those who wrote about black America was that they distorted the black past. If you would tell me who I am, he has said repeatedly, at least find out who I have been. "Consult the text." For the artist as well as the social scientist, the text of black American life is contained largely in black language and lore.

During his three years at Tuskegee, Ellison stared down the old southern conceptions of black life. He played hookey from the old guard at Tuskegee and clung to the ambitions and ideals developed in Oklahoma City. By seeking out the New Negroes of Tuskegee, Ellison continued to mature, in spite of the general atmosphere of intellectual timidity at the college. He wanted to define himself and black American life in the broadest possible contexts: his formulations now included Eliot and Handel, Alain Locke and the rowdy blues.

Because of a mix-up about his scholarship at the end of his third year, Ellison found himself without the forty-dollar tuition fee for the coming year and no other money to live on. He decided that rather than work in Alabama, where it would be difficult to save money for the fall term, he would venture north. What he had heard and read made New York sound like a romantic place, and he looked forward to getting a job there. And perhaps he could also satisfy his desire to tackle life from other angles. Though she recognized that music was his first love, Eva

Hamlin was enthusiastic about Ellison's prospects as a sculptor; to encourage him, she presented him with a letter of introduction to Augusta Savage, a black sculptor who lived in Harlem.[73] Without realizing that he was "dropping out," Ellison took a train from Alabama headed north to Harlem, New York.

2

Up North

Aside from the winter spent in Dayton, Ohio, the war years in the
Merchant Marines, and the two years in Rome as a guest of the
American Academy of Arts and Letters (1955-1957), Ellison
has lived in New York since 1936. Although he first journeyed north
specifically to study sculpture and to earn money as a musician for his last
year at Tuskegee, he was also lured to New York by a magical promise of
greater freedom. "New York," he said, "was one of the great cities
prominent in the Negro American myth of freedom, a myth which goes
back very far into Negro American experience. In our spirituals it was the
North Star and places in the North which symbolized Freedom and to
that extent I expected certain things from New York."[1] He expected
New York to be a fulfillment of "the irrepressible belief in some Mecca of
equality." Literature depicted Harlem as "a glamorous place, a place
where wonderful music existed and where there was a great tradition of
Negro American style and elegance."[2]

In *Invisible Man*, the protagonist informs the outspoken veteran of the
Golden Day bar that he is on his way to New York, and the vet becomes
quite excited:

"New York!" he said. "That's not a place, it's a dream. When I was
your age it was Chicago. Now all the little black boys run away to
New York. Out of the fire into the melting pot. I can see you after
you've lived in Harlem for three months. Your speech will change,
you'll talk a lot about 'college,' you'll attend lectures at the Men's

House . . . you might even meet a few white folks. And listen," he said, leaning close to whisper, "you might even dance with a white girl!"[3]

In "Harlem Is Nowhere" (1948), Ellison deals with the trauma suffered by many southern blacks who migrated north. As many new arrivals soon found out, Harlem was by no means the Freedom Land heralded in folklore. "To live in Harlem is to dwell in the very bowels of the city . . . a ruin . . . overcrowded and exploited politically and economically." The black newcomer to Harlem arrives at the very "scene and symbol of the Negro's perpetual alienation in the land of his birth." The troubled psychology of Harlem blacks "arises from the impact between urban slum conditions and folk sensibilities." The abrupt shift from feudal South to "the vortex of industrialism" in the North and the "resulting clash of cultural factors" account for the extremes of Harlem—the burgeoning creativity and the madness, the vaulting optimism and the deep despair.[4]

When the black southerner moves north, he surrenders certain emotional and cultural supports:

> He leaves a relatively static social situation in which he has developed those techniques for survival which Faulkner refers to as "endurance," and an ease of movement within explosive situations which makes Hemingway's definition of courage, "grace under pressure," appear mere swagger . . . He surrenders the protection of his peasant cynicism—his refusal to hope for the fulfillment of hopeless hopes—and his sense of being "at home in the world" gained from confronting and accepting (for day-to-day living, at least) the obscene absurdity of his predicament. Further, he leaves religion . . . family . . . and a body of folklore—tested in life-and-death terms against his daily experiences with nature and the Southern white man—that serve him as a guide to action.[5]

Away from the southern black milieu the black man finds himself "thrown back upon his own 'slum-shocked' institutions."

Yet, if many blacks have been broken and bent by Harlem, if one sees "white-haired adults crawl in the feudal darkness of their childhood, if [Harlem] is the scene of the folk-Negro's death agony, it is also the setting of his transcendence." In Harlem "you see the transformation of the Southern idiom into a Northern idiom . . . Harlem is a place where our folklore is preserved, and transformed. It is the place where the body of our Negro myth and legend thrives. It is a place where our styles, musical styles, the many styles of Negro life, find continuity and metamorphosis."[6] Millions of blacks brought their institutions and their optimism to the cities of the North. And the emerging northern black culture did provide some sense of continuity for black newcomers from the South.

In 1936 Harlem was still emerging fast as the black American cultural capital (as James Weldon Johnson has termed it), attractive to artists and intellectuals, black and white. Ellison recalls that before World War II, when the police began to tell whites to beware the large black New York neighborhood, Harlem was known as a tremendously rich and open cultural center. In the thirties and forties Ellison could be found browsing at the 135th Street Library and at Lewis Michaux's bookstore, located then on Seventh Avenue at 125th Street. He would save his nickels and dimes to get to the Savoy once or twice a week. The Savoy Ballroom "was thriving and people were coming to Harlem from all over the world. The great European and American composers were coming there to listen to jazz—Stravinski, Poulenc. The great jazz bands were coming there. Great dancers were being created there."[7] Twice a week also, often with Langston Hughes, Ellison went to shows at Harlem's Apollo Theatre. By 1940, Ellison and his wife lived next door to Teddy Wilson, and after Wilson's job at the Café Society downtown they would go to after-hours hangouts where musicians jammed: to Sidney Bechet's place, where Wilson or Art Tatum would hold down the house piano, to the Rhythm Club, to Clark Monroe's Uptown House, or to a place where the waiters sang as they served drinks. Around the corner on 137th Street was the Red Rooster, and on 116th was Jimmy Daniel's club, where an international set mingled with the usual Harlem crowd. "Jazz was part of a total culture, at least among Afro-Americans," said Ellison. And jazzmen were heroes.[8]

During the 1940s heyday of the jazz club Minton's, Ellison was among those "who shared, night after night, the mysterious spell created by the talk, the laughter, grease paint, powder, perfume, sweat, alcohol and food—all blended and simmering, like a stew on the restaurant range, and brought to a sustained moment of elusive meaning by the timbres and accents of musical instruments locked in passionate recitative."[9] There Ellison would listen to some musicians he had heard back in Oklahoma City: Charles Christian, Lester Young, Hot Lips Page, Ben Webster, along with creators of the bop idiom, Charlie Parker, Thelonious Monk, Dizzy Gillespie, Bud Powell, and Charlie Mingus. There too Ellison would run into his friend from Oklahoma City, Jimmy Rushing, who had also moved to New York. Hour-long conversations and visits with Rushing when he was not on the road kept Ellison in close contact with the inside world of jazz and blues and with friends across the country, particularly those in Oklahoma City.

There was also promising theater in Harlem during the thirties and for- ties. In June 1936, when Ellison came to town, the WPA Negro Theatre Project's production of *Macbeth*, directed by twenty-one-year-old Orson Welles with an all-black cast that included Jack Carter, was attracting standing-room crowds to Harlem's Lafayette Theatre. *Turpentine*, the Federal Theatre's second production in Harlem, opened the same month; noted for its social realism, this play about difficulties faced by workers in Florida's swamplands indicated the Harlem group's intention both to at- tempt serious drama and to avoid black stereotypes. When the WPA Theatre Project folded, the Negro Playwright's Company and the Cabaret Theatre Arts Committee maintained high standards, presenting polished, socially conscious plays at the Lafayette and the Lincoln. In a *New Masses* review of the Negro Playwright's Company production of Theodore Ward's radical play, "Big White Fog," Ellison expressed his optimism: "With this production a fresh source of incalculable possibilities has begun to pour its strength into the stream of the American theatre."[10]

Ellison did not get steady work in New York as a trumpeter as he had hoped. In fact, he performed only one public engagement there, and it was to be his last as a professional musician: he played the trumpet parts for a modern dance recital by Anna Sokolow. He still wanted to write symphonies, however, and studied for about a year with Wallingford Riegger. For a moment fate seemed to pull Ellison up to the very summit of the world of jazz. In 1936 a friend took him to the Edgecomb Avenue apartment of Duke Ellington, who remembered seeing Ellison at Tuskegee. The bandleader invited Ellison to the following day's rehearsal, but then had to cancel the invitation. Not wanting to be presumptuous about joining one of America's best bands, Ellison said no more about the matter and it was dropped.[11] By the late thirties, when he became im- mersed in fiction writing, he put down the trumpet permanently, refus- ing even to attend concerts for fear of being diverted.[12]

In 1936 the Depression was still raging and Ellison had trouble finding work of any kind. At first, still trying to earn enough cash to return to Tuskegee, he worked behind the food bar of the Harlem YMCA, where he had a room. Having waited tables in Oklahoma City, he had polish as a barman and held that job off and on for almost a year. Many odd jobs followed. One of the most instructive and interesting was a position as substitute receptionist and file clerk for the psychiatrist Harry Stack Sullivan. This job lasted only a short while, but the experience was quite valuable: as he was filing, Ellison would glance through the case histories of some of the famous people Sullivan was treating. This spurred Ellison to reread Freud on dreams and to study modern psychology with increased interest. When he began writing fiction, and studying authors who had presented dreams in their fiction—especially Dostoevsky, who "taught the novelist how to use the dream"—Ellison realized how much his stint with Sullivan had contributed.[13]

In 1936 and 1937 Ellison also worked in various factories around town, and later he worked as a free-lance photographer and builder of hi-fi systems. There were lengthy stretches, too, when he could get no work at all and spent nights on wooden benches in St. Nicholas Park below City College or on the daybed in a friend's living room.[14]

The sculptor Augusta Savage explained that her duties on a WPA arts project made it impossible for her to instruct him. So Alain Locke and Langston Hughes, enthusiastic about Ellison's possibilities in sculpture, suggested that he work with another Harlem artist, Richmond Barthé. Ellison studied with Barthé for about a year before abandoning sculpture in 1936.

Contact with the literary world was quickly made. Ellison had met Langston Hughes quite by chance on his second day in Harlem.[15] Through Hughes he met Richard Wright, and a friendship between Wright and Ellison blossomed. Though Wright was older and more secure in his identity as an artist, the two men were basically in the same predicament: they were radically inclined black intellectuals with southern backgrounds trying to survive in New York and struggling to make art in the midst of the Great Depression. They talked endlessly about politics and art, drank, and exchanged jokes and stories.[16]

Wright was candid about his belief that Ellison had started too late to develop into a serious writer, but he was impressed with his friend's ability to discuss literature in such detail and urged him to write a short story for *New Challenge*. Ellison begged off. He was, after all, a musician and lacked writing experience. Wright "forced his hand" by asking simply for a short review of Waters Edward Turpin's newly published novel *These Low Grounds*.[17] With this review, entitled "Creative and Cultural Lag," which appeared in the Fall 1937 issue of *New Challenge*, Ellison took the "fatal step" on the road to becoming a writer. He found it satisfying to be published in a magazine of national circulation, alongside such writers as Wright, Margaret Walker, Sterling Brown, Owen Dodson, Norman MacLeod, and Frank Marshall Davis.

When Wright asked Ellison to contribute a short story for the Winter 1937 number of *New Challenge*, Ellison agreed. Using his knowledge of hoboing on trains, he wrote "Heine's Bull," his first short story. Although it was overly influenced by Hemingway, it impressed Wright and got as far as galleys (which Ellison has retained for his scrapbook). In the magazine's final draft new poems by Margaret Walker and others superseded "Heine's Bull" and the story was dropped. The Communist Party's sudden withdrawal of support of the magazine, and problems between the magazine's editors, Dorothy West and Marion Minus, caused the Winter 1937 issue to fold unpublished anyway, and *New Challenge* did not appear again.

In February 1937 Ellison received the shattering news that his mother, who had moved to Dayton, had died there suddenly. He rushed to Dayton for her funeral. In a haunting prose-poem called "February," which appeared in *Saturday Review*, 1955, Ellison recalls his mother's death and the awesome Dayton winter during the recession of 1937:

> February is a brook, birds, an apple tree—a day spent alone in the country. Unemployed, tired of reading, and weary of grieving the loss of my mother, I'd gone into the woods to forget. So that now all Februaries have the aura of that early morning coldness, the ghost of quail tracks on the snow-powdered brook which I brushed aside as I broke the brook to drink; and how the little quail tracks went up the ice, precise and delicate, into the darker places of the bank-ledge undisturbed.[19]

To Ellison, February 1937 was a time of desperate struggle to gain some perspective on the tragedy of losing his mother. It also involved the larger struggle to confront the reality of change, death, and decay:

> February is climbing up a hill into the full glare of the early sun, alone in all that immensity of snowscape with distant Dayton drowsing wavery to my eyes like distant horns. It's walking through a park-like grove, the tall trees stark, the knee-high snow wind-blown and pathless, to a decaying shed sheltering a fine old horsedrawn sleigh, carved and scrolled with traces of gold leaf clinging to its flaking wood.[20]

Ellison's statement in "February" that he survived by his gun through ice, snow, and homelessness is no mere figure of speech. Ellison and his brother Herbert both arrived in Dayton almost completely out of money. Nights, when the temperature skidded toward zero, they slept in a car parked in a garage with both cardoors open. They kept themselves alive by hunting quail, which they either ate or sold to local General Motors officials.[21] Although the Ellison brothers had hunted since childhood in

Oklahoma, never had it been such a serious enterprise. Luckily, by reading Hemingway's descriptions of leading a bird in flight, Ellison became an excellent hunter during those lean months in Dayton. Obviously Hemingway's imagery impressed Ellison very much; years later he said, "When Hemingway describes something, believe him. He's been there."[22]

In Ohio, Ellison began writing "in earnest." After hunting all day, he practiced his writing and studied Joyce, Dostoevsky, Stein, and Hemingway—especially Hemingway, recalls Ellison. "I read him to learn his sentence structure and how to organize a story." To get a feel for his language, Ellison copied in longhand some of Hemingway's stories. And he began to read as never before, realizing that "I didn't really learn to read until I began to write." Hemingway, whose stories and reports from abroad Ellison had first admired while waiting for haircuts in Oklahoma City barbershops, was his "true father-as-artist," he says. Before returning to New York, Ellison wrote and discarded several stories. He even started a novel, part of which was published under the title "Slick Gonna Learn." This effort was helpful, he later said, because it taught him that he did not yet know enough to write a novel. Although under the spell of Marxist ideology, he would soon (temporarily) repudiate Hemingway's fiction as too defeatist and apolitical, Ellison's first published stories and essays bear the definite influence of Hemingway, as well as his other mentor, Richard Wright.

Ellison returned to New York weary and distraught. One issue was decided, however: all of his creative energies would be channeled into becoming a good writer. He began to arrange his life so that writing would be his main focus—"to stake my energy against the possibility of failing." Out of money but determined to continue to practice his writing, Ellison became a beneficiary of the New Deal's Federal Writers' Program.

Because of the conservatism and racism of several state Project directors, in the early days of the Federal Writers' Project blacks encountered great difficulty getting hired. Furthermore, since at that time very few Negro writers were actually earning a living from their publications, it was not easy for them to prove they were professionals.[23] Luckily, the Project's Editor of Negro Affairs, Sterling A. Brown, appointed in 1936, and the "Black Cabinet" (Ralph Bunche, John Preston Davis, William Hastie, and Robert Weaver) were pushing for more Negro writers to be hired by the Project nationally. Thus, with the added help of Richard Wright, Ellison landed a Project job almost as soon as he arrived back in the city in 1938.[24]

Ellison's experience on the Federal Writers' Project (1938-1942) provided enough money to live on, $103.50 monthly, and a good deal more than money. Besides rescuing him from the despair of unemployment, working on the Project stocked Ellison with "information and insights about [his] country during a highly formative period of [his] literary life."[25] On the Project Ellison was in touch with seasoned, professional writers as well as beginners like himself. In this high-spirited, productive company, he began to find his personal "voice" in fiction. In the process he grappled with questions that were to provide the dominant themes in his writing: Who is the American? Who is the black American? How does a person's past relate to his identity? What role does folk art play? Ellison became a highly conscious writer during his years on the Federal Writers' Project.

He pursued his Project assignments with the same diligence he had given to his musical studies. One of his first jobs, which was on a manuscript called "Famous New York Trials," gave him the opportunity to learn something of the history of New York's political and legal systems. He spent days at the New York Court of General Sessions, reading transcripts of court cases and collections of crime reports. This handling of "raw materials" was quite exciting to Ellison, and it proved instructive to him as an apprentice writer. Even when the research was tedious, he found interest in the drama and ritual of the courtroom: here were forms to consider as materials for fiction.[26]

Along with about twenty other black employees of the New York Project, Ellison spent many months in the Schomberg Library digging up material for *The Negro in New York*. As a member of that research team, Ellison wrote a series of short memoranda (200 to 2,000 words in length) dealing with prominent black New Yorkers and with historical incidents involving the black community. From June 9, 1938, to June 29, 1942 — almost his entire time on the Project — Ellison submitted papers on such topics as "Negro Instructors in New York Institutions of Higher Learning," "Jupiter Hammond," and "Great Riots of New York; Complete Account of the Four Days of Draft Riot of 1863."[27] These essays, which were carefully footnoted and replete with facts, offered interpretation as well as supportive data in prose that often reflected the balance and grandeur of Ellison's later prose, but which as often lacked his characteristic precision of language and verve.

From 1938 to 1940 Ellison also worked under the supervision of Nicholas Wirth, one of the most ingenious Project leaders of New York's "Living Lore Unit." This group of twenty-seven writers sought to recount the story of New York City in the words of New Yorkers. They were occupied in documenting "urban and industrial folklore." The team's work, assembled (but not published) under the title "Chase the White Horse," testified to their conviction that a vital part of American history existed in the tales, toasts, boasts, songs, and rhymes of American folklore.[28]

In an effort to trace the origins of the lore, Ellison would ask his Harlem children "informants" where they had learned particular pieces. These inquiries were generally fruitless; the children often simply did not recall where they had picked up a game or song. Almost never, Ellison noted, were southern parents or relatives named as game or song teachers. Ellison was convinced, nonetheless, that some—perhaps most—of the Harlem lore had been transplanted directly from the South and Southwest. Even when the Harlem lore seemed indigenous, Ellison often spotted the southern source. Sometimes he could recognize a remnant of a saying or rhyme he had heard in the South reduced to a "mumble" or nonsense phrase in Harlem. "Out of the rural context in which the story or rhyme had originated," the *meanings* of the folk art changed and, at times, appeared to dissolve entirely. Even reduced to mumbles, however, the folklore often retained ritual significance and suggested a tradition, a bridge to the South and to the past. "That's what the people have to work out of," he has said. "This tradition goes way back to the South, and some of it goes back to Africa."[29]

Ellison also visited hundreds of Harlem apartments and public places, where he collected stories by exchanging them with adults. This process of interviewing and transcribing sharpened Ellison's ear for idiosyncrasies of speech and gave him practice in getting particular speech patterns onto paper. He wrote the transcribed Harlem stories from the viewpoint and in the idiom of the people who told them. During the interviews he often was able to get a story on paper "by using a kind of Hemingway typography, by using the repetitions." He has said: "I couldn't quite get the tone of the sounds in but I could get some of the patterns and get an idea of what it was like."[30]

One especially fascinating report from interviewer Ellison was submitted on June 14, 1938. Standing on 135th Street and Lenox Avenue, Leo Gurley told Ellison about "Sweet-the-Monkey." Gurley began his story with what folklorists call a signature: "I hope to God to kill me if this aint the truth. All you got to do is go down to Florence, South Carolina and ask most anybody you meet and they'll tell you its the truth." Gurley's "Sweet-the-Monkey" in some respects resembles the narrator of *Invisible Man's* prologue, as here:

> It was this way: Sweet could make hisself invisible. You don't believe it? Well here's how he done it. Sweet-the-monkey cut open

a black cat and took out its heart. Climbed a tree backwards and cursed God. After that he could do anything. The white folks would wake up in the morning and find their stuff gone. He cleaned out the stores. He cleaned up the houses. Hell, he even cleaned out the dam bank! He was the boldest *black* sonofabitch ever been down that way. And couldn't nobody do nothing to him. *Because* they couldn't never see im when he done it. He didn't need the money. Fact is, most of the time he broke into places he wouldn't take nothing. Lots a times he just did it to show 'em he could. Hell, he had everybody in that lil old town scaird as hell; black folks and white folks . . . He wont let hisself be seen.[31]

Many of the rhymes, jokes, and peculiarities of speech which enrich Ellison's fiction were drawn from his experience in Oklahoma and Alabama; many others were drawn from notes he made while researching and interviewing in Harlem for the Federal Writers' Project. Beyond simply copying bits of already collected folklore into his fiction, Ellison developed a working knowledge of Afro-American rhymes, games, and stories. Moreover, he refined his sense of the folkloric context: the moments and the settings in which persons, particularly Afro-Americans, were likely to use the stylized speech of folklore. He studied text as well as context. In his fiction, therefore, the lore is more than local color; it is ritualistic and reflective of a whole lifestyle.

For example, in *Invisible Man* the protagonist tells a black man on the street to "take it easy" and the man replies with an ebullient "boast," here serving an initiatory purpose:

Oh, I'll do that. All it takes to get along in this here man's town is a little shit, grit, and mother-wit. And, man, I was bawn with all three. In fact, I'maseventhsonofaseventhsonbawnwithacauloverbotheyesandraisedonblackcatboneshighjohntheconqueror andgreasygreens . . . I'll verse you but I won't curse you -My name is Peter Wheatstraw I'm the Devil's only son-in-law, so roll 'em . . . My name is Blue and I'm coming at you with a pitchfork. Fe Fi Fo Fum. Who wants to shoot the Devil one, Lord God Stingeroy! . . . Look me up sometimes, I'm a piano player and a rounder, a whiskey drinker and a pavement pounder. I'll teach you some good bad habits. You'll need 'em.[32]

On the Federal Arts Project, writers studied folklore along with practicing the literary craft needed to transpose the lore into written literature. Project worker Ellison collected lore and studied history by day, and wrote his own fiction by night. The Project provided some of the impetus for writers' rediscovery of the American language, a process that intensified greatly in the thirties. During the Project years, Ellison became very conscious of language and folklore as keys to the past and to personal identity. "The character of a people," he has said, "is revealed in their speech." For him, the heightened consciousness of a historical perspective provided by the Project's structured examination of language and folklore planted seeds that helped his writing grow beyond the limits of literary realism. If Harlem proved a somewhat tarnished "Mecca of Equality," it did offer to young Ellison exciting opportunities for artistic growth.

3

Lure of the Left

T
he stimulus that existed in New York during the thirties," Ellison recalls, "was by no means limited to art; it was also connected with politics; it was part of the *esprit de corps* developed in the country after we had endured the Depression for a few years. It had to do with my discovering New York and the unfamiliar areas of society newly available to me."[1]

Ellison's New York friends encouraged his leftward leanings. Wright was an active member of the Communist Party when they met. Having served as secretary of the John Reed Club in Chicago, he was considered a party spokesman. Hughes was a charter member of the radical American Writers' Congress and had been writing leftist articles, fiction, and poetry for almost ten years when Ellison was introduced to him. In 1937 Hughes traveled to Russia, which he depicted in reports for the *Chicago Defender* as a haven of interracial cooperation. Though never a member of the Communist Party, Hughes often wrote and spoke in behalf of party issues.[2]

Ellison sometimes attended social gatherings to honor Spanish or German antifascists or an American about to journey secretly to Spain and enlist in the Abraham Lincoln Brigade. Some of these functions, staged in the plush homes of rich leftist supporters, were attended by such exempla of radical American letters as Granville Hicks, Isador Scheider, Kenneth Fearing, Clifford Odets, William Rollins, Jr., and Malcolm Cowley.[3]

Ellison also picketed and wrote articles in support of Communist Party issues, but he always distrusted the party's tendency to lift politics above the concerns of literature. Above all, he clung to his belief in the transcendent value of artistic technique. How, after all, could a writer pinpoint the *real* vices of society and their most devastating effects on man's soul and body if he had not mastered his craft? Ellison also insisted on historical and psychological credibility in fiction. How could a writer produce a realistic novel without a solid grounding in human psychology and history? How could he deal with black American life without at least an acquaintance with black language and folk art? As a student of Eliot as well as Marx, Ellison continued to believe that an artist must study the philosophy, history, and especially the literature of the past.[4]

As early as 1940, Ellison found himself increasingly unwilling to portray the black American as the spirit-broken product of the outside forces set against him. He was beginning to envisage black characters who were able to understand their environment and to master it by positive action or by the magic of art. By 1940 too, Ellison realized that his view of fiction was quite different from that of Wright and other realists. His concern with the strengths of the black character, with style, with folklore, and with history as "a repository of values" eclipsed his enchantment with black proletarians, scarred, battered, and on the run. Beneath the brittle surface of even his first reviews in the thirties, one detects an uneasiness with ideological evaluations of literature. By the fifties, he would blast the Left and declare that certain kinds of literary realism revealed "everything except the nature of man."[5]

From 1937 to 1944 Ellison wrote over twenty book reviews for such radical periodicals as *New Challenge, Direction, Negro Quarterly*, and *New Masses*. Most of these were done for *New Masses* which, in 1940, printed at least one of Ellison's reviews every month. These first reviews reflect a leftist persuasion, which becomes, at points, explicitly Marxist.

Mirroring the Communist Party position of the day, Ellison's criticism often described black Americans as citizens of a state or nation (like a Russian soviet) within the United States. The literature of black Americans (the subject of about half of his reviews in the thirties and forties) was, Ellison believed, an emerging national literature that should serve to heighten the revolutionary consciousness of the black populace. The black writer should not instill in his audience mere "race consciousness," however, but awareness of class. Ideally the revolutionary black writer inspired black working people to unite with workers of other "nationalities" against the bourgeoisie, white and black. On the whole, black writers had failed in their revolutionary calling.

In the thirties, Ellison joined the chorus of critics calling for realism as the literary form appropriate for the radical writer. He hailed the photographic clarity of such realists as Steinbeck and Wright, who vividly portrayed workers trampled and forgotten on the farms and factory lines of America. Although these writers spotlighted particular regions and circumstances, they also tapped universal themes.

While writing for the *New Masses*, Ellison deprecated the New Negro Movement and failed to see his own links with certain of its positive aspects. What had started, he wrote, as a potentially black nationalistic and revolutionary movement became contaminated by "bourgeois ideology." Riots and lynchings after the world war unleashed a shock wave of militancy among the black masses. The New Negro writers, however, deceived by the "rain of stocks, bonds and dollar bills" in the twenties and anxious to please their rich white patrons, failed to articulate the defiant mood of their working-class brethren. And the New Negro's writing was not only ideologically unsound, but it suffered from technical backwardness. "Aside from ignoring the folk source of all vital Negro art," wrote Ellison, "the fiction of the group was chiefly lyrical, and for the most part was unaware of the technical experimentation and direction being taken by . . . such writers as Joyce, Stein, and Hemingway."[6]

With the crash of 1929, according to Ellison, "Negro middle class ideals were swept away in a flood of unemployment, poverty, and the suppression of civil liberties brought on by the depression." The Depression also further spurred the development of black working-class consciousness:

> The depression years, the movement for relief, the rise of the CIO with the attending increases in union activity among Negroes, the Herndon and Scottsboro cases, the fight against the poll tax—all made for the emergence of a new proletarian consciousness among black people. Along with this came the Federal Arts Projects and the stimulus which they gave to Negro cultural activity. The grinding impact of the depression upon the aroused Negro people was transforming its folk consciousness into a working class awareness.[7]

In such a world, the meaninglessness of bourgeois writing became obvious and "the writer who had stood aloof from the people, confining himself to transmitting the small, thin, compromising voice of the black middle class, found himself drowned out in the mighty roar of the masses."

Recognizing the weaknesses of their New Negro antecedents, black writers who arrived on the scene in the thirties wanted to employ styles and themes to stimulate the protest movement of the masses and assist in the birth of their radical consciousness. These writers felt an urgent responsibility to "come to grips with and record those forces of the period that were moving the black farmers and workers to unprecedented activity."[8]

Although the Depression years brought tremendous difficulties to Americans, they were also, in Ellison's words, "great times for literature." They were times for "the conscious writer" to study society's laws and to examine its citizens' emotions "stripped naked." Furthermore, the writer could perceive the great American themes of tomorrow shining "beyond the present chaos." The black writer's particular duty was to overcome the handicap of living in a racist and capitalist Babylon and to teach his readers to do the same. His grandest responsibility, said Ellison, echoing Joyce's phrase, was "to create the consciousness of his oppressed nation."[9]

"Creative and Cultural Lag," Ellison's review of black writer Waters Edward Turpin's epic novel *These Low Grounds*, was written at the behest of Richard Wright. This first review is startling in that it reflects so thoroughly the black leftist sensibilities of the times and yet embodies so many of the literary values Ellison retained in decades to come. Even then stamped with the balanced and formal Ellison style, this review gives a good idea of what he meant by the term "realism."

Turpin's novel depicts four generations of a black family from the Civil War to the thirties and introduces types of characters "often neglected by the 'New Negro' school of writers":

> house servants, farmers, barbers, bawdy house keepers, church functionaries, cooks, stage entertainers, and a Negro army officer of the World War, along with contemporary young Negro college men, women and teachers . . . along with . . . the roustabouts, sudsbusters, bellboys, shoe-shine boys, coal men, ditch diggers and such.[10]

Turpin was wise to concentrate on the coastal region of Maryland, Ellison thought. In so doing, he showed a "willingness to explore the rich deep materials of the Negro . . . In this region life emerges sharp and clear in its outlines, forceful and blunt in its impact, and as real as good rich black earth, and as free of superficialities."

Turpin's inattention to politics and history, however, weaken the novel's realism. For example, the characters are "carried through the period of Reconstruction with no mention of the fact." At a time when

throughout the world writers are "alert to social and historical processes
. . . no writer can afford to remain untouched by the activity around
him." The black writer needs an especially acute awareness of his situation so that he can "transcend his immediate environment and grasp the
historical process as a whole, and his group's reaction to it." He must
deepen his readers' awareness of themselves as actors in an international
drama and as workers of the world. Turpin did not have enough awareness of history's unrelenting movement toward world revolution.

Turpin's novel, according to Ellison, betrayed a flawed technique as
well as a dim historical and political perspective. Furthermore, "Turpin
might profit by a closer acquaintance with the techniques of his contem-
poraries since their problems are his, and their achievements similar to
those he seeks." The characters are well chosen but are described in such
dead language that they appear "stillborn":

> With a greater development in technique, Turpin could have given
> us more than one level of writing. He would have entered into the
> consciousness of his characters to give us a fuller picture of human
> beings. People like [those characters] *know* that life for Negroes in
> their situation is not as simple as Turpin would have us believe, and
> a closer examination of their consciousness would have thrown into
> relief more of the social and emotional factors present. (p. 91).

By linking realism and writing craft, Ellison differed with many revolutionary writers, who believed that "raw" writing by and for the blue-
collar masses would inevitably surpass the "effete scribblings" of drawing-
room academics like Eliot and James.

In his first reviews, which reflect the influence of Richard Wright and
Sterling Brown (no doubt the strongest proponent of realistic portrayal of
black characters in literature), Ellison demonstrated his sustained interest
in realistic and historical black fiction. In years to come, he would continue to advise writers to sharpen their writing technique, to acquaint
themselves with history and psychology, and to resist the temptation of
presenting mere black stereotypes. Only the well-informed and skillful
writer could present a sharply focused—a truly realistic—picture of black
experience.

On September 24, 1940, Ellison's review of Langston Hughes's
biography *The Big Sea* appeared in *New Masses* under the title "Stormy
Weather." In this, his longest and most searching literary essay up to that
time, Ellison hailed Hughes's early pioneering work in black revolutionary poetry but expressed disappointment in *The Big Sea's* simplistic

style and superficial characterizations. Clearly, Ellison's ideas of literary realism had broadened since his 1937 review of *These Low Grounds*.

In "Stormy Weather" Ellison began to emphasize the crucial importance of folklore in literature. He argued that Hughes was among the very small group of New Negro writers who based their work on folk sources, and who hence survived the bourgeois wave of writing in the twenties as well as the shattering impact of the Great Crash. "Declining the ideological world of the Negro bourgeoisie," Ellison wrote, Hughes "gained his artistic soul."

> While his contemporaries expressed the limited strivings of this class, Hughes' vision carried him down into the black masses to seek his literary roots. The crystallized folk experience of the blues, spirituals and folk tales became the stuff of his poetry. And when the flood of 1929 wrecked the artistic houses of his fellows, his was balanced firm upon its folk foundation.[11]

Hughes was one of the first to sense that the black worker spoke a "language of protest," a black urban idiom, and that "the speech pattern of this new language had long been present in Negro life, recorded in the crystallized protest of American Negro folklore." His poetry reflected the transformation of rural folk expression into urban folk expression, which by the thirties was fast becoming "the basis of a new proletarian art."

The Big Sea, however, was not explicit enough for Ellison in its realism or radicalism. Its use of understatement as a narrative pose was "charming in its simplicity" but risked the possibility of being misunderstood:

> Many *New Masses* readers will question whether this [understatement] is a style suitable for the autobiography of a Negro writer of Hughes' importance; the national and class position of the writer should guide his selection of techniques and method, should influence his style. In the style of *The Big Sea* too much attention is apt to be given to the esthetic aspects of experience at the expense of its deeper meanings. Nor—this being a world in which few assumptions can be taken for granted—can the writer who depends upon understatement to convey these meanings be certain that they do not escape the reader. To be effective the Negro writer must be explicit; thus realistic; thus dramatic. (p. 20)

Ellison has remained somewhat suspicious of understatement in fiction. In a 1946 review he attacked his former model Hemingway for using the technique of understatement as a deceptive mask; beneath his terse prose,

Hemingway was taking defeatist, self-indulgent, reactionary positions. As late as 1953, when accepting the National Book Award, Ellison explained that he chose not to assume the narrative stance of the hard-boiled novel, "with its dedication to physical violence, social cynicism and understatement. Understatement depends, after all, upon commonly held assumptions and my minority status rendered all such assumptions questionable."

Ellison also criticized Hughes's self-portrayal as a picaresque figure rather than as a tough-minded activist whose self-awareness developed with experience. Using the terminology of André Malraux, Ellison observed that by projecting himself as a picaresque character,

> Hughes avoids analysis and deeper comment, and, in some instances, a deeper unity is lost. This is the unity which is formed by the mind's brooding over experience and transforming it into conscious thought. Negro writing needs this unity, through which the writer clarifies the experiences of the reader and allows him to recreate himself. (p. 20)

In a proper autobiography, wrote Ellison, the black writer is responsible for revealing to his readers the process whereby he gained his artistic consciousness in a world in which "most of the odds are against his doing so." In the South, "the attainment of such a consciousness is in itself a revolutionary act." The black writer's duty is to recognize that "the spread of this consciousness, added to the passion and sensitivity of the Negro people . . . will help create a new way of life in the United States" (p. 21).

The desire for a *conscious* protagonist in American literature has remained a trademark of Ellison's.[12] Lacking such a figure, a novel's political significance sometimes becomes opaque and its view of mankind too pessimistic. In 1942, reviewing William Attaway's *Blood on the Forge*, Ellison commended the author's presentation of southern-born blacks as harried and confused in the concrete mazes of the urban North. He pointed out that the artistic vision is incomplete, however, without the presence of a character whose consciousness is reborn in the North:

> Conceptually, Attaway grasped the destruction of the folk, but missed its rebirth on a higher level. The writer did not see that while the folk individual was being liquidated in the crucible of steel, he was also undergoing a fusion of new elements. Nor did Attaway see that the individual which emerged, blended of old and new, was better fitted for the problems of the industrial environ-

ment. As a result the author is so struck by the despair of his material that he fails to see any ground for hope in his material. Yet hope is there.[13]

Ellison's early desire for conscious heroes in American writing signals his eventual break with many of his literary and political friends, including Richard Wright.

When Ellison began writing for publication, clearly he was modeling his criticism and fiction after Richard Wright's. "Blueprint for Negro Writings," Wright's literary manifesto of 1937,[14] influenced the younger writer tremendously. Ellison's own major critical treatises of this period, "Recent Negro Fiction" and "Stormy Weather," both contain elaborations on Wright's "Blueprint" thesis, although these works are not as explicitly Marxist. In "Blueprint" Wright argues that the black writer's responsibility is to awaken the black masses to "the nationalist implications of their lives."[15] But no facile chauvinism is advanced here. Writing from a radical perspective and using modern techniques, the writer's further responsibility is to aid his readers to transcend mere nationalism and to achieve the international, revolutionary viewpoint of the Marxist. Certainly Ellison adhered to the spirit of these formulas in his own first published critical pieces and short stories. In his essay "Recent Negro Fiction" (1940) Ellison commended Wright's collection of stories, *Uncle Tom's Children*; as "Blueprint" demanded, these stories were valuable both as literature and as radical political statements. Of the characters in *Uncle Tom's Children* Ellison wrote:

> They are three-dimensional people, possessing an emotional and psychological complexity never before achieved in American Negro writing. Taking for its characters Negro men and women at bay in the oppressive Southern environment, the book represents one of the few instances in which an American Negro writer has successfully delineated the universals embodied in Negro experience. The result is an imaginative exploration of Southern Negro types.[16]

Especially impressive to Ellison was that certain of Wright's "Negro types" approached their fate consciously and through political conviction.

"Recent Negro Fiction" also hailed *Native Son* as one of the finest American novels of its time:

> In Wright's *Native Son* we have the first philosophical novel by an American Negro. This work possesses an artistry, penetration of

thought, and sheer emotional power that places it in the front rank of American fiction. Indeed, except for its characters and subject matter, it seems hardly identifiable with previous Negro fiction; but this, however, only in a superficial sense concealing factors of vital importance to the understanding of Negro writing.[17]

In this article, Ellison lauded *Native Son*'s technical excellence. Oddly enough, however, Ellison found nothing specific to praise in the novel and turned his review into a personal accolade of Wright as a man of distinction.

Wright, said Ellison, exemplified the high possibilities in black life. His books testified to "an artistic sensibility overcoming the social and cultural isolation of Negro life and moving into a world of unlimited intellectual and imaginative possibilities." A large part of the reason Wright was able to crash through racial barriers was that he was drawn to literary and political radicalism. His achievement of radical artistic consciousness amounted to a "rebirth equal only to the attainment of positions of advanced trade union leadership of Negro workers."[18]

General and fleeting, the praise *Native Son* received in "Recent Negro Fiction" was nonetheless almost its last from Ralph Ellison. In his major critical essays of 1946, 1957, and 1967—extended pieces in which Ellison surveyed the historical forms and functions of the American novel—he omitted serious mention of *Native Son* and Wright's other novels. In several interviews and in his response to Irving Howe's "Black Boys and Native Sons," however, Ellison did broach the subject of *Native Son*'s value. Whether because of his need to "kill off" an overbearing senior colleague and competitor (not to say literary parent),[19] or to shed one of his own tight-fitting literary skins, in his fifties and sixties commentaries Ellison berated *Native Son*'s realism and radicalism in sharp, icy terms.

Although Ellison recognized that *Native Son*'s Bigger Thomas represented humanity smoldering under the ashes of oppression and despair, he never could accept Bigger as an adequate portrait of the black American. To Ellison, this character was little more than an ideological formulation, a fragment of sociological mortar fired at the guilty conscience of white America. Ellison came to view him as a cousin of the romanticized types of the New Negro school and of Turpin's flat characters in *These Low Grounds*. Blacks themselves knew that black life was not as dimensionless and dull as Wright said. *Native Son* was too deterministic and anchored by Marxist ideology:

In *Native Son* [Ellison wrote in 1964] Wright began with the ideological proposition that what whites think of the Negro's reality is more important than what Negroes themselves know it to be. Hence Bigger Thomas was presented as a near-subhuman indictment of white oppression. He was designed to shock whites out of their apathy and end the circumstances out of which Wright insisted Bigger emerged. Here environment is all—and interestingly enough, environment conceived solely in terms of the physical, the non-conscious. Well, cut off my legs and call me Shorty! Kill my parents and throw me at the mercy of the court as an orphan! Wright could imagine Bigger, but Bigger could not possibly imagine Richard Wright. Wright saw to that.[20]

Bigger failed to represent vital essences in black experience and in universal human experience, and the character fell far short of being the conscious hero Ellison was calling for in his criticism of the forties. And though *Native Son* was bursting with the latest sociological findings and radical political perspectives, it seemed to present a shrunken, hardened view of blHck life, a view that was not, finaings and radical political perspectives, it seemed to present a shrunken, hardened view of black life, a view that was not, finally, *realistic*.

"Black Boy's Blues" is most notable for its argument that if Wright's autobiography was influenced by other studies of human personality, such as Joyce's *Portrait*, Dostoevsky's *House of the Dead*, and Nehru's *Toward Freedom*, its form is also shaped by the black American blues. Here Ellison explained that if the blues record life's pain, they also hint of the "possibility of conquering it through sheer toughness of spirit." Echoing Unamuno's philosophy of the "tragic sense of life," Ellison went on to define blues as

an assertion of the irrepressibly human over all circumstances whether created by others or by one's own human failings. They . . . consistently remind us of our limitations while encouraging us to see how far we can actually go . . . They are a corrective, an attempt to draw a line upon man's own limitless assertion . . . an impulse to keep the painful details of existence in one's aching consciousness, to finger its jagged grain and to transcend it not by the consolation of philosophy but by squeezing from it a near-tragic, near-comic lyricism. As a form the blues is an autobiographical chronicle of personal catastrophe expressed lyrically.[21]

In this review, Ellison also pointed out that the sharp-edged environment itself is the true subject of *Black Boy*: "Here it is not the individual that is the immediate focus, as in Joyce's *Stephen Hero*, but that upon which sensibility was nourished."[22] Defending in this instance Wright's strong emphasis on environment, Ellison wrote that "in the South the sensibilities of both blacks and whites are inhibited by the rigidly defined environment." He extended the definition of the environment in an interesting way: "man cannot express that which does not exist—either in the form of dreams, ideas or realities—in his environment."[23]

A passage from *Black Boy* which has proven troublesome to many of Wright's reviewers was quoted by Ellison in "Richard Wright's Blues":

> "Whenever I thought of the essential bleakness of black life in America, I knew that Negroes had never been allowed to catch the full spirit of Western Civilization, that they lived somehow in it but not of it. And when I brooded upon the cultural barrenness of black life, I wondered if clean, positive tenderness, love, honor, loyalty and the capacity to remember were native to man. I wondered if these human qualities were not fostered, won, struggled and suffered for, preserved in ritual from one generation to another."[24]

In 1945, Ellison defended even this statement: "How could the South, recognized as a major part of the backward third of the nation, nurture in the black, most brutalized section of its population, those forms of human relationships achievable only in the most highly developed areas of civilization?" Wright's statement was not uttered in despair, said Ellison. The author was only

> pointing out what should be obvious (especially to his Marxist critics) that Negro sensibility is historically conditioned; that Western culture must be won, confronted like the animal in a Spanish bullfight, dominated by the red shawl of codified experience and brought heaving to its knees.[25]

Eighteen years later Ellison ended his public defenses of *Black Boy*. As if smarting from acute "anxiety of influence," Ellison sharply attacked Wright's first autobiography as too harsh an indictment of black life and argued that, like *Native Son*, the autobiography was hollowed out to conform to Marxist ideology. In the later article, Ellison quoted the passage from *Black Boy* in which Wright presented a Jamesian catalogue of characteristics missing from black civilization:

> "After I had outlived the shocks of childhood, after the habit of reflection had been born in me, I used to mull over the strange absence of rea kindness in Negroes, how unstable was our

tenderness, how lacking in genuine passion we were, how void of great hope, how timid our joy, how bare our traditions, how hollow our memories, how lacking we were in those intangible sentiments that bind man to man and how shallow was even our despair. After I had learned other ways of life I used to brood upon the unconscious irony of those who felt that Negroes led so passionate an existence! I saw that what had been taken for our emotional strength was our negative confusions, our flights, our fears, our frenzy under pressure."[26]

"How awful," wrote Ellison, "that Wright found the facile answers of Marxism before he learned to use literature as a means for discovering the forms of American Negro humanity." When he made the decision to stress ideology and the power of negative aspects of environment rather than the individual's ability to overcome them, that was "doubtlessly . . . the beginning of Wright's exile." In response to Irving Howe, a staunch Wright defender who charged Ellison with being "literary to a fault" in *Invisible Man*, Ellison wrote, "Thank God I have never been so literary" as to question the value of black humanity.[27]

Although his first writings were strongly influenced by Wright, as the forties wore on, Ellison began to discover his own themes and styles. Ellison came to fear that his old mentor was more interested in politics than in art. Also he thought Wright "too driven or deprived or depraved" to know about many of the things ("weather, guns, dogs, horse, love *and* hate and impossible circumstances which to the courageous and dedicated could be turned into benefits and victories") which interested him and which he found in other writers, such as Hemingway.[28] Furthermore, he felt that Wright knew too little about the deeper meanings and the irrepressibly playful language of folklore and the blues.

Perhaps most important, Ellison wanted to depict black American life in a more positive light than Wright had done. Bored with what he found to be the tight outlines of the deterministic world painted by Wright, Ellison opted for the magic world of possibility he found outside the boundaries of literary realism. When, as a student of literature and a writer, Ellison plunged "back into the shadow of the past where time hovers ghostlike" and surveyed the totality of black American life as expressed in literature and folklore, he perceived richness and a promise of heroism where, in his view, Wright and many authors of the thirties saw only the awesome environment and despair.

Still, it should be pointed out that Ellison—disdainful of the idea of being considered "the new Richard Wright"—pursued his artistic individuality so vigorously that at a certain stage in his career he seems to have begun *looking* for points of direct departure from the compelling and eloquently described world of the older writer. Ellison even seems to have stopped being able to read Wright seriously. If we had no more commentary on Wright's fictional world than Ellison's, we might forget that *Black Boy* and *Native Son* are works full of ironies, allusions, complexities of characterization; that these works sound the American mainstream and find it now shallow and polluted, now deep and wonderfully mysterious. We would forget too that *Invisible Man* springs not full-formed from a single writer's experience—no novel does. It comes from Dostoevsky, Joyce, Hemingway; and, no less so, from Richard Wright whose *Native Son*, "The Man Who Lived Underground," and *Black Boy* (that first-person "blues" narrative about a bright boy who endures everything, including a battle royal) seem to have been at Ellison's elbow as he was creating *Invisible Man*.

Ellison wrote a number of political tracts in the thirties and forties—propaganda pieces he has called them[29]—which are of interest particularly for their antirealist strain, and for the shift of focus we can see in them from the environment to the individual who manages to endure in heroic fashion. In 1967 Ellison explained his perspective on black American heroism, a viewpoint that was developing in the thirties and forties:

> I . . . point to the heroic component of our experience for these seem to me truths which we [blacks] have long lived by but which we must now recognize consciously. And I am not denying the negative things which have happened to us and which continue to happen . . . But literature teaches us that mankind has always defined itself *against* the negatives thrown it by both society and the universe. It is the human will, human hope, and human effort which make the difference. Let's not forget that the great tragedies not only treat of negative matters, of violence, brutalities, defeats, but they treat them within a context of man's will to act, to challenge reality and to snatch triumph from the teeth of destruction.[30]

There is little heroic action in Ellison's first protest article for *New Masses*, "Judge Lynch in New York," in August 1939 (which appeared in *Negro Digest* a year later, revised and shortened), a sharp attack on the antiblack and antisemitic actions of Father Coughlin and his "Christian

Front" followers.[31] With its Hemingway-like attention to narrative detail and use of choppy sentences with phrases linked by conjunction after conjunction, "Judge Lynch in New York" is a carefully written story depicting black boys whose hard times in New York seem to leave them no choice except to organize and to fight back. The article itself proved to be an effective weapon of protest. Shortly after it appeared, a wave of protest was directed against the police precinct involved, and one day the station chiefs came to the front door of Ellison's Hamilton Street apartment. "At first I was upset," he recalls, "but then I realized that since these guys had come to my *apartment* instead of having me dragged to the *station*, they were not out to beat me up. It meant my writing had been effective and they had come to me for information."[32]

Reporting for *New Masses* on the Third National Negro Congress held in the spring of 1940, Ellison drove with five friends to Washington, D.C. In the resulting protest article, "A Congress Jim Crow Didn't Attend," Ellison accentuated leftist issues of the day: exploitation of workers, segregated housing, segregated public facilities, lynching. Trade unionism, black nationalism, and (since the black "nation" as Ellison envisioned it would cooperate with other American groups) integration were offered as solutions to the problems of black Americans. In this article Ellison also concentrated on the heroics of particular leaders of the Movement. "Suddenly I realized that the age of the Negro hero had returned to American life."[33]

For "A Congress Jim Crow Didn't Attend" Ellison used a deadpan tone, short sentences, and understatement to indicate a sense of barely controlled excitement and tension:

> We drove all night to beat the crowd . . . Fog hung over the Delaware roads, over the fields and creeks, so that we could not tell water from grass, except in spots where the fog had lifted . . . coming out of some town the driver failed to see a road marker and almost wrecked the car. It shook us awake and we talked to keep the driver alert. (p. 8)

When they saw some soldiers outside Baltimore, Ellison "asked where they were going and was told there was an army camp near by. Someone said that I would find out 'soon enough' and I laughed and said that I was a black Yank and was not coming."

The National Negro Congress hall and residences seemed to provide a grand setting for heroic action against a backdrop of American economic and moral bankruptcy. Washington was the capital of legalized Jim Crow where blacks were boxed into a corner of the city and where downtown restaurants were strictly segregated. But "stretched out beneath the long shadow of Washington's monument," convention delegates, protesting discrimination in hotel accommodations, pitched tents "like those discovered by Steinbeck's Joads." The Congress' auditorium was appropriately Olympian:

> The carpet is thick and deep blue, the ceiling high and soothing to the eyes. In front, on both sides of the speakers' platform, there are gigantic columns that seem to pull you upward, out of yourself, as your eyes follow them aloft. The auditorium had that overwhelming air usually associated with huge churches, and I remembered what André Malraux once said about the factory becoming for the workers what the cathedral was, and that they must come to see in it not ideal gods, but human power struggling against the earth . . . The building is dedicated to labor. I hoped that what was to happen there during the Congress would help bring nearer that transformation of which Malraux wrote . . . It *was*, for the three days of the Convention, sacred ground. (p. 6)

Upon the Congress' sacred ground blacks and whites, young and old, farmers and city people mingled to voice their opposition to racist and capitalist exploitation.

After the convention's official speech making subsided, Ellison searched the corridors for "those from down where being militant, being a man, carries a threat of dispossession, of flogging, of rape charges, of lynching death . . . those whose very presence means a danger faced and a fear conquered, and danger to be faced again" (pp. 6-7). James McMillan, a preacher and coalminer from Kentucky who had "felt the sting of a lynch-rope around his neck and lived to tell about it," was one of these. "His first question is, 'What's being done about the Anti-Lynching Bill?' " There were steelworkers and farmers and "a tall man in a cattleman's hat" who said, "All my life I been wanting to see some of our Negro leaders go down there to Congress and let them know how we felt about things. Didn't think I'd live to see it, but it happened." John P. Davis and Ben Davis "got [reactionary Congressman Martin] Dies told." "That's why I'm here this morning," said the man in the cattleman's hat. The convention's most outstanding figures, however, were Owen Whitfield (described by Ellison in an earlier *New Masses* article, "Camp Lost Colony"), a tall black woman from Arkansas, and Hank Johnson from Chicago.

Whitfield talked to the group with the skill of a country preacher, and the farm people responded "Amen!" and "It's the truth!" Ellison noted that Whitfield's "was not a speech from above" like the address of A. Phillip Randolph, whom Ellison at that time found to be a timid and pretentious "red-baiter" (p. 6). In a Whitmanesque burst of enthusiasm, Ellison wrote that "Whitfield is of the earth and his speech is of the earth, and I said 'Amen' with the farmers." This black man spoke "with pride of his Missouri people" of Camp Lost Colony, and "the audience is with him when he lashes out at leaders who avoid positive action out of fear of their 'status' . . . His is the pride of one who knows what it means to fight and win. He made the nation listen to the voices of his people" (p. 3).

The Arkansas woman, with strands of gray hair showing from beneath her straw hat, was president of her local CIO-affiliated union of 260 members. Unused to speaking into a microphone, she had to be shown how to stand before it. Using his ability to capture speech patterns without resorting to obstructive phonetical transcription (a skill he was working on while doing interviews for the Writers' Project), Ellison quoted the woman's plain talk:

> Ladies and gentlemen, I'm here to tell youall that we in Arkansas is having a tight time. Folks down there is working for sixty and seventy cents a day. Folk with kids, I mean. Now youall know that ain't enough fo' no folks with children to be gitting. I come up here to tell youall about it; and to ask youall if there's *anything* youall can do fo' us down in Arkansas, please to do it. I was proud to come. I mean I was proud to come to this Congress. I was proud my people sent me. You know, we got other people down there who wants to see the hard tasks done. But they's shaky. They's scaird they'd be moved off the land. Well, I tell 'em that they moving every day anyhow! . . . They bet' not harm me. An' if they was to kill me, they'd have to *bury* me. So I'm just on they hands. I'm looking for better conditions for my people. (pp. 7-8)

Where, wondered Ellison, did this woman acquire her "calm dignity"? After her speech he asked if religion were her secret. "Well, son," she replied, "we use to go to the graveyard and preach to folks 'bout heaven.' But I done found out that the way to serve Christ is by helping folks here on earth" (p. 8).

Hank Johnson, a CIO organizer from Chicago, represented an example of an urban hero. Speaking against black participation in the world war, he said, "How can I defend America right or wrong? I am as good an American as anybody, but what would I do if I went down round my home in Austin, Texas, and reported some spies, and got myself lynched?" Johnson's manner and words impressed Ellison greatly. Here was a black southerner who had moved north and been transformed by the Movement:

> What Hank Johnson did to me is hard to convey. I have seen many of my friends frustrated in their efforts to create themselves. They are boys full of protest and indignation which has no social outlet. They are unhappy working at jobs they hate, living under restrictions they hate. Hank Johnson was like one of them *transformed*. He is full of indignation but indignation that has found a direction. When he spoke all the violence that America has made our Negro heritage was flowing from him transformed into a will to change a civilization. (p. 8)

Hank Johnson probably provided one of the models for the narrator of *Invisible Man*, particularly at the point when the Invisible Man declares that he feels suddenly more human and transformed because of his membership in the radical group, the Brotherhood.

In "A Congress Jim Crow Didn't Attend," Ellison excitedly announced that transformed blacks like Whitfield, Johnson, and the Arkansas woman represented "a new pole of leadership . . . among the Negro people and the National Negro Congress is their organization." When the resolution to join forces with the CIO was brought before the Congress, and A. Phillip Randolph (whom the far-left faction had successfully ousted from the chairmanship) protested that such a coalition would invite controversy, the transformed blacks shouted back from the floor. "Peonage," one delegate yelled, "Anti-Lynch Bill, poll tax, these are our issues in American life, and some of us will have to die for them! Yes, we want to join with the CIO! We cannot stop for controversy." Ellison wrote that there "in the faces of my people I saw strength. There with the whites in the audience I saw the positive forces of civilization and the best guarantee of America's future" (p. 8).

At a time when the undertow of Ellison's disagreement with left-wing politics was already strong, the Communist Party's war policies drove Ellison and many other blacks with similar political convictions away from the ranks of the organized Left. When, as Ellison pointed out in 1944, the party lent its "shame-faced support" to the segregated United States armed forces, many blacks became bitterly doubtful of the supposedly radical group's goodwill toward minorities. The party also made the error of ignoring the fact that "little Hitlers" (Ellison's term for white

American racists) plagued blacks at home; for blacks the war against fascism had to continue on the home front as well as overseas. When the party attacked this position as "narrowly nationalistic," it seemed to Ellison that Russian foreign policy had more sway in the American party than did the exigencies of its local black members. In an interview over twenty years later, Ellison commented: "The Communists recognized no plurality of interests and were really responding to the necessities of Soviet foreign policy, and when the war came home, Negroes got caught and were made expedient in the shifting of policy."[34]

That many blacks left the party resulted too from what Ellison has termed a "paternalistic relationship" between white party leaders and black members. In his acerbic 1944 review of Myrdal's *An American Dilemma*, Ellison said that the Community Party was no more sincere in its interest in black issues than was the New Deal administration. But "sincerity," he observed, "is not a quality one expects from a political party, not even revolutionary ones. To question their sincerity makes room for the old idea of paternalism, and the corny notion that these groups have an obligation to do something *for* the Negro."[35]

In *Invisible Man* the protagonist's decision to give up his wholehearted support for the Brotherhood is based on his discovery that the radical group is capable of selfish trickery and burdened with racism, the old American disease. The Brotherhood viciously sacrifices Harlem's interests for the sake of "international" goals and tries to mold the Invisible Man into their conception of The Good Negro: one passively willing to use his energy and his art (his oratory) exactly as the party commands. The Brotherhood is the Community Party, to a large degree. But Ellison also wanted the Brotherhood to be seen in a larger context: the Communist Party was not the only group of white American political activists to betray their black countrymen or to use blacks and their art for narrow political ends. Ellison's experience with the Communists made it clear to him, however, that this pattern of black betrayal continued to be manifest throughout contemporary American society.

In 1942 Ellison quit the Federal Writers' Project to become managing editor of *The Negro Quarterly*, and he worked on its staff for one year, leaving just before the journal folded. Angelo Herndon, just breaking away from the Communists, was editor of this "Review of Negro Life and Culture," which featured leftist artists and scholars, black and white. Sterling A. Brown, Herbert Aptheker, Richard Wright, Normon McLeod, J. Saunders Redding, E. Franklin Frazier, Owen Dodson, and Stanley Edgar Hyman all contributed to the journal during its brief existence; it lasted only four issues before collapsing. For *The Negro Quar-*

terly Ellison wrote a review of William Attaway's novel *Blood on the Forge*, and an unsigned editorial comment, which obliquely criticized the Communist Party; it also advocated that black leaders concentrate more on the interests and needs of blacks.

In the editorial comment, Ellison called for black unity and self-determination. He warned that when black leadership is provided from outside the black community,

> Negro people are exploited by others; either for the good ends of democratic groups or for the bad ends of fascist groups . . . As long as Negroes fail to centralize their power, they will always play the role of sacrificial goat, they will always be "expendable." Freedom, after all, cannot be imported or acquired through an act of philanthropy, it must be won.[36]

In this comment, as in several of Ellison's early political writings, the artist inadvertently upstages the political analyst. Black leaders, he argued, must realize that the secret to the consolidation of black power resides in their ability to analyze and use the lore and language of black Americans. Without understanding Afro-American myths and symbols, no black leader can lead with success, regardless of his program's merits.

> Much in Negro life remains a mystery; perhaps the zoot suit conceals profound political meanings; perhaps the symmetrical frenzy of the Lindy-hop conceals clues to great potential power—if only Negro leaders would solve this riddle. On this knowledge depends the effectiveness of any slogan or tactic . . . They will be accepted by the Negro masses only to the extent that they are helped to see the bright star of their hopes through the fog of their daily experiences. The problem is psychological; it will be solved only by a Negro leadership that is aware of the psychological attitude and incipient forms of action which the black masses reveal in their emotion-charged myths, symbols and wartime folklore. (p. 300)

Ellison called here for a more efficient propaganda effort by black leaders and for their increased sympathy with the political interests of the black masses. He also expressed his growing awareness that artists need not join a party or carry a banner: folk art has political and even universal meanings. He went on to explore the relation of folklore, politics, and literature most enthusiastically in his own early short stories, his apprentice work.

4

Apprenticeship

The years 1939 to 1944 were an apprenticeship for Ellison who, in a *New York Post* feature story of 1943, was bylined as "a short story writer." He published eight stories during this crucial five-year span, and his writing grew in eloquence and complexity from story to story. He wrote many more stories than he tried to publish, looking upon them as practice pieces, "five-finger exercises." Operating in an experimental attitude, Ellison would start writing a story by jotting down a few themes and then try to develop them into plots, scenes, images, and characters.

His first short stories ("Slick Gonna Learn" and "The Birthmark") are in the realistic and naturalistic mold and highlighted the "jagged edges" of the black American environment. And these first stories offer explicitly political resolutions to the dilemmas they pose. As early as 1940, however, as Ellison began to focus on his own Oklahoma background, his vision was not so much that of a political realist as a "regionalist": his first Buster and Riley stories ("Afternoon," "Mister Toussan," and "That I Had the Wings") explore the language, folklore, and unique features of a southwestern town as seen by two curious and daring black boys. "In a Strange Country" is a transitional wartime story, important because of its heightened technical complexity. Also, here a protagonist first declares his inexorable *Americanness* as well as his unmistakable blackness.

"Flying Home" and "King of the Bingo Game" are more than apprentice pieces. In these works Ellison discovered his surrealist or "antirealist" voice and managed to integrate folklore, ritual, politics, history, and an absurdist vision of American experience in a way that may be termed Ellisonian. The two stories center on the individual and his efforts to cope with a world become machine-mad and meaningless; in both, a black protagonist struggles to confront the question, Who am I? Thus Ellison's pre-*Invisible Man* stories become increasingly engaging and multidimensional as the author's interest shifts: the power of the environment to maim the politically unaware black American gives way to the power of the black American, once aware of his black and American traditions and values, to overcome.

Ellison began "Slick Gonna Learn" in Dayton, while he was poring over stories by his favorite writers and studying their styles. Despite Ellison's disclaimers, this story bears the definite influence not only of Hemingway but of the Farrell and Drieser school of naturalism, especially its star pupil, Richard Wright. Appearing with the note, "From an Unpublished First Novel," and containing a one-paragraph "Author's Synopsis" of the plot preceding the story's action, this first published story was useful to the twenty-five-year-old writer. Though he would soon repudiate many of its attitudes toward life and literature, "Slick Gonna Learn" at least taught Ellison that he did not yet know how to organize a novel.

Set in the Deep South, the situation of "Slick Gonna Learn" is in places typical of the proletarian stories of the thirties, where crisp political themes and plots verge on melodrama and slapstick. Just when his pregnant wife most urgently needs a doctor's care, Slick is laid off his job at the Hopkins plant and is left with only a few dollars to his name. Desperate for cash, he finds himself in a crap game and his hand is cold. When he loses his last two dollars and asks Bostic, a local pimp, for a five-dollar loan, Bostic refuses. The pimp then suggests that Slick's wife might earn his money back for him: "If it's goodnough to marry, it's goodnough to sell." Blind with fury, Slick attacks both Bostic and a white policeman on the scene. For striking a white man, Slick finds himself in court.[1]

"You niggers are always fighting, aren't you, boy," remarks the judge. "Boy," he then asks, "are you working?" When Slick answers "Nawsuh," the judge wants to know: "Did you *ever* work?" Slick explains that he has just been laid off at the plant. "Are you married, or just living with one of those high yellas over there on the West Side?" When in reply to this barbed question Slick fails, momentarily, to add the customary "-suh," the judge takes offense until Slick makes the correction. "I thought you had forgotten yourself," he says. Discovering that Slick's wife is pregnant, the judge says, "Leave it to the niggers to have kids." Having blandly assaulted his defendant with this chain of racial taunts, he releases Slick from custody.

As in several Wright stories and novels, the protagonist achieves a sense of his power and worth as a human being through violence. Hitting the officer in the midst of confusion is an action unconsciously willed by Slick; as such it produces a healthy solution, at least psychologically, to the dilemma of "living Jim Crow." And when he is released from the courtroom a free man despite his tabooed crime, Slick swaggers with a supercharged sense of his manhood. "Slick was startled. For a moment he had forgotten [the policeman] at his side. He came to a sudden stop. He had knocked the hell out of a white man and gotten away with it! The *law* had let him go. Something seemed to surge in his mind."

Another central theme of "Slick" is that the protagonist must learn to view his predicament not only in a racial context, but from the perspective of the incipient class revolution. The firing of Slick precipitates the story's crisis. And the judge doesn't send Slick to jail in order to avoid attracting the attention of city reporters, in town to investigate the Hopkins plant layoffs. Seeing Slick released from court unpunished, the police take matters into their own hands and gang Slick on his way home in the rain. But suddenly the car radio begins to squawk: "Car number eleven proceed to the Hopkins plant immediately. Riot call. East gate of factory yard threatened by strikers. Disperse mob." Thwarted again, the policemen kick Slick a few times and leave him in a ditch dodging their gunfire—saved again by the workers.

Black and white workers' cooperation is dramatized in the story's final scene. Stumbling down the highway in the rain, Slick is hailed by a white truck driver who thinks the limping man has been hit by a car. When he sees the white man's truck pulling to a halt, Slick thinks, "Oh no, *another* one." But the driver turns out to be genuinely humane. "I don't usually pick up riders, lose my job if I did," the white man says. "But hell! a man is still a man and it's nasty as hell tonight." The story ends in a moment of Slick's confusion and perception: " 'Them white dawgs!' he thought. He turned and watched the man bent over the steering wheel, studying his face and tried to connect him with the experiences of the day as the truck roared through the rain to the city" (p. 16).

Clearly Slick is not truly "slick" but *lucky* to have lived through the day. His task is to learn the connections between his personal rebellions and those of his white and black working-class brethren. Concerted struggle would lead, Ellison hoped, to world revolution.

Also stamped in the naturalistic mold is "The Birthmark," Ellison's second published story. Originally published in *New Masses* and reprinted in *Negro World Digest*, it was listed by John O'Brien as one of the best stories of 1940. The action of this lynching story is again stark and violent; and again the political meanings preside. A black youngster named Willie has been lynched. His brother Matt and sister Clara, instructed that the boy has been hit accidentally by a car, are summoned to identify the body. Like "Slick Gonna Learn," this story deals with the harshness of black life in the segregated South. It raises questions that southern blacks had to face daily: How do you receive your inevitable dose of injustice? Passively? At what Cost to your pride and humanity? Violently? At what cost to your health? And, taking its title from a tale by Hawthorne, this story also causes us to wonder what the birthmark is. What is the cost of its removal?

Outwardly Matt seems very passive. Whites order him about and refer to him as "boy." In order to identify the body on the highway, Matt searches for the birthmark on Willie's stomach and sees that the youth has been castrated. "Don't no car do nothing like that," he remarks. For Matt's impudence a policeman smashes him in the back with his gun barrel and yells, "We don't have no lynchings in this state no more!" Furthermore, he adds, Matt and Clara had better remember that fact " 'cause a car might hit *you*. Understand what I mean?" He glares at Matt, who feels suddenly castrated himself and strains to control his anger. "*If he only didn't have that gun*," he thinks, watching the policeman. But knowing that if he starts a fight it would probably mean his own death and possibly Clara's, Matt says, "Yes suh . . . I understand suh."[2] Clara, on the other hand, is enraged. "They lynched Willie, Matt," she shouts. "They done lynched our little brother . . . I know what I'm saying. I ain't gonna be the same after this, Matt, and I want to see it all so's I'll never forget why." Perhaps, she says, if the family had been more outspoken in the past, Willie would be alive.

Both "Slick Gonna Learn" and "The Birthmark" involve black characters who are terrorized by a viciously racist society. Described by a distant narrator in reportorial terms, these characters are not especially particularized in speech, dress, or manner. As in most black proletarian stories, they appear as ordinary representatives of the black masses caught in the courtrooms and squad cars and on the highways of southern towns. Much of the dialogue occurs at close, hot range between poor, innocent blacks and mean white lawmen.

Although in these stories one hears the Hemingway-like staccato sentences and repetitions, the action is often much more explicit than

Hemingway's; it is, indeed, overstated (in the manner of Wright) in order to shock readers out of their complacency. Whereas in Hemingway's "Hills Like White Elephants," for example, readers are made to piece together for themselves the story's plot and meaning, Ellison leads his readers straight to the gruesome scene of the murder in "The Birthmark": "The flesh was hacked and pounded as though it had been beaten with hammers . . . The ribs had been caved in. The flesh was bruised and torn . . . Below his navel . . . was only a bloody mound of torn flesh and hair." The significance of this tale could never be mistaken.

Overt political ideology also informs Ellison's first two stories. As in much of Wright's early work, "Slick" and "Birthmark" urge readers to join leftist political organizations to combat racial and capitalist injustices. Ellison portrays black Americans as the hapless, angry victims of social abuse, trapped in the cul-de-sacs of their environment; their birthmark, like Willie's, is a scar of castration. It is also the mark of blackness, which covers their bodies and limits their freedom in the New World. Ritually, the lynching of Willie signifies white society's deadly attempt to remove America's black blemish, to get shut of the Negro. According to young Ellison, the solution—if one exists—is to channel black rage into clearly defined political action.

Ellison wrote three Buster-Riley stories in the forties and another, "A Coupla Scalped Indians," in 1956; Buster also turns up in a story published in 1970, "Song of Innocence." These stories (some of which are subtitled "offshoots" or forerunners of novels) involve two nine- or ten-year-old black boys, Buster and Riley, who grow up in an Oklahoma town. The first of these, "Afternoon," marks a departure for the author in that it has no clear political brunt. Buster and Riley are rambunctious, curious boys who explore their world and resist their families' attempts to control them. In theme and tone the story reminds one of Mark Twain.

Like Aunt Polly and other stalwart parental figures (especially the women) in Mark Twain's fiction, Buster's and Riley's parents uphold their community's traditional (and usually most conservative) values. The boys grudgingly accept some of these values (witness their guilt when they fail to obey their parents), and they duck others. Ellison has pointed out that if the women in his fiction possess a certain harshness, it is a tender harshness; they temper and prepare their sons for a difficult life as black men.[3] Sometimes, too, the harshness of Ellison's black maternal figures reflects the meanness of their circumstances.

Riley's mother, who has no husband at home, works hard both around her own house and for the white folks. She calls Riley a lazy rascal for failing to help her with the wash and for claiming not to know she needs him. Her voice hits him "like a slap in the face": " 'You didnt know! Lawd, I dont know why I had to have a chile like you. I work my fingers to the bone to keep you looking decent and thats the way you 'preciates it. You didnt know!' " Feeling guilty, Buster stands in the kitchen, "looking like a dying calf," until his mother tells him to go out to play and to leave her alone. Buster senses that something more than his irresponsibility has caused his mother to snap at him, and he quickly obeys her now. He knows that "she was like this whenever something went wrong with her and the white folks . . . Let them white folks make her mad," he tells Riley, "and I catch hell."[4]

Riley, whose home life is much rougher than Buster's, also feels that his parents' white employers cause them to flare up against him. He tells Buster that one night his father became so possessed by rage that the old man intended to whip his son with a piece of wire. Another evening he was prepared to tie Riley in a gunny sack and smoke him like a ham. Like Huck Finn's vagabond father, Riley's father is so mean, observes Riley, "he even hates hisself." His crazy violence is due, we are told, to his slave mentality. Riley's mother saves the boy from being cut up and "smoked": "My ole lady stopped 'im. Told 'im he bet' not . . . She said, 'Dont you come treating no child of mine like no slave. Your Ma mighta raised you like a slave, but I aint raising him like that an you bet' not harm a hair of his head' " (p. 36).

Through their identification with certain mighty heroes from fact, folklore, and fiction, Buster and Riley feel capable of overcoming all antagonists. "You just wait til I get big," says Riley. "I'm gonna beat the hell outta my ole man. I'm gonna learn how to box like Jack Johnson just so I can beat his ass." Jack Johnson, "first colored heavyweight champion of the whole wide world . . . fast as a cat . . . better even than Joe Louis," is one hero Riley has heard of, ironically, from his father, who sometimes sings:

> If it hadn't a been
> for the referee
> Jack Johnson woulda killed
> Jim Jefferie. (p. 36)

Jack Johnson could conquer "the whole wide world": not only fathers but white folks too.[5] "Wonder where he is now," says Buster. "I don't know," answers Riley, "up North in New York, I guess. But I bet *wherever* he is, ain't nobody messing with him" (p. 36).

Buster and Riley are given rebel, "mannish" strength from an old folk hero. "Mister Rabbit" the trickster comes to Buster's mind, and the two boys chant a kind of song of praise:

> Well, I met Mister Rabbit
> down by the pea vine
> 'An I asked him where's he gwine
> Well he said Just kiss my behind
> And he skipped on down the pea vine. (p. 30)

Like Mark Twain's Huck and Tom, Buster and Riley are very superstitious. And, similarly, superstition is more than ignorant hokus-pokus; it provides Buster and Riley a means for comprehending and humanizing the world they live in. Their exchange concerning a dead alley cat shows the Twain influence very strongly:

> Buster suddenly stopped and grabbed his nose.
> "Look at that ole dead cat!"
> "Aint on my mama's table."
> "Mine neither!"
> "You better spit on it, else you'll have it for supper," Buster said.
> They spat on the maggot-ridden body and moved on.
> "Always a lots a dead cats in the alley. Wonder why?"
> "Dogs get em, I guess."
> "My dog ate so many dead cats once he went crazy and died," said Riley.
> "I don't like cats. They too sly."
> "Sho stinks!"
> "I'm holding my breath."
> "Me too." (pp. 30-31)

In "Afternoon" Ellison seems to have decided that his naturalistic stories, concentrating on the brutalities of existence and on the moment of violent confrontation, missed some vital aspects of life as he himself had lived it. Buster and Riley note things that Slick, Matt, and Clara, besieged by the terrors of their predicaments, cannot. They hear the hum of electricity in the telephone wires and smell the creosote of black paint on the poles. They are fascinated by the sharp cackling of hens and by the sound of someone diligently practicing scales on a piano. They hear the drumming of woodpeckers and the thumping of oilwells. Buster watches the tiny globe of milk that glistens on his toe when he breaks a sprig of milkweed between his bare toes.

Buster and Riley, whose names together announce their sturdiness and high-spiritedness, are aware of social injustices; but they test the values of their society and dare it *not* to make a place for them.

Tightly woven and powerful, "Mister Toussan" (1941) is the finest of the Buster-Riley stories. It concerns a white man, Mr. Rogan, who refuses to allow the boys to eat cherries from his tree. Folklore, overheard and traded by Buster and Riley, pulls their thoughts into flight, to freedom and deliverance on the coat-tails of a folk hero. Like "Afternoon," this story represents an implicit criticism of the naturalists, who often tended to consider folklore as the escapist and ignorant mutterings of defeated men and women.

The spiritual "All God's Chillun," sung by Riley's mother above the noise of the machine she uses to sew for the white folks, fortifies the boys' conviction that they have a kind of sacred right to the cherries. She sings:

> I got wings, you got wings,
> All God's chillun got a-wings
> When I git to heaven gonna put on my wings
> Gonna shout all ovah God's heaven.[6]

The boys themselves express this yearning for freedom in secular terms. Buster says that if he had wings,

> "Shucks, I'd outfly an eagle, I wouldn't stop flying till I was a million, billion, trillion, zillion miles away from this ole town."
> "Where'd you go, man?"
> "Up North, maybe to Chicago."
> "Man, if I had wings I wouldn't never settle down."
> "Me, neither, with wings you could go anywhere, even up to the sun, if it wasn't too hot . . ."
> ". . . I'd go to New York. . . ."
> "Even around the stars. . . ."
> "Or Dee-troit, Michigan. . . ."
> "You could git some cheese off the moon and some milk from the Milkyway. . . ."
> "I bet I'd loop-the-loop. . . ."
> "An parachute." (pp. 142-143)

Buster and Riley's exclamations and brags link the heaven of the spiritual to other mythic realms, and to the promised land of the north-bound, free-rambling bluesman.

The boys dream too about a flight through time and tell the tale of "Mister Toussan," inflating the Haitian revolution of 1781 and Toussaint L'Ouverture's part in it to gigantic dimensions. In fact, this stretched version of the incident serves to remind us that, at the time of the actual Haitian revolt, the tale of the black revolutionary grew into a kind of folktale and spread like wildfire among American slaves.[7]

The theme of the "Toussan" tale-within-a-tale affirms the black folk (and, of course, the universal) values of bravery and independence; also its very form, based on the call/response pattern in sermons, songs, and stories, constitutes a celebration of black American culture. At the start of the tale, Riley answers Buster, who preaches with fire and tempo, beginning his lesson by quoting his source, in this case his favorite schoolteacher.

> "Really, man, she said that Toussan and his men got up on one of them African mountains and shot down them peckerwood soldiers fass as they'd try to come up . . ."
> "Why good-God-amighty!" yelled Riley.
> "Oh boy, they shot 'em down!" chanted Buster.
> "Tell me about it, man!"
> "And they throwed 'em off the mountain . . ."
> ". . . Goool-leee! . . ."
> ". . . And Toussan drove 'em cross the sand . . ."
> ". . . And where'd ole Toussan run 'em?"
> "Down to the water, man . . ."
> "To the river water . . ."
> ". . . Where some great big old boats was waiting for 'em . . ."
> "Go on, Buster!"
> "An' Toussan shot into them boats . . . Boy, till them peckerwoods hollered 'Please, please, *Please*, Mister Toussan . . .'"
> "We'll be good," broke in Riley.
> "Thass right, man," said Buster excitedly. He clapped his hands and kicked his heels against the earth, his black face glowing in a burst of rhythmic joy.
> ". . . He said in his big, deep voice, 'You all peckerwoods better be good, 'cause this is Sweet Papa Toussan talking and my nigguhs is crazy about white meat!' " (pp. 144, 146-147)

That the facts of the story are less important than its heroic and folk mode is indicated when Riley (who knew absolutely nothing a moment before about Toussaint L'Ouverture, but who is quite conversant in black vernacular forms) finishes telling it:

"Come on, watch me do it now, Buster. Now I bet old Toussan looked down at them white folks standing just about like this and said in a soft easy voice: 'Aint I done begged you white folks to quit messin' with me?' "

Riley completes the story by leaping to his feet and fencing artfully with five imaginary soldiers before he runs each through with his imaginary sword. "Yeah," confirms Buster, "Thass 'bout the way it was."

Buster and Riley are—to say the least—dubious historians of the Haitian revolt, but they are excellent storytellers. They bobble the facts (assuming, for example, that Haiti is in Africa), but they convey the spirit and essence of the *tale*: a black hero has stepped forward to fight and deliver his people from white dominance. In their stylized version of the revolutionary story, they conjure "Good . . . clean . . . mean . . . sooopreme Sweet Papa Toussan" in the image of the mighty High John the Conqueror and the children's game hero, King of the Mountain. This Sweet Papa is even based on the God, Jesus, Daniel, and Moses of many black sacred folk forms: heroes battling against all odds for their people's freedom. To save the Chosen People (who, in many black spirituals and sermons, appear as black Americans in the Egyptland of America), God of the Old Testament sank Pharoah's army in the depths of the Red Sea. "Pharoah's army got drownded," goes one spiritual, "Oh Mary, don't you weep." In another, "Every Time I Feel the Spirit," God threatens his wayward children:

> Upon the mountain my Lord spoke,
> Out of his mouth came fire and smoke.
> In the valley on my knees,
> Asked my Lord, Have mercy, please.[8]

Like the awesome God of the spirituals, Mister Toussan comes down the mountain to deliver his people from bondage. Toussan was "a fightin' son-of-a-gun, wasn't he, man"? says Riley. "Oh yes," answers Buster, "he didn't stand for no foolishness."

To increase the folkloric effect of "Mister Toussan," this short story begins and ends with signatory rhymes. It opens with:

> Once upon a time
> The goose drink wine
> Monkey chew tobacco
> And he spit white lime. (p. 140)

The story ends when Riley dances barefoot, chanting:

> Iron is iron
> And tin is tin
> And that's the way . . .
> The story . . . ends. (p. 151)

Just before this final rhyme, Buster suggests that they sneak around the back of Rogan's house to steal some cherries. The boys' identification with Toussan, as well as with Africa and angels, moves them to action. They have a right to break away from unjust societal restrictions: to assert their human rights over Rogan's property rights. According to *The Negro in New York*, the Haitian revolutionary's success "fired the imagination of the sorebeset blacks and gave them encouragement. More important still, the Haitian revolt gave welcome birth to a race-consciousness among Negroes of the world."[9] Certainly as it came down to Buster and Riley, the Toussan story inspired elaborate "lying" and a renewed desire to be free—even, if necessary, to steal freedom.

"That I Had the Wings," based on a childhood experience involving Ellison, his brother Herbert, and Frank Mead, a neighbor in Oklahoma City, appeared in the magazine *Common Ground* in 1943. In this story, Riley has been confined to his backyard for the day because he fell off the church roof chasing pigeons the day before. Completely unpenitent for this devilment, Riley convinces Buster that they can teach Ole Bill the rooster to fly. Here again it is Riley (or any of us little guys) against authority: "As always Aunt Kate has made him feel guilty, as though he had done something wrong which he could never remember." Birds and flight again are central metaphors. And once more Riley and Buster get a sense of power through a folk hero—for that is what they transform Ole Bill into—and through images in folk rhymes.

Riley's identification with a baby bird's first attempt to fly inspires him to recite a "wicked verse."

> If I was the President
> Of these United States
> I'd eat good chocolate candy bars
> An swing on the White House gates—
> Great-God-a-mighty man—
> I'd swing on them White House gates.[10]

Poor Aunt Kate hears Riley and is aghast. The boy's sacrilegious expression of racially taboo ambitions and wild disregard for white power symbols is senseless, sinful, and perhaps even a danger to himself and his family: "The Lawd don't like it an white folks wouldn't neither" (p. 31). In place of the wicked rhyme she suggests the church song, "If I Had the Wings of a Dove." But Riley accepts neither Aunt Kate's judgment of him nor her song. Instead he mutters a parody:

> If I had the wings of a dove, Aunt Kate,
> I'd eat up all the candy, Lawd,
> An tear down the White House gate. (p. 32)

Once started with his sinful versifying, Riley bites his lip with fear of divine punishment, but the words dance in his mind as he mocks another spiritual: "Amazin grace, how sweet the sound. A bullfrog slapped my grandma down." These parodies do more than protect him from the limited vision of experience proffered by the ex-slave, Kate. As they allow for the expression and thus the dispersion of doubt, the parodies even strengthen true belief. Ironically, they also voice the truly aggressive, optimistic spirit of the church songs they seem to deride. It is Riley whose project for the day reflects his desire to soar beyond what seem to be life's tightening possibilities. "Buster," he says, "don't you wish somebody would teach you and me to fly?"

Riley comments to his friend Buster that if he were reincarnated, he would like to come back just like Ole Bill, the family's boss-rooster. Ole Bill "can whup anything whut wears feathers . . . When he gits his spurs into another chicken, he jus rides on to the promis' lan'." Ole Bill, he continues, can strut "like a big fat preacher." When the boys hear the rooster start to crow, they chant a call-and-response song of praise to him:

> "Man, man! He's the fightin'est, crowin'est rooster in the whole wide world!"
> "Listen to that son-of-a-gun!"
> "Aaaw, sing it, Bill!"
> "Man, thass lil Gabriel!"
> "Shucks, he's the Louie Armstrong of the chickens!"
> "Blowing his golden trumpet, Lawd . . ."
> "An tellin all the roosters they better be good . . ."
> "Cause he won't stan for no foolishness . . ."
> "Ole Bill says, Tell all the dogs, an tell all the cats, they better be good or go join the bats . . . cause the mighty Ole Bill's in town."

"Naw, naw, man. He's the Louie Armstrong of the chicken playin 'Hold That Tiger'. . . ."
"Yeah telling that tiger not to act no fool. . . ."
"Thass it, hittin high *p*. . . ."
"Boy, ain't no *p* on no horn. It's *do re me*," sang Riley.
"Yeah, 'tis. When Louie plays it, 'tis. It's *do re me fa sol la ti* and *p* too!" (p. 33)

Like Stakolee, High John the Conqueror, and other badmen of black American folklore, Ole Bill is a brash and good-looking fighter. Associated with heroes of jazz, sports, and folklore, both secular and sacred ("lil Gabriel" appears in many spirituals, notably in "That Great Gettin' Up Mornin'"), Ole Bill himself acquires heroic status. He inspires the boys to be as stylish, freewheeling, and as fearlessly masculine as himself.

After a painfully abortive attempt to force Ole Bill to fly, the boys harness some baby chicks in tiny parachutes and prepare to eject them as "in them airplane movies." At the most critical moment in the chick-flying experiment, Aunt Kate spots Buster on the chicken-house roof and calls loudly, "GIT DOWN FROM THERE SUH!!!" Riley turns to face her and freezes, "caught between two magnets," while the birds sail to their deaths.

Like the other Buster-Riley pieces, "That I Had the Wings" is a parabolic story rich in folk forms. The boys are encouraged by their sur-roundings—transformed by the magic of folklore—to take chances. They distill from their experience a "usable past," traditional attitudes and styles that broaden their scope as black boys. In this initiation into manhood the boys try to defy the limitations of barnyard animals and to assert themselves over the mythically masculine Ole Bill. Clearly this is a ritual preparation for youngsters who, as blacks, will have to defy what seem like impossible odds against them. Buster and Riley also symboli-cally *reject* elements of Afro-American tradition. Next time they will pay even less attention to the timid and conservative Aunt Kate, no matter how she glares and curses. Even though, of course, she is right—chickens can't fly—in ritual terms her lesson is not only superficial but harmful; for in a sense she is teaching the boys that they, as blacks, cannot hope to fly, to better their condition, or to soar in imagination.

In 1943 Ellison joined the Merchant Marines, in part because he had belonged to the National Maritime Union since 1936, when he picketed for them, but mainly because he "wanted to contribute to the war, but didn't want to be in a Jim Crow army."[11]

While still in the service, Ellison was awarded a Rosenwald Fellowship to write a novel. In fact, he already had one outlined: a wartime book in which a black pilot is shot down, captured by the Nazis, and placed in a detention camp where he is the highest-ranking officer; the Nazi guards try to take advantage of the situation by pitting the white Americans against their black commander.[12] Ellison continued working on this novel even after he began *Invisible Man* in 1945. It never achieved enough unity to satisfy its maker, though, and only one section was published, "Flying Home." "In a Strange Country," which concerns a young black serviceman in the midst of world war, also seems to be an offshoot of the abandoned novel. Taking its title from a story by Ernest Hemingway, "In a Strange Country" features Ellison's first truly sophisticated adult character, Parker, a black man familiar with Russian folk music and Shakespeare. In the course of this slight narrative (much less ambitious than "King of the Bingo Game" and "Flying Home," which also appeared in 1944), Parker makes discoveries about his absurd and dangerous position as a black GI overseas, where his white American comrades greet him by shrieking, "It's a nigger!" and beating him until his eye is swollen. This is Ellison's first of many intelligent but "innocent" black characters wandering in the midst of a nightmare world where friend is foe and foreign is familiar.[13]

In this story, the answer to the complicated question of identity is a *musical* one. Parker makes the connection between his experiences back home at jam sessions involving white and black jazz musicians with the hearty renditions of folk and patriotic songs by a group of friendly Welshmen:

> Parker smiled, aware suddenly of an expansiveness that he had known before only at mixed jam sessions. When we jam, sir, we're Jamocrats! He liked these Welsh. Not even on the ship, where the common danger and a fighting union made for a degree of understanding, did he approach white men so closely.
>
> For that's a unity of economics, he said to himself. And this is a unity of music, a "gut language," the food of love. ". . . *Dear Wales. I salute thee. I kiss the lips of thy proud spirit through the fair sounds of thy songs . . . I believe in music!*" Well! *And in what's happening here tonight.* (pp. 90-91)

Music, here, is Ellison's metaphor for democracy and love.

And the music provides more than escapism or hollow sentimentality. When his hosts salute him with the American national anthem, Parker is shaken by a wave of conflicting sensations: he feels disgust, guilt, embarrassment, and finally relief:

> And suddenly he recognized the melody and felt that his knees would give way. It was as though he had been pushed into the horrible and foreboding country of dreams and they were enticing him into some unwilled and degrading act, from which only his failure to remember the words would save him. It was all unreal, yet it seemed to have happened before. Only now the melody seemed charged with some vast new meaning which that part of him that wanted to sing could not fit with the old familiar words. (p. 93)

Entering his character's consciousness more deeply than in any previous story, Ellison catches a sense of the complex absurdity of Parker's experience. Suddenly, "that part of him that wanted to sing" responds to the American anthem: "For the first time in your whole life, he thought with dreamlike wonder, the words are not ironic" (p. 93).

Like Buster and Riley and the Invisible Man, Parker's confusion is abated by music—in this case not a black folk parody or a spiritual, but by Welsh songs and the American national anthem. Through music and the realization that jazz reflects not just American style but American ideals, he is purged of alienation from himself and his country. He is shocked into recognizing that despite his disgust at the whites who jump him—despite the burdensome reality of racism—his identity is that of "Jamocrat" and "black Yank." Through music he solves the problem of his identity, at least for the moment: "I am a Jamocrat!" This solution recalls the reported response of saxophonist Charlie Parker (who might have inspired this tale) to a question concerning his religious affiliation: "I am a devout musician."[14]

Constructed like "Mister Toussan" as a story-within-a-story, "Flying Home" deals with two thwarted flights: that of the black pilot Todd, whose plane collides with a buzzard and crashes in a field in Macon County; and that of Jefferson, who comes to Todd's rescue and who in his "tale told for true" sails from heaven back to the hell of Alabama. Jefferson's uproarious folktale, catalogued by collectors as early as 1919, eases the pain of Todd's ankle—injured in a plane crash—and his wait for a doctor's help. It also serves an initiatory function for the starry-eyed greenhorn, Todd, who, like Jefferson's heavenly flier, must eventually confront the evils of Jim Crow Alabama, however high he has flown. In this brilliantly layered story—an excellent fictional companion piece to the Swing Era's popular tune, "Flying Home"—a variety of other folk motifs direct the young pilot on his looping flight home.

The critic Walter Blair writes that comic folklore aids the American's attempts to adjust himself to "totally new ways of living" as well as to "amazing differences between himself and his neighbors."[15] In a lecture on American humor, Ellison points out, too, that funny tales provide escape, entertainment, and instruction. "Americans began," he says, "to tell stories which emphasize the uncertain nature of existence in the new world, and as we did so, we allowed ourselves some relief from the pain of discovering that our bright hopes were going to be frustrated."[16] Thus we have tall tales about the flintiness of farmland thought to be bursting with mile-high cornstalks; the corrosion of buried treasure; the brutality and sorcery of the Indians. Thus, too, in the land of the brave and free, we have humorous tales about the hatred and the casual violence of surly white men against men black and red.

Jefferson's tale, listed by Richard Dorson as "Colored Man in Heaven,"[17] provides Todd with a perspective for viewing his plight as a black flier in training whose plane has been knocked down by buzzards (called "jimcrow birds") onto the land of a racist white man, Graves. The folkloric lesson also concerns the segregated air force of World War II, during which the question of whether or not to trust black fliers in combat was raised for the first time. Implied, too, is the more general problem of how to face a violently segregated society—or, yet more generally, how to confront a man-made world full of sorrow and death. From the tale Todd learns to laugh at the fact that his brightest and loftiest hopes may at last be grounded by greedy jimcrow birds.

Like many Afro-American humorous tales, the "Colored Man in Heaven" joke accepts for the moment as true certain black stereotypes.[18] As soon as he gets to heaven, Jefferson (the created hero of his own story) raises a ruckus by speeding so fast that he scares the white angels and "knocked the tips offa some stars." Some of the heavenly "boys" even claim that Jefferson, flying with just one wing, stirred up a storm in Alabama and caused some lynchings. "Like colored folks will do," he forgets the warnings from St. Peter, "who finally loses patience with the "flying fool" and sends him back to Alabama. But Jefferson has the last word: "Well, he says, "You done took my wings. And you puttin' me out. You got charge of things so's I can't do nothin' about it. But you got to admit just this: While I was up here I was the flyingest sonofabitch what ever hit heaven!"[19] Far from expressing self-hatred, this tale turns the black stereotype of the unmanageable, forgetful, smart-mouthing black man inside out. As an in-group black joke, "Colored Man in

Heaven" takes the teeth from racist charges by accepting them as true and then laughing at their foolishness. If he does "act up" in heaven, at least while there he is the "flyingest" of the heavenly fliers.

This tale also gives historical perspective to the dilemma of living in Jim Crow America.[20] Jefferson finds that black angels in Zion do not fly because they are required to wear heavy harnesses. Jefferson refuses to be encumbered, though, and discovers that he can "loop-the-loop . . . smooth as a bird," even with one wing. His swooping patterns earn him a dressing down by St. Peter in front of smirking white angels. And finally Jefferson is thrown back into segregated Alabama. Similarly, not only were blacks in the "heaven" of America burdened with the heavy harness of slavery; but at the abrupt end of Reconstruction the political freedoms tentatively offered were snatched back. Blacks were returned to a society full of restrictions based on race. By the 1940s, black men were trained to fly planes at Tuskegee airfield, but for a long time black air force pilots (like Todd) were barred from combat duty. Knocked back by "jim crows," Todd must learn the old survival technique of laughing at—or somehow distancing himself from—a situation with snarled historical roots.

This tale is also part of a greenhorn's ritual into a complex and violent society. Todd's greenness is reflected in his undue optimisn about his chances of flying in combat. Why does he want to fly? Because "it's as good a way to fight and die as I know," he tells Jefferson. Asked if he has ever been troubled by whites who don't want blacks to be pilots, Todd tightens up and says, "No—no one has ever bothered us." To this the older man says, "Well, they'd like to." In Jefferson's tale even St. Peter and God Himself seem involved in the conspiracy to keep blacks harnessed. After hearing this story, Todd becomes angry at what seem like personal references; but he relaxes as he sees that symbolically he too has been knocked down from the heaven of his fantasies. In the end he is freer of illusions; he is more shrewd and wary. In a sense he has "crossed over" into the fallen realm of adulthood. As he is carried from the field by Jefferson and his son, "a new current of communication flowed between the man and boy and himself . . . And it was as though he had been lifted out of his isolation, back into the world of man" (p. 483).

A variety of other folk motifs operate in this rich and compressed story. To pass the time, Jefferson tells a tale about jimcrows and "hosses." Jimcrows, he says,

don't eat nothing what's alive . . . They the damndest birds. Once I seen a hoss all stretched out like he was sick, you know. So I hollers, "Gid up from there, suh! Just to make sho!" An, doggone, son, if I don't see two ole jimcrows come flying right up outta that hoss's insides! Yessuh! The sun was shinin' on 'em and they couldn't a been no greasier if they'd been eating barbecue! (p. 474)

Again Jefferson tells of a cruel world where things are even worse than they seem. As the black song game says:

> "Did the Buzzards come?" "Yes, ma'm!"
> "Fer to pick the bones?" "Yes, ma'm!"

Todd begins to sense the uncertainty of appearences when he considers that his life's direction seems determined by "some sealed orders, couched in ever more technical and mysterious terms." Like the yokel who carried a sealed note saying "keep this nigger boy running" (the secret orders for the greenhorn of *Invisible Man*), Todd needs to realize that the possibility that his "errand" as a pilot is that of a country fool.

The story concludes when Todd hears a mockingbird's song and sees a buzzard circling in the sun "like a bird of flaming gold." But in this tale of rebirth, it is Afro-American folklore (as it intersects with classical mythology) and Jefferson, the tradition-bearer, that save the day. Todd learns to laugh at the limitations implicit in his situation in America. While Jefferson explains to Todd that he has to face the white killer, Graves (as well as his fate as a man born to die), Todd comprehends, suddenly, how Jefferson himself has managed to endure previous encounters with violence. With his eyes opened by Jefferson's folk art, Todd sees the old man from a new perspective:

> What was it Jefferson held in his hand? It was a little black man, another Jefferson! A little black Jefferson that shook with fits of belly-laughter while the other Jefferson looked on with detachment. Then Jefferson looked up from the thing in his hand and turned to speak. (p. 483)

The old man also has gained his clarity of vision by distancing himself from himself and his predicament through the magic of his folk art. As Kenneth Burke has observed, "the comic frame should enable people to be observers of themselves while acting. Its ultimate would not be passiveness, but maximum consciousness. One would 'transcend' himself by noting his own foibles."[21]

When Graves finally arrives, he seizes and kicks Todd, and directs some white doctors to lash him into a straightjacket. But our protaganist demonstrates that he has absorbed the lesson Jefferson has been preaching all afternoon. Instead of reacting with shame or blind fury, Todd begins to laugh: "blasts of hot, hysterical laughter tore from his chest, causing his eyes to pop and he felt that the veins in his neck would surely burst" (p. 483). Having achieved a new perspective on the situation, "part of him stood behind it all, watching the surprise in Graves' red face and his own hysteria." Todd's laughter saves his life; the white men do not feel particularly threatened by a guffawing black fellow who doesn't resist their cruel action. Thus released, Todd looks at Jefferson and knows that the old black man's values are redemptive. He knows that "somehow he had been his sole salvation in an insane world of outrage and humiliation" (p. 483).

The last story Ellison published before he began to work fulltime on *Invisible Man* was "King of the Bingo Game" (1944). This compelling story, the first one in which Ellison felt he had discovered his own fictional voice, synthesizes much that the writer learned as an apprentice, and it foreshadows certain of *Invisible Man's* most memorable forms and themes. As in "Slick Gonna Learn," the protaganist here is an unemployed young black man whose wife's need for medical care has made him desperate for money. His predicament has analogies in every previous Ellison story; a young black man fights for freedom in a land tightly gripped by authority figures (Aunt Kate, Rogan, Graves, tight-eyed white cops). It is in this surrealistic story, however, with its dreamlike shifts of time and levels of consciousness, that the struggle is seen in its most abstracted form. The unnamed hero realizes, in an epiphany, that his battle for freedom and identity must be waged not against individuals or even groups, but against no less than history and fate.

The King is Ellison's first character to sense the frightening absurdity of everyday American life. Yesterday he saw a woman walking into the bright street with a bedbug on her neck. He dozes in a theater and imagines himself as a boy in the South, chased by a train that had jumped the track to pursue him, "and all the white people laughing as he ran screaming." He sees himself as "a long thin black wire that was being stretched and wound upon the bingo wheel." His nose begins to bleed, and he feels "as though the rush of blood to his head would burst out in baseball seams of small red droplets, like a head beaten by police clubs." It is in this wildly imagistic realm, where past and present, dreaming and waking converge, that the King, like the Invisible Man, sees the visions that may spell salvation.

Buster and Riley find that southern folk culture—despite its sudden violence—provides clear and stable definitions of black manhood. Up north, however, the King discovers that the values he learned in Rocky Mountain, North Carolina, do not apply. He is hungry and thirsty, but he knows better than to ask strangers in a movie theater for food and drink. "Up here it was different. Ask somebody for something, and they'd think you were crazy."[22] When the King stands perplexed on the bingo stage, not only does the white emcee laugh at him ("So you decided to come down off that mountain to the U.S."); so do the blacks. "Ole Jack thinks he done found the end of the rainbow," someone shouts. As his emotions crescendo, the audience claps and shouts in derisive mockery:

> *Shoot the liquor to him, Jim, boy!*
> *Clap-clap-clap*
> *Well a-calla the cop*
> *He's blowing his top!*
> *Shoot the liquor to him, Jim, boy!* (31)

With no encouraging spiritual or anthem, with no guide like Jefferson to remind him of the way home, this hero must make his way alone. "He felt alone, but that was somehow right," he thinks. With southern folk culture and consciousness half forgotten and shattered in the North, the King must rely on his personal creativity and resilience to win freedom and identity.

He tangles with his *fate*, which seems to have been irreversibly determined long before he was born. Standing before the bingo wheel, he feels that he has "moved into the spell of some strange, mysterious" being, that he is blinded by the wheel's lights and awe-struck by its power:

> He felt vaguely that his whole life was determined by the Bingo wheel; not only that which would happen now . . . but all that had gone before, since his birth, and his mother's birth and the birth of his father. It had always been there, even though he had not been aware of it, handing out the unlucky cards and numbers of his days. (p. 31)

Here he echoes a question posed by the Invisible Man: What if history is a gambler?

If so, the King feels he must do more than hope his lucky number comes up; he must subvert the process that has left him and his generations luckless. His unwillingness to stop turning the bingo wheel symbolizes this forthright subversion. By refusing to play the game he has been fated to lose, he discovers who he is. First he realizes that he has lost the old identity: "Somehow he had forgotten his own name. It was a sad, lost feeling to lose your name, and a crazy thing to do . . . 'Who am I?' he screamed" (32). Then "he was reborn. For as long as he pressed the button he was The-man-who-pressed-the-button-who-held-the-prize-who-was-the-King-of-Bingo." Like the Invisible Man, the King frees himself when he discovers that he has been a sleepwalker, a fool, naive enough to accept unquestioningly the judgments handed down by an indifferent bingo wheel of fate, of circumstance, of history. Like the Invisible Man, he sees the cruelty of the culture and society that have shaped his personality; the vision frees him of his illusions. The instant before he is run off the stage, he *is* in control of his fate. Moreover, he is symbolically reborn, a new person better able to deal with life's absurd and dreadful turns. Before the curtain is rung down on him, he hears the taunts and laughter in the theater but, foreshadowing the steely determination of Jim Trueblood in *Invisible Man*, the King says, "Well, let 'em laugh. I'll do what I gotta do."

In 1945, physically exhausted by hard work and by a grueling Merchant Marine voyage, and absolutely through with the unfinished war novel, Ellison went to recuperate at a friend's place in Wakesfield, Vermont. Certain ideas seemed to come into focus there. He had been reading Lord Raglan's *The Hero*, a study of historical and mythic heroes, and he had been thinking about leadership in the Afro-American community. Why, he wondered, did black leaders so often seem uncommitted to their black constituents? Why did they so often seem dependent not on the will of blacks but on the largesse of white patrons? Along with these questions, of course, Ellison was concerned with a sheaf of intellectual issues, and with the persistent problem of finding a literary form flexible enough to contain his wild and shifting vision of the American hodgepodge of cultures and characters. His apprentice years in New York helped determine his decision to write a novel about black identity, heroism, and history, and to write it in a style "unburdened" by naturalism.

One morning in 1945, still in Vermont, Ellison scribbled the words, "I am an invisible man" — which turned out to be his novel's first sentence. He recalls that he played with the idea and "started to reject it, but it intrigued me, and I began to put other things with it. And pretty soon I had a novel going, and I began to work out of a conceptual outline on it. And as fast as I could work out the concepts, the incidents started flowing in on me." Back in New York, Ellison spent time writing in his apartment on St. Nicholas Avenue, but he also got up every morning and headed downtown to work like other businessmen. Using a friend's office at 608 Fifth Avenue, Ellison put in at least eight hours a day before he returned to his home on the edge of Harlem.

He worked on the novel for seven years, publishing it in 1952. To many critics, *Invisible Man* seemed like a miraculous first work. But his years as an apprentice writer prepared him for the book. His first published fiction, "Slick Gonna Learn," was conceived as part of a novel. By the forties, with "Flying Home" and "King of the Bingo Game," he had discovered a voice and the set of questions and concerns that were timeless but were nonetheless *his*. By the mid-forties he had absorbed the lessons of Mark Twain, Hemingway, Wright, and the social realists; and he had experimented with the narrative devices of many writers — especially James, Faulkner, Dostoevsky, and Joyce. The sentence "I am an invisible man" started him on a project into which he could pour all he had learned in his years as a craftsman perfecting his trade.

5

Invisible Man: Black and Blue

Published in 1952, Ralph Ellison's *Invisible Man* has been acclaimed by a growing line of commentators writing in diverse critical tongues: formalists, structuralists, psychological critics, folklore and myth critics.[1] Despite the high-beamed scrutinies, however, *Invisible Man* retains its mysterious power to rock us with laughter and terror. As if in defiance of the single-minded critic, Ellison drew symbols and rhetorical schemes from any and every source he felt would enrich the texture and meaning of his first novel's prose. Sophocles, Homer, Dostoevsky, Bergson, Freud, Jung, Raglan, Burke, Eliot, Joyce, Wright, and Malraux; spirituals, blues, and minstrels' jokes; personal experiences rendered symbolically—all figure in *Invisible Man*. Some allusions and symbol clusters trail off like wistful jazz riffs; some recur and provide the novel with structure. No one formula, though, can explain this capacious novel, which owes as much to the symbolist tradition of Melville and Hawthorne as it does to the vernacular tradition of Mark Twain and Hemingway. Without seeking, then, to unfasten every trapdoor of *Invisible Man*, I would like to examine an important aspect of the book, an aspect treated fleetingly by even Ellison's most apt critics: its uses of black American folk art.

An intricate pattern of folk forms is woven through the fabric of *Invisible Man*. Ellison makes use of a Mother Goose rhyme, "Who Killed Cock Robin," transforming it into a mock dirge, "They Picked Poor Robin Clean." "Three Blind Mice" appears in a Brotherhood political speech, and "London Bridge Is Falling Down" and "Hickery Dickery Dock" also turn up. Archetypal tricksters and heroes are stretched and mocked. By using these varied sources, Ellison makes the point that black Americans have an extraordinarily broad cultural heritage that expands beyond political and social boundaries in sometimes surprising ways.

Several critics, following Ellison's hints, have singled out folklore as the cornerstone of *Invisible Man*. Leon Forrest and Susan L. Blake have pointed out the complex interplay of mythic and folkloric patterns in the novel.[2] Floyd Horowitz has discovered the novel's use of patterns from the Brer Rabbit and Brer Bear cycle of black American folk stories.[3] He does not account for the fact that the Invisible Man himself at times plays the role of the fleet rabbit, outrunning the whole field at the end, but Horowitz's early commentary on structure was ground-breaking. The Invisible Man is constantly cast in the role of the thick-headed Brer Bear, stumbling time and time again into traps deftly set by Brer Rabbit in his various aliases: Bledsoe, Norton, Emerson, Brockway, Jack.

Verbal games abound in the novel. Critics have noted that the snappy patter of the blueprint carrier who claims to be "Peter Wheatstraw the Devil's Son-In-Law" is framed in the form of an American boast, a folk form as old as the roaring of such ring-tailed folk heroes as Boone, Crockett, and Mike Fink: half-alligator, half-bulldog, half-rattlesnake. It should be noted too that Peter Wheatstraw, whose name, like that of Stakolee and High John, associates him with black folk heroism, appears in *Invisible Man* as a uniquely black badman whose language and style of performance transmute his American boast into an Afro-American one.[4] Some attention has been given to Ellison's uses of the "dozens" and "signifying," those games of verbal competition in which one's opponent and, in the case of the dozens, one's family (especially one's mother) are assaulted with polished insults.[5]

Although George Kent's casual uses of the terms "folk" and "folklore" weaken the impact of his argument, his main point remains: *Invisible Man* is built on folk foundations.[6] Furthermore, the Invisible Man's gradual move from innocence to experience and from repression to expression is spurred by folk forms. His acceptance of black folklore keeps him from losing touch with his identity in the fast and maddening world of the North. In time he sees that without his folk tradition, without the "mother wit" inherited from the past struggles of black Americans, he truly is an Invisible Man, a calculation rolling helter-skelter in social space.

The use of black folklore enabled Ellison to achieve the "magical" stylistic effects he had been seeking in his fiction for ten years. Not only did the folkloric allusions provide the work with a richness of texture and a solid structure; they also propelled its themes and images into a swirling dream world beyond that of social realism.

In addition to the analogues to the Brer Rabbit and Brer Bear tales, Ellison employs several folk motifs to give structure to *Invisible Man*. The Invisible Man's archetypal movement from darkness to light is treated ironically by the author who, in an interview, says:

> In my novel, the narrator's development is one through blackness to light; that is, from ignorance to enlightenment: invisibility to visibility. He leaves the South and goes North; this, as you will notice in reading Negro folktales, is always the road to freedom—the movement upward. You have the same thing again when he leaves his underground cave for the open.[7]

Underlying the black-white motif is a play on the notion of blackness as evil, whiteness as good. The twist here is that the Invisible Man finds his enlightenment as he finds his blackness; his "movement upward" is also a plunge into a dark manhole. According to black folklore and history, though, this underground trail does lead to freedomland.

The rhyme from black Americana and from vaudeville recurs in the novel: "If you're white, you're right; if you're brown, stick around; if you're black, get back."[8] The veteran from the Golden Day warns the Invisible Man against believing in this terse refrain, but Bledsoe tells him that white *is* right and he had better not forget it. Louis Brockway, the old badger-faced black man, wins a special bonus for thinking up the motto for the Optic White Paint Factory, "If it's Optic White, it's the right white." Ellison also plays with the idea, based on a standard joke, that one reason people keep bumping into the Invisible Man is that in the dark the black boy is just too black to see.[9] And this despite the notion that blacks were "perfect slaves" because their skin color made for "high visibility."

Symbolically, the novel involves a series of elaborate greenhorn's initiations that test and temper the Invisible Man for black life in America. Thus he suffers the battle royal where, as in many folktales (as well as in black fiction, autobiography, and biography), black boys are pressed into fighting one another for the amusement of white men. This nightmarish game not only highlights the caste lines in the segregated South, but prepares the greenhorn Invisible Man for the unpredictibility and viciousness of American life. Thus, too, he is victimized by the cynical college president Julius Bledsoe who, after requiring the Invisible Man to leave school, gives him sealed letters of recommendation secretly asking potential white employers to "help him continue in the direction of that promise which, like the horizon, recedes ever brightly and distantly beyond the hopeful traveler" (p. 145). This classic "fool's errand" is foreshadowed in the young man's earlier dream about his grandfather, who tells him to read aloud the gold engraved words in a letter he has been carrying: "To Whom It May Concern: Keep This Nigger Boy Running." The greenhorn's initiation is universal; it was part of the stock in trade for the Yankee humorists of the eighteenth and nineteenth centuries. In an Afro-American context, however, the razzings of the black yokel assume special meanings: they teach him to brace himself for the foibles and caprices of humankind—and especially for those city slickers or country sharpies who hate his race. Enfolded here too (as Leon Forrest and Robert Hemenway have pointed out) is a crucial survival lesson: learn to read!

The novel's central metaphor of running is influenced by patterns from black American folklore.[10] The narrator's grandfather, who stands for the past the young man does not understand or accept, speaks several sets of magic words that start him on his odyssey, set him "running." Running in the manner of various folk figures, one step ahead of destruction, the narrator scampers like a rabbit from scene to scene. Probably one source of this running motif is the black folk rhyme, also adopted by white minstrels in black-face, known as "Run, Nigger, Run." One version of this goes as follows:

> Run, nigger run; de patter-roller catch you;
> Run, nigger, run, it's almost day.
> Run, nigger, run, de patter-roller catch you;
> Run, nigger, run, and try to get away.
>
> Dis nigger run, he run his best,
> Stuck his head in a hornet's nest,
> Jumped de fence and run fru de paster;
> White man run, but nigger run faster.
>
> Dat nigger run, dat nigger flew,
> Dat nigger tore his short in two.[11]

Thus in this slavery-born folk rhyme blacks could laugh both at themselves and at the dread patrollers. Ellison elaborates on the running motif by making a joke of the Invisible Man's flight as he is pursued by "patter-rollers" of a different sort: by Bledsoe, Norton, Brockway,

Wrestrum, and Jack who, like a slave patrol, threaten his freedom at every turn.[12]

During his reefer-inspired dream in the prologue, the Invisible Man encounters a woman moaning and singing. She stops her song to tell the young man her story. She was a slave who bore her master several sons. Loving her children, she came to love their father, even though he never made good his promise to set them free. One day, when she realized her sons were angry and old enough to kill their father, she poisoned him and he withered away "like a frost-bit apple" (p. 14). This story is based on the "folk secular" sometimes called "Promises of Freedom":

> My ole Mistiss promise me
> W'en she died, she'd set me free.
> She lived so long dat 'er head got bal'
> An' she give out 'n the notion a dyin' at all . . .
>
> Ole Mosser lakwise promise me
> W'en he died, he'd set me free
> But ole Mosser go an' make his will
> Fer to leave me a-plowin' still . . .
>
> Yes, my ole Mosser promise me;
> But 'his papers' didn't leave me free.
> A dose of pizen he'ped 'im along
> May the Devil preach 'is funeral song.[13]

This piece, subtly blended into the novel, increases the work's surreal effect while it also provides a historical dimension. The Invisible Man, like a slave, must confront modern "Mossers" and "Mistisses," with their own dubious promises of freedom.

Another folk character dating from slavery days, Brer Dog, also shows up in the novel. In Afro-American lore the dog is an enigmatic and deceptive fellow who is usually outdone by the rabbit, his natural enemy.[14] In the novel as in the folklore, the dog may earnestly pledge to be the rabbit's friend, but the careful rabbit is never convinced.

According to one tale, the rabbits and the dogs hold a convention at which the dogs agreed "to leave off runnin' rabbits." Later on, though, walking through the woods with a dog, the ever "suscautious" rabbit hears a pack of dogs in the distance and takes off. He explains, "De rabbits didn't go to school much and he didn't learn but three letters, but that's trust no mistake; Run every time de bush shake."[15] Similarly, throughout the novel the dog is a threatening figure who nonetheless can be over-

come. Brother Tarp, we are told, is guarded on the chain gang by a team
of dogs, but gradually he befriends them and is able to escape.

The dog has made his way north too, it appears. Peter Wheatstraw,
singing "Feet Like a Monkey Blues" on the street in Harlem, hollers
about his woman with legs "like a mad bulldog." Furthermore, the
Harlem dog is on the prowl and dangerous. In part of a ritual of recognition,[16] Wheatstraw, sensing the Invisible Man is from the South, says,
"What I want to know is, is you got the *dog*?" Still going for middle-
class respectability, the hero does not immediately understand. But
Wheatstraw is persistent:

> Oh, goddog, daddy-o. Who got the damn dog? Now I know you
> from down home, how come you trying to act like you never heard
> that before! Hell, ain't nobody out here this morning but us col-
> ored—Why you trying to deny me? . . . Is you got him, or ain't
> you? (p. 153)

When finally the Invisible Man remembers his lines and says, "No, not
this morning," a grin spreads over Wheatstraw's face. Then discoursing
on Brer Dog and Brer Bear, Wheatstraw gives the Invisible Man his view
of the way things are in Harlem:

> "Damn, man! I thought sure *you* had him," he said, pretending to
> disbelieve me . . . "Well maybe it's the other way round," he said.
> "Maybe he got holt to you."
> "Maybe," I said.
> "If he is, you lucky it's just a dog—'cause, man, I tell you I
> believe it's a bear that's got holt to me . . . Hell, yes! *The* bear.
> Caint you see these patches where he's been clawing at my behind?
> . . . Man, this Harlem ain't nothing but a bear's den. But I tell you
> one thing . . . it's the best place in the world for you and me, and if
> times don't get better soon I'm going to grab that bear and turn
> him every way but loose." (p. 153)

Harlem may be a bear's den or a mad dog's house but, naturally, "Peter
Wheatstraw the Devil's Son-In-Law" knows that he will get by as long as
he has "a little shit, grit and mother-wit." Having remained conscious of
his southern folk roots, he is well prepared for Harlem's bears or "dog-
days."

Waiting to give his first address as a Brotherhood spokesman, the Invisible Man recalls his own experience with Brer Dog. As a child he stood
outside a chicken-wire fence watching Master, the bulldog, and was

afraid to touch him even though, panting in the heat, the dog "seemed to grin back at me like a fat good-natured man, the saliva roping silvery from his jowls." Master was a likable but untrustworthy old fellow: he wore the same expression and growled the same low note whether calmly "snapping flies" or "tearing an intruder to shreds" (p. 293).

Brother Jack, who at the end of the novel our hero calls "Marse Jack," is as much the *dog* as he is the rabbit of Afro-American folklore. Accordingly, Jack the Dog seems to be peaceful and trustworthy, but is not. Early on, the Invisible Man senses that Brother Jack was "in some ways . . . like a toy bull terrier" (p. 293). Here is a warning, submerged in folklore, that our hero, who has repressed his "mother-wit," does not comprehend until very late in the game.

Invisible Man has been rightly labeled a "blues novel."[17] In Albert Murray's words:

> *Invisible Man* was *par excellence* the literary extension of the blues. It was as if Ellison had taken an everyday twelve bar blues tune (by a man from down South sitting in a manhole up North singing and signifying about how he got there) and scored it for full orchestra . . . It had new dimensions of rhetorical resonance (based on lying and signifying) . . . It was a first rate novel, a blues odyssey, a tall tale . . . And like the blues, and echoing the irrepressibility of America itself, it ended on a note of promise, ironic and ambiguous, but a note of promise still. The blues with no aid from existentialism have always known that there were no clear-cut solutions for the human situation.[18]

Like Louis Armstrong, scat-singing and blowing blues trumpet, the Invisible Man struggles to cope with change after change through the magic of his words. In this sense, he is not so much an antihero as a comic hero striving for (to use Murray's term to describe the American character) "blues-heroism." The "blues hero," Murray says, represents qualities perfected by the blues soloist. For him,

> Improvisation is the ultimate human (i.e., heroic) endowment . . . Even as flexibility or the ability to swing (or to perform with grace under pressure) is the key to . . . the charisma of the hero, and even as infinite alertness-become-dexterity is the functional source of the magic of all master craftsmen, so may skill in the art of improvisation be that which both will enable contemporary man to be at home with his sometimes tolerable but never quite certain condition

of *not* being at home in the world and will also dispose him to regard his obstacles and frustrations as well as his achievements in terms of adventures and romance.[19]

Like a blues singer, the Invisible Man recounts his story with style, irony, and a sense of absurdity, viewing his trials and glories in terms of adventure and romance.

Blues language and rhythms resound throughout *Invisible Man*. The novel begins and ends with reference to Louis Armstrong's blues. In the prologue, the narrator declares that, to compensate for his invisibility, he has strung his underground hole with 1369 light bulbs and, though he already owns one radio-phonograph, he wants four more in order to hear his favorite blues properly. In mock patriotic fashion, the narrator wants to eat his favorite dessert of vanilla ice cream (white) and sloe gin (red) while listening to Armstrong's plaintive blues, "What Did I Do To Be So Black and Blue?"

Armstrong's blues, improvised just a fraction behind and then ahead of the beat, seem to express something fundamental about the narrator's Afro-American sense of timing:

> Invisibility, let me explain, gives one a slightly different sense of time, you're never quite on the beat. Sometimes you're ahead and sometimes behind. Instead of the swift and imperceptible flowing of time, you are aware of its nodes, those points where time stands still or from which it leaps ahead. And you slip into the breaks and look around. That's what you hear vaguely in Louis' music.[20]

This lagging behind time is in keeping with CPT (colored people's time), the old joke on "traditional" Afro-American lateness.[21] The ability to slide artfully in and out of tempo, Ellison implies, also can be a weapon. The yokel of the prologue defeats the fast-footworking machine-timed boxer by simply stepping "inside of his opponent's sense of time" (pp. 11-12).

In the prologue, Ellison indicates that by tuning into the most profound meanings of the blues one is put in touch with certain fundamental aspects of Afro-American history and culture. The Invisible Man stumbles awkwardly "in the spaces between the notes" of Armstrong's blues and "not only entered the music but descended, like Dante, into its depths" (p. 12). Deep between the beams of blues sound, he encounters a series of black folk forms: a spiritual, a folk story, a sermon, a blues-like moan. When he finally ascends from this strange "underworld of sound," he hears Louis Armstrong innocently state the theme of the novel, inquiring (in the words of the Fats Waller song): "What did I do/To be so black/And blue?"[22]

The blues resound through many scenes in the first chapters of the novel. At times they seep almost imperceptibly into the action and increase its resonance by capturing the mood of the narrator. After departing from Rabb Hall (a stronghold of Brer Rabbit?), where Dr. Bledsoe tells our hero he has two days to pack his things and leave the dream campus, the Invisible Man wanders blankly across the school lawn, his stomach feeling achy. The blues, trailing in the distance, offer notes of sympathy: "From somewhere across the quiet of the campus the sound of an old guitar-blues plucked from an out-of-tune piano drifted toward me like a lazy, shimmering wave, like the echoed whistle of a lonely train, and my head went over again, against a tree this time, and I could hear it splattering the flowering vines" (p. 130).

Jim Trueblood's blues also prove soothing. They give eloquent and cathartic expression to his absurd situation (pointed out by some critics as an oedipal as well as an existential crisis). Living on a country road far away from the "beautiful college" in an "old log cabin with its chinks filled with chalk-white clay," he tells his story over and over until he nearly sings it. Before his disgrace (he impregnated both his wife and his daughter), the college people occasionally had invited Trueblood to sing in the chapel for the white guests. But having brought shame upon "the whole race" by his misdeeds, Trueblood is the target of the college leaders' sharp hatred. Nonetheless, Trueblood manages to face up to his outrageously "blue" situation. Even after his wife has slashed him in the head, renounced and abandoned him, as well as marshaled community sentiment against him, Trueblood collects his strength and continues on courageously. He identifies with "the boss quail bird": "Like a good man, what he gotta do, he *do*." He also recalls his own heritage rooted in spirituals and the blues. Recounting the situation, Trueblood's speech achieves a kind of blues cadence:

> I thinks and thinks, until I thinks my brain go'n bust, 'bout how I'm guilty and how I ain't guilty. I don't eat nothin' and I don't drink nothin' and cain't sleep at night. Finally, one night, way early in the mornin', I looks up and sees the stars and I starts singin'. I don't mean to, I didn't think 'bout it, just start singin'. I don't know what it was, some kinda church song, I guess. All I know is I *ends up* singin' the blues. I sings me some blues that night ain't never been sang before, and while I'm singin' them blues I makes up

my mind that I ain't nobody but myself and ain't nothin' I can do
but let whatever is gonna happen, happen. (p. 63)

In his solitude, after releasing "some kinda church song" that dissolves
into a blues, the black sharecropper finds himself able to face his family
and community with renewed strength. Somehow the blues provide just
the vehicle for coming to terms with the twisted and painful details of
Trueblood's situation; by expressing himself in this "near tragic, near
lyric" form, he conquers his fearful guilt. In the presence of Norton, the
white college trustee, the Invisible Man is "torn between humiliation and
fascination" at the farmer's story.[23] But our young and ambitious hero is
more interested, at this juncture, in winning a tip from Norton than in
learning about the strengths and mysteries of his culture.

Like the exchange about the dog, the blues occasionally remind the
narrator of the black folk heritage he has tried, in his hot pursuit of
middle-class prestige and power, to rise above. Booted out of college, the
Invisible Man journeys to New York where the situation appears to favor
his desire to forget the past. The folklore, however, trails him north. He
tramps snappily from trustee to trustee, believing in their benevolence
and Bledsoe's,[24] when suddenly he hears Wheatstraw wailing his strange
blues. In his clear ringing voice Wheatstraw serves up the Invisible Man a
comic and absurd vision of the world he lives in. Belting out the words of
Count Basie's and Jimmy Rushing's "Boogie Woogie Blues,"[25] the man
appears to describe a weird-looking but good-loving woman:

> She's got feet like a monkey
> Legs like a frog—Lawd, Lawd!
> But when she starts to loving me
> I holler Whoooo, God-dog!
> Cause I loves my baabay,
> Better than I do myself . . .
>
> She's got feet like a monkeeee
> Legs
> Legs, Legs like a maad
> Bulldog.

A college man now and up north too, the Invisible Man deems this blues
lyric repulsive; it is rowdy and contradictory, stocked with references to
the enigmatic, black-belt-born folk figures of the frog, the monkey, and
the bulldog.

Nonetheless, the Invisible Man finds the blues, the like of which he has
heard since childhood, oddly fascinating. In his own blues-tinged reflec-

tions, he senses not only a complex artistry at work in the blues, but a previously unnoticed degree of personal affirmation:

> I strode along, hearing the cartman's song become a lonesome, broad-toned whistle now that flowered at the end of each phrase into a tremulous, blue-toned chord. And in its flutter and swoop I heard the sound of a railroad train highballing it, lonely across the lonely night . . . He was a man who could whistle a three-toned chord. (p. 156)

And although, as in the case of Trueblood's story, he wonders if it is truly pride or disgust that he feels about the bluesman and the "flutter and swoop" of his song, he suddenly thinks, "God damn . . . they're a hell of a people!"[26] Peter Wheatstraw, strolling in Harlem, helps the slow-to-learn hero make a vital connection: southern black folk experience must not be discarded in the North. The bluesman's warning to the young man is significant: Youngblood, he says in his way, do not deny me.

The Harlem bluesman's song also prepares the hero for the disappointment he must face when he learns that Bledsoe and the trustees have conspired to "keep him running." Here the blues not only serve as an antidote for pain but seem to describe with humorous exaggeration the quality of his luck: "Feet like a monkey, Legs like a maaad bulldog!"

Mary Rambo, along with Trueblood, Wheatstraw, Brother Tarp, and Dupre, is one of the novel's stalwart black figures called by one critic "folk characters." Mary runs the roominghouse in Harlem where the Invisible Man stays after leaving the factory hospital in a daze. Of Mary, Ellison has written, "Imagine what this country would be without its Marys . . . Imagine, indeed, what the American Negro would be without the Marys of our ever-expanding Harlems."[27] Mary's name may have been suggested by the biblical Mary as well as the Mary of Lonnie Johnson's blues song, "She's My Mary." Were he disposed to shout a blues, the Invisible Man could have shouted about Mary Rambo:

> She was my Mary, when this whole world turned me down,
> She was my father, mother, sister, brother; she helped me to carry on
> And she will still be my Mary, when everything goes wrong.[28]

Wisely, Mary Rambo has transported the southern black blues to the urban North. She sings the blues and uses blues lyrics in her speech. As if to pass along the source of her strength to the hero, weak and worn from the factory hospital ordeal, when Mary puts him to bed, she quietly sings,

"If I don't think I'm sinking, look what a hole I'm in" (p. 221). The next line of this traditional blues, "If you don't think I love you, look what a fool I've been,"[29] remains unstated, but a southern black boy like the narrator would know it and be soothed. Much later in the novel, when at last he is freed of his illusions, he expresses himself in the language of the blues, echoing Mary's song. His ordeals, he says, were painful but at least they "showed me the hole I was in" (p. 495).

Throughout the novel, even when money is scarce, Mary remains as loving as the Mary of the Bible and of Johnson's blues. Like Trueblood she is braced and enlivened with hope by singing the blues. During a particularly difficult time, when the Invisible Man's rent is long overdue and the air is heavy with the smell of cabbage (omen of bad times) for the second day in a row, Mary sings a "troubled song" in a voice paradoxically clear and untroubled. She sings "Back Water Blues," which like many blues songs tells (in mournful yet *swinging* terms) of a natural disaster. The song, written by Bessie Smith, floated through the hallways of Mary's rooming house:

When it rain five days an' de skies turned dark as night
When it rain five days an' de skies turned dark as night
Then trouble taken place in the lowland that night.

I woke up this mornin', can't even get outa mah do'
I woke up this mornin', can't even get outa mah do'
That's enough trouble to make a po' girl wonder where she wanna gu . . .

Backwater blues done cause me to pack mah things an' go
Backwater blues done cause me to pack mah things an' go
Cause mah house fell down an' I cain' live there no mo'.[30]

Bessie's blues sung by Mary Rambo remind the Invisible Man of his responsibility as a black-youth-of-promise to relieve his people's suffering. "Back Water Blues" stings him with the knowledge that times are hard and makes him feel guilty for not having a job. After hearing Mary's mournful song, he rushes headlong into the Brotherhood job offered that afternoon by Brother Jack.

By the time the Invisible Man lands the position as the Brotherhood Harlem leader, not only does he seem aware of the political value of such "folk forms" as jazz-tempoed marching bands[31] (he organizes the Hot Foot Squad to march for the party), but like Trueblood and Mary he has also learned to derive personal strength from the blues and to sense their humor. As he contemplates clearing a block in Harlem of its ramshackle fences and filth, his plans are mocked by reality: "And just then a paper bag sailed from a window to my left and burst like a silent grenade, scattering garbage into the trees and pancaking to earth with a soggy, exhausted plop!" His hopes nonetheless are rekindled when he considers in the words of so many blues songs, "The sun will shine in those backyards someday" (p. 328).[32]

After the death of his Brotherhood protégé, Tod, the Invisible Man contemplates black urban folk experience with heightened insight into its importance. Realizing that he has followed the Brotherhood line in discounting ordinary blacks as irredeemably outside the groove of history, "dead on the city pavements" (as Jack says), he wonders who will be their "historians." The policeman who fired the fatal shots was the only historian Tod ever had. Who will tell Tod's story? The blues provides a kind of history,[33] he notes—but how adequate is its version of Harlem's story? Hearing a languid blues coming from a record shop, the hero pauses to think: "Was this the true history of the times, a mood blared by trumpets, trombones, saxophones and drums, a song with turgid, inadequate words?" (p. 383). The Invisible Man's doubts are not the author's; the blues, at once terse and "turgid," do express the complexity of the American scene with special effectiveness. And blues singers *are* historians in the sense that they, like all artists, project the lasting themes, forms, and images of their culture. Escuedero, Ellison observed in an interview, can recapitulate the history of Spain with a simple arabesque of his fingers. The same is true of the skilled blues artist, footnoting his history with blue notes and field hollers.

The Invisible Man's discovery of P. B. Rineheart's existence heightens his sense that he has been missing some important aspects of Harlem's history. Rineheart is the archetypal trickster, providing the Invisible Man with an escape from his pursuers.[34] He is also a skillful and devious master of improvisation against an insane urban backdrop; he is the strutting badman of many blues, a blues-villain, so to speak. He takes his name from various sources, including a rallying cry for mob action at Harvard College and a blues by Jimmy Rushing:

> *Rineheart, Rineheart*
> *It's so lonesome up here*
> *On Beacon Hill.*[35]

Implied here is that, if the Invisible Man had stayed in touch with the folk rather than the downtown Brotherhood, he would have known about such Harlem characters as Rineheart and about the American character in general, resilient and deft in crouching behind whatever costume and mask a given situation demands.[36] Furthermore, he would know more about the sometimes chaotic realities behind appearances—the "heart" of experience as well as the "rine."

In search of the dimensions of black life previously overlooked and undervalued, the narrator ducks into a Harlem bar, the Jolly Dollar, wearing his Rineheart hat-and-shades disguise. As if in anticipation of the trouble he will encounter at the bar—in trying out his disguise on his comrade, he and Brother Hambro square off to fight—and in anticipation of the mad confusion of the incipient riot, the juke joint's blues and dancers give an eerie and hellish sensation:

> A crowd of men and women moiled like nightmare figures in the smoke-green haze. The juke box was dinning and it was like looking into the depths of a murky cave. And now someone moved aside and looking down along the curve of the bar past the bobbing heads and shoulders I saw the juke box, lit up like a bad dream of the Fiery Furnace shouting:

> > *Jelly, Jelly*
> > *Jelly,*
> > *All night long.*

Here this shouter's blues, "Jelly, Jelly,"[37] one version of which was written by Billy Eckstein and Earl Hines, erupts from the back of the bar and contains a premonition of the violence to come. Before long the riot will shake Harlem "like a bad dream" raging "all night long."

When the riot does explode, the absurdity and terrible hilarity of the scene on the streets are best expressed by a tubby black woman who has seated herself atop an abandoned Borden's milkwagon. Laughing drunkenly, she drinks frothy beer from a large jug and, sloshing it on her gingham pinafore, dips free liquor for all comers. As she passes around the beer, she belts out a vendor's blues[38] passionately and with blues-shouter's timber:

> > *If it hadn't been for the referee*
> > *Joe Louis woulda killed*
> > *Jim Jefferie*
> > *Free beer!*

Invisible Man closes with words from an aphorism and from the old New Orleans blues song (a version of which was recorded by Louis Armstrong), "Buddy Bolden's Blues."[39] Contemplating this song, the Invisible Man decides that he must emerge from his manhole to confront all aspects of his experience, even those previously shunned and repressed.

> I must come out, I must emerge. And there's still a conflict within me: With Louis Armstrong one half of me says, "Open the window and let the foul air out," while the other half says "It was good green corn before the harvest." Of course Louis was kidding, he wouldn't have thrown old Bad Air out, because it would have broken up the music and the dance, when it was the good music that came from the bell of old Bad Air's horn that counted. Old Bad Air is still around with his music and his dancing and his diversity, and I'll be up and around with mine. (pp. 502-503)

By the end of the novel the Invisible Man is speaking an idiom infused by the blues. Comforted, inspired, warned, and instructed, he learns to cherish the tradition out of which they were created. By the time he sits down to write his memoir, he has gained something of the ironical perspective of the blues. He has learned, too, from the blues of the wisdom of his forefathers, the humor, bitterness, love, disappointment, and the will to endure. Through acceptance of the blues, the narrator moves from shame to pride in his tradition. "I am not ashamed of my grandparents for having been slaves," he records. "I am only ashamed of myself for having at one time been ashamed" (p. 19).

In their discussions of *Invisible Man*'s folk allusions, few critics have included spirituals and gospel music. Like the blues allusions, the many subtle references to sacred folk music serve to enrich the weave of the novel's prose. Church forms also dominate certain scenes. As with the blues, the hero starts out ashamed of the "primitive" sacred forms and is not freed of his illusions until he recognizes their beauty and wisdom and their value as a bridge to the past.

The Invisible Man's dream-vision between the "Black and Blue" notes that sound through the prologue takes him to a place where a black woman sings a somber spiritual. Her song reflects the "hybrid" (though black American)[40] nature of the singer's and culture of her style of singing; the spiritual is "as full of Weltschmerz as flamenco" (p. 12). Singing it grants a certain freedom, she explains to our hero. "*Old woman,*" he asks her, "*What is this freedom you love so well?*" It lies in loving, not hating, she says, and also in the power of self-expression: "*I guess now it ain't nothing but knowing how to say what I got up in my head*" (p. 14).

The young man is most ashamed and contemptuous of black church music while he is in the South. At school, during spring festival when the white millionaire trustees descend to be courted and ceremonialized, the sacred forms are exploited as entertainments. As the Invisible Man moves toward his chapel seat, he hears voices "mechanically raised" in song by students with faces "frozen in solemn masks." Purged of genuine emotion, the hard-faced singers answer the powerful whites' demand for a sign of black docility. Like the songs performed at minstrel shows, the spirituals seem to constitute "an ultimatum accepted and ritualized, an allegiance recited for the peace it imparted" (p. 100). To that extent, says the narrator, the songs were loved by the students, "loved as the defeated come to love the symbols of their conquerors. A gesture of acceptance, of terms laid down and reluctantly approved" (p. 100). Thus in tribute (or mock tribute) did Bledsoe strike up his favorite spiritual, "Live-a Humble."[41] For the benefit of the rich white guests the students stiffly sing, "Lead Me To a Rock That Is Higher Than I," again seeming to conform to the minstrel-show idea that blacks are contented and self-effacingly humble.

Jim Trueblood and his country quartet of gospel songsters, brought forward to entertain white guests at the school, also cause the students to wilt with shame. The collegians hold Trueblood and all the local "black peasants" in strict contempt but tolerate their "primitivism" on occasion for the good of their school's coffers:

> We were embarrassed by the earthy harmonies they sang but since the visitors were awed we dared not laugh at the crude, high, plaintively animal sounds Jim Trueblood made as he led the quartet . . . How all of us at the college hated the black-belt people . . . during those days! We were trying to lift them up and they, like Trueblood, did everything it seemed to pull us down. (p. 47)

At times, even in the presence of the white financiers, the meaning of the sacred music penetrates the congregation. Though repressed by the upward-bound blacks, the folk music continues to have a grip on their imagination. Before Homer A. Barbee's chapel address to the students and millionaires, a thin brown girl serenades the gathering *a cappella*. Beginning softly, the girl appears possessed by her song, her voice "a disembodied force that sought to enter her, to violate her, shaking her, rocking her rhythmically, as though it had become the source of her being, rather than the fluid web of her own creation" (pp. 105-106). Before the eyes of the congregation, she appears as a vessel of "contained, controlled and sublimated anguish," expressing the bottled-up feelings of her black classmates. While the words of the song reverberate indistinctly in the chapel air, the song's impact on the hero is definite; it expresses a mood that is "sorrowful, vague and ethereal." Like certain spirituals, her song "throbbed with nostalgia, regret and repentance." At its conclusion, the Invisible Man sits with a lump in his throat as even the white guests exchange smiles of appreciation.

Homer A. Barbee, a black preacher from Chicago, delivers the epic story of the college's Founder using certain black sermonic devices.[42] In his speech he clarifies some of the genuine meanings of Afro-American sacred folk music. Chanting, Barbee recalls how when the Founder first showed signs of failing health, a church song, a "long black song of blood and bones," was raised:

> Meaning HOPE!
> Of hardship and pain:
> Meaning FAITH!
> Of humbleness and absurdity:
> Meaning ENDURANCE!
> Of ceaseless struggle in darkness, meaning:
> TRIUMPH.

Within spirituals and gospel songs exists a celebration of the power to endure even the worst seasons of distress. This music gave the local blacks a means of expressing their terrible sorrow at the Founder's death: "The people came to sing the old songs and to express their unspeakable sorrow . . . singing unashamedly their black folks' songs of sorrow, moving painfully, overflowing the curving walks, weeping and wailing . . . and their low murmuring voices like the moans of winds in a wilderness" (p. 118).

At the close of the dramatic eulogy (where, incidentally, one finds—though mocked—virtually all of Lord Raglan's prescriptions for the legendary hero),[43] the white guests are momentarily forgotten by the students. Led by Bledsoe, they raise a moan of sorrow for the Founder. "This time," notes the narrator, "it was music sincerely felt, not rendered for the guests, but for themselves; a song of hope and exultation" (p. 120).

Overwhelmed with grief at his dismissal from the college, the Invisible Man rushes from the auditorium. Dvorak's New World Symphony is played by the school orchestra. And although he has been ashamed of the gospel music and spirituals performed there, he dimly senses that out of these folk forms come symphonies, novels, and dance suites. In New World Symphony, the hero "kept hearing 'Swing Low Sweet Chariot' resounding through its dominant theme[44] — my mother's and my grandfather's favorite spiritual. It was more than I could stand" (p. 121). Hearing strains of the spiritual also makes him feel guilty since, by his blunders, he has smashed his family's hope that he would finish college.

Like the blues, spirituals help awaken the Invisible Man to the value of his folk heritage. In the factory hospital, where the cyclops-eyed doctors attempt to sever the hero's sense of identity, to blunt the progress of a case "developing over three hundred years," he is rescued by his stubborn memory of folk forms, including spirituals. Shut in the nickel and glass box, he feels self-alienated; in a flash of pain he "seemed to go away" and the lights before his eyes "receded like a taillight racing down a dark country road. I couldn't follow" (p. 204). As his vision clears, the Invisible Man seems to see a trumpet man like the one in the epilogue who blows good music through bad air: "The air seemed to grow thick with fine white gnats, filling my eyes, boiling so thickly that the dark trumpeter breached them in and expelled them through the bell of his gold horn, a live white cloud mixing with the tones upon the torpid air" (pp. 204-205). Blowing his golden horn in the gnat-heavy air, the trumpet player, like Gabriel of the spirituals, renders in a sweet voice above the mocking obligattos of a mockingbird, the old church song "The Holy City." Suddenly the young man appears to come to himself, defying the intentions of the factory hospital doctors. "I came back," he says.

Out of the hospital, the Invisible Man receives a steady stream of motherly encouragement from Mary. Alluding to Mahalia Jackson's gospel song, she tells him that he has a responsibility to help other blacks to "move on up a little higher."[45] Here the double meaning of the spirituals and gospel songs is made plain. Mary does not mean only that the young man should move on up from the downward road of sin; she is also speaking of social betterment in this land.

The Brotherhood, on the other hand, shuns all reminders of cultural differences and opposes all evidences of "petty individualism." The Invisible Man gradually rejects this part of their doctrine, however, as he discovers that only through acceptance of his own heritage can he be free. When a crisis arises in his Brotherhood work — he receives an anonymous threatening note — he thinks about the past. Is he being betrayed by a jealous white enemy of the organization? A rival black politician? Does the answer lie in the past? He talks with old Brother Tarp, who looks at him for a strange moment through his grandfather's eyes. He spent nineteen years on a chain gang for saying no to a white man. After their conversation, the Invisible Man hears a "throaty voice singing with a mixture of laughter and solemnity":

> Don't come early in the morning
> Neither in the heat of the day
> But come in the sweet cool of the
> Evening to wash my sins away.

Hearing this church song, he "plunged down a well of years" and "a series of memories" bob up. Clearly the solution to the problem of who sent the note does lie in the past. The gospel verse and Brother Tarp's words warn that history *repeats*. Jack, as we later learn, actually sent the note, paralleling the action of the white man against Brother Tarp. As usual, however, the Invisible Man misses the point, thinking, "There was no time for memory, for all its images were of times passed" (p. 338).

Not until Tod's funeral does the Invisible Man become fully conscious of the transcendent value of black sacred folk music. As he speculates whether or not the crowd gathered around Tod's casket is moved by love or hate or political militancy, he hears two men spontaneously lifting a spiritual, "Many Thousand Gone." The song's words contain a stern renunciation of slave life, described in the starkest of terms:

> No more auction block for me
> No more, no more,
> No more auction block for me,
> Many thousand gone . . .
>
> No more peck of corn for me
> No more, no more,
> No more peck of corn for me
> Many thousand gone.
>
> No more driver's lash for me
> No more, no more,
> No more driver's lash for me
> Many thousand gone.[46]

One man sings the song in a plaintive, husky voice and the other, who plays baritone sax in the band that has assembled, fumbles for the key and then takes up the tune in a high, sweet tone. The song touches something deep in the crowd. Paradoxically, as Brother Jack has said (but does not mean), the masses *do* "toss up" a leader, just as they will choose Dupre to lead in the destruction of a Harlem rat-trap during the riot. Feeling a "twinge of envy," the Invisible Man looks at the man who unashamedly intones the old song:

> It was a worn, old, yellow face and his eyes were closed and I could see a knife welt around his upturned neck as his throat threw out the song. He sang with his whole body, phrasing each verse as naturally as he walked, his voice rising above all the others, blending with that of the lucid horn. I watched him now, wet-eyed, the sun hot upon my head, and I felt a wonder at the singing mass. (pp. 391-392)

For the first time, he is conscious of the wonder and depth of feeling conveyed by the spiritual. And although the song speaks of redemption from the evils of slavery, somehow it transcends the particular moment. He contemplates his own response and that of the crowd:

> I was listening to something within myself, and for a second I heard the shattering stroke of my heart. Something deep had shaken the crowd, and the old man and the man with the horn had done it. They had touched something deeper than protest, or religion . . . All were touched; the song had aroused us all. It was not the words, for they were the same old slave-born words; it was as though he'd changed the emotion beneath the words while yet the old longing, resigned, transcendent emotion still sounded above, now deepened by that something for which the theory of the Brotherhood had given me no name. (p. 392)

He looks around: even the whites are singing.

The song's emotion frees the Invisible Man from his self-alienation and fortifies a sense of continuity within his tradition. Moreover, it aids him in realizing that within himself and within his tradition there are forms of expression to which all men may respond. Significantly, though the Brotherhood terms the funeral for Tod a "circus side show," the Invisible Man, for once, defends his true feelings about the event. He sees at last that in a guise of objectivity and political scientism, the leaders of the Brotherhood (like Bledsoe and the college trustees) despise the blacks whose interests they pretend to serve.

As in many major American novels, the sermon plays an important part in *Invisible Man*.[47] In the prologue, the Invisible Man hears a black preacher sermonizing at high pitch. Choosing as his sermon topic "The

Blackness of Blackness" (echoing the Bible), the preacher shouts, "*Now blackness is ... an' blackness ain't ...*" He continues, chanting, "*Black will git you ... an' black won't ... It do ... an' it don't.*" Conjuring and then undercutting the biblical story of Jonah (echoing the theme of several spirituals as well as the sermon used by Melville in *Moby Dick*), the preacher says that black "*will get you, glory, glory, Oh my Lawd, in the WHALE'S BELLY.*" "*Preach it, dear brother,*" the congregation answers. "*An' make you tempt ... Old Aunt Nelly! ... Black will make you ... or black will unmake you*" (pp. 12-13). Here, as in many fables and myths, magic words (like those of the narrator's grandfather) confound our hero. What, given all these contradictions and ironies, *does* blackness mean? For the Invisible Man part of the answer lies, as we have seen, in his acceptance of the black folk form in which the question is posed.

Though no other sermons per se exist in the novel, in several instances characters employ the styles of black preachers. Homer A. Barbee claps his hands and chants in sermonic style. And inevitably, when the Invisible Man begins making public addresses for the Brotherhood, he uses black church techniques. His improvised speech on the steps of the dispossessed old couple's apartment house rings with the spirited repetitions of the sermon. In his first speech as the Brotherhood's Harlem leader, he depends on shouted responses from the audience, as a black preacher does. Most tellingly, in this speech, again improvised, he gives an eloquent testimonial:

> "May I confess?" I shouted ... "You are my friends. We share a common disinheritance, and it's said that confession is good for the soul ... *Something strange and miraculous and transforming is taking place in me right now ... as I stand here before you!* ... Let me describe it. It is something odd. It's something that I'm sure I'd never experience anywhere else in the world ... I feel ... I feel ... I feel, I feel suddenly that I have become *more human* ... I feel that after a long and desperate and uncommonly blind journey, I have come home." (pp. 299-300)

And although the home he speaks of is, on one level, the political one, the Brotherhood, his style of speech recalls the home of the spirituals: a heavenly home or a state of mind that brings peace. The hero's conversion to the Brotherhood is stated in terms often used to describe spiritual salvation.

Folk forms also permeate the scene in the factory hospital where the narrator's sudden remembrance of a spiritual shields him from the planned annihilation of his identity. As he strains to recall who he is, the words of his grandmother's mock spiritual also come back to him:

> *Godamighty made a monkey*
> *Godamighty made a whale*
> *And Godamighty made a 'gator*
> *With hickeys all over his tail.*

The doctors, after examining the young man, believe that their dehumanization process (which, like the program of the Brotherhood, is designed to nullify his past and individual will) is a huge success. Though he says nothing, the Invisible Man thwarts their plan as he remembers another childhood rhyme:

> *Did you ever see Miss Margaret boil water?*
> *She hisses such a beautiful stream*
> *Seventeen miles and a quarter*
> *You can't see her pot for her steam.*

He also remembers Buckeye the Rabbit, a familiar figure in black folklore the doctors have only the vaguest knowledge of. Brer Rabbit, of course, could escape from the silly machine with no difficulty at all. Suddenly "giddy with the delight of self-discovery," the Invisible Man recalls a childhood song about the rabbit:

> *Buckeye the Rabbit*
> *Shake it, shake it*
> *Buckeye the Rabbit*
> *Break it, break it.*

In a flash, the Invisible Man feels that somehow he is the folkloric rabbit, able to escape the modern-day briar patch of the hospital.

The dozens also save the Invisible Man from destruction in the factory hospital. At a time when he seems able to remember neither his own name nor his mother's, the game of the dozens places him on the correct track. "WHO WAS YOUR MOTHER?" the doctor inquires. "Feeling a quick dislike," the Invisible Man thinks, "half in amusement, I don't play the dozens. And how's your old lady today?" (pp. 210-211). When the examiner asks, "BOY, WHO WAS BRER RABBIT?" the reply rushes to the hero's mind, "He was your mother's back door man" (p. 211). The doctors interpret the young man's silence as total success for the machine. In truth, however, the Invisible Man does not lose his identity; he falls back upon it in wonderment.

Throughout the novel, as the hero grows in self-awareness, his use of signifying and dozens multiplies. At first he hurls stylized insults (he signifies) at his foes only in his imagination. In his mind's eye, he sees himself watching President Bledsoe in New York, then advancing upon the pompous "educator" to accuse him of eating chitterlings in private. He would snatch out "a foot or two of chitterlings, raw, uncleaned and dripping sticky circles on the floor" and shake them in Bledsoe's face, shouting insults: "Bledsoe, you're a shameless chitterling eater! I accuse you of relishing hog bowels! Ha! And not only do you eat them, you sneak and eat them in private when you think you're unobserved! You're a sneaking chitterling lover! I accuse you of indulging in a filthy habit" (pp. 230-231). At this point in the daydream the Invisible Man imagines himself forcing Bledsoe to lug out his concealed yards of raw Thitterlings, mustard greense daydream the Invisible Man imagines himself forcing Bledsoe to lug out his concealed yards of raw chitterlings, mustard greens, racks of pig ears, and black-eyed peas, with their "dull accusing eyes." "Why," thinks the Invisible Man, moving closer to the dozens vein of humor, "it would be worse than if I accused him of raping an old woman of ninety-nine years, weighing ninety pounds . . . blind in one eye and lame in the hip." Such a disclosure of outright "field niggerism" causes Bledsoe's exile to wash dishes in a New York automat. In the South he would be unable to land a job on a honey wagon.

As he walks the streets in Harlem, the Invisible Man's southern politeness and meekness gradually dissolve into the dozens and signifying. When he throws the Sambo bank-doll into a trash can,[48] a light-skinned black woman, revealing extreme prejudice against her southern cousins, rudely tells the young man to fetch it and move on. "You field niggers from the South . . . are ruining things" for better colored people, she tells him. Steeped in good home training, the Invisible Man protests politely and then, with disgust, reaches through the garbage to retrieve the bank. "It serves you right," the woman says. This time, signifying words are on his lips. "That's enough out of you, you piece of yellow gone to waste . . . I've done what you wanted me to do; another word and I'll do what *I* want to do" (p. 285). Even the descriptive prose has a signifying-like edge when it turns upon the woman: she is a small lady whose coat sleeves hang limp like atrophied arms, "a short woman with a pince-nez on her chin, her hair pinned up in knots" (p. 284).

When Louis Brockway, the paint factory Uncle Tom, insults the Invisible Man and even bites him on the shoulder, the younger man jumps on him with a few old, signifying insults he has heard his grandfather use: "Why, you old-fashioned, slavery-time, mammy-made, handkerchief-headed bastard . . . Does this paint go to your head? Are you drinking it?" (p. 198). In disgust, he looks at the greasy old man with his pockets slicked shut with black slime and thinks, Tar Baby!

The heated differences between the Invisible Man and the other members of the Brotherhood, particularly Brother Jack, break into swift dozens and signifying play. At the meeting where Brother Wrestrum (whose very name, like Tobitt's—two bits—is a dozens-like play on words) accuses him of treachery, the Invisible Man asks if the organization truly believes the absurd charges. "Is everyone reading Dick Tracy these days?" demands Jack. "Oh, yes," says the Invisible Man. "Yes, I am. I'm interested in all manner of odd behavior" (p. 350). In the climactic confrontation with Brother Jack, in which the Invisible Man perceives that the group's leader is coolly willing to sacrifice the black community in behalf of "larger interests," dozens crackle from the hero's end of the table. Paralleling the southern town leaders who at the battle royal challenge the Invisible Man for a slip of the tongue, "social equality," Jack questions the hero's assertion of "personal responsibility." Jack is answered—or nearly so—in the language of the dirty dozens:

> "We went ahead on my personal responsibility," I said. Brother Jack's eyes narrowed. "What was that?" he said. "Your what?"
>
> "My personal responsibility," I said.
>
> "His personal responsibility," Brother Jack said. "Did you hear that, Brothers? Did I hear him correctly. Where did you get it, Brother?" he said. "This is astounding, where did you get it?"
>
> "From your ma—"I started and caught myself in time. "From the committee," I said. (p. 400)

Realizing that talking about Jack's mama would be misunderstood and unappreciated, the Invisible Man holds off. "Wouldn't it be better if they called you Marse Jack?" he says (p. 409).

As this brisk exchange proceeds, white Brother Tobitt gets into the act and is also confronted in dozens terms. Why, he asks, was Tod eulogized by the Invisible Man at "that side show of a funeral"? The hero forces a harsh smile and inquires, "How could there be a side show without you as the star attraction, who'd draw the two bitts admission, Brother Twobitts?" (pp. 402-403). Challenged further by Tobitt about the funeral, the Invisible Man asks: "And what is the source of your great contribution to the movement, Brother? A career in burlesque? And of your profound knowledge of Negroes? Are you from an old plantation family? Does your black mammy shuffle nightly through your dreams?" (p. 404). Learning that Tobitt has "a fine Negro" wife, the Invisible Man says his source is too narrow.

The hero goes on to tell Tobitt what he himself has learned at great pain—that for anyone to know what is happening in the black community, he must check with ordinary community people. He advises: "Ask your wife to take you around to the gin mills and the barber shops and the juke joints and the churches, Brother. Yes, and the beauty parlors on Saturdays when they're frying hair. A whole unrecorded history is spoken then" (p. 407). The Invisible Man speaks here from the experience gained after Tod's death. In one of the novel's most powerful scenes, he ponders the importance of black folk art and ordinary blacks he has forgotten and taken for granted. He sees some black boys in a subway station and considers their styles and habits.

> Yes, I thought, what about those os us who shoot up from the South into the busy city like wild jacks-in-the-box broken loose from our springs—so sudden that our gait becomes like that of deep-sea divers suffering from the bends? What about those fellows waiting still and silent there on the platform . . . standing noisy in their very silence; harsh as a cry of terror in their quietness? . . . Walking stiffly with swinging shoulders in their well-pressed, too-hot-for-summer suits, their collars high and tight about their necks, their identical hats of cheap black felt set upon the crowns of their heads with a severe formality above their hard conked hair? It was as though I'd never seen their like before. (p. 380)

The Brotherhood has taught him that such men are "out of time," unimportant. Suppose, though, that such men were of supreme value? The idea strikes him suddenly:

> Who knew (and I now began to tremble so violently I had to lean against a refuse can)—who knew but that they were the saviors, the true leaders, the bearers of something precious. The stewards of something uncomfortable, burdensome, which they hated because, living outside the realm of history, there was no one to applaud their value and they themselves failed to understand it. What if Brother Jack were wrong? What if history was a gambler, instead of a force in a laboratory experiment, and these boys his ace in the hole? . . . his big surprise! (p. 381)

The Invisible Man's realization of the value of the black masses is important in several ways. It is in line with the democratic ideal that people have fundamental rights, including that of participation in the political process. No downtown Brotherhood (however left-wing) has the right to make categorical decisions for the people uptown. The Invisible Man also sees that black people, though ignored and abused by the majority, have managed to maintain their own unique sense of life and integrity; he has no reason to be ashamed of his grandparents. Finally he understands that he is one of the "jacks-in-the-box": he is an individual but connected to a tradition. By the end of the novel he is moved by a spiritual ("Many Thousand Gone"), quotes a blues ("Buddy Bolden's Blues"), and talks in the language of the dirty dozens. He sees at last that he is one of "the bearers of something precious." He feels "as though I carried a heavy stone, the weight of a mountain on my shoulders" (p. 383). True to this image, the novel ends with the Invisible Man's conscious need to play a heroic role, to help blacks "move on up a little higher."

Invisible Man is not a historical novel, of course, but it deals with the past as a burden and as a stepping stone to the future. The hero discovers that history moves not like an arrow or an objective, scientific argument, but like a boomerang: swiftly, cyclically, and dangerously. He sees that when he is not conscious of the past, he is liable to be slammed in the head with it again when it circles back. As the novel unfolds, the Invisible Man learns that by accepting and evaluating all parts of his experience, smooth and ragged, loved and unloved, he is able to "look around corners" into the future:

> And now all past humiliations became precious parts of my experience, and for the first time . . . I began to accept my past and, as I accepted it, I felt memories welling up within me. It was as though I'd learned suddenly to look around corners; images of past humiliations flickered through my head and I saw that they were more than separate experiences. They were me; they defined me. I was my experiences and my experiences were me, and no blind men, no matter how powerful they became, even if they conquered the world, could take that, or change one single itch, taunt, laugh, cry, scar, ache, rage or pain of it. (p. 439)

At the beginning of the novel, the Invisible Man presents himself as a kind of Afro-American Jonathan, a "green" yokel pushed into the clownhouse of American society. He starts out ignorant of his society, his past, himself. By the end of the book he accepts his southern black folk past and sees that ordinary blacks like his grandfather, Trueblood, Mary, Tarp, Dupre, the unnamed boys in the subway, and himself are of ultimate value, no matter what the Bledsoes and Jacks say. Jarred to consciousness by folklore (among other things), the Invisible Man realizes that the tested wisdom expressed in spirituals, blues, dozens, and stories is a vital part of his experience. At last he comprehends that whatever he might do to be "so black and blue," he is, simply, who he is.

6

Visions and Revisions

Once Ellison finally approved the galley sheets of *Invisible Man*, he felt spent emotionally and artistically. Even before *Invisible Man* actually was published, however, he had begun jotting down ideas for a new novel, so that if the first one failed he would be too busy to worry. In 1952 he said he had a new novel "on the bench." Asked in 1953, shortly after the National Book Award ceremonies, what his next book would be about, he suggested that it might be a kind of elaboration of the first: "I don't feel that I have exhausted the theme of invisibility."[1] Indeed, he felt he could salvage some of the material edited out of *Invisible Man*, if he could find a proper form. "Out of the Hospital and Under the Bar" (1963), featuring the Invisible Man and Mary Rambo, was one such section. And although it may never have been part of the original novel, "Did You Ever Dream Lucky?" (1954) also involved *Invisible Man*'s Mary Rambo. For "A Coupla Scalped Indians" (1956), Ellison looked back into the world of Buster and Riley, whose antics had inspired several stories of the forties. While he struggled with the new novel, Ellison published these three fine offshoots and extensions of previous work, each exploring again how the naive youngster or newcomer readies himself or herself for adult life in the American maze.

For Ellison, smoothly conveying the protagonist from one scene to another posed one of the most difficult technical problems in writing *Invisible Man*. He wrote at least two versions of the "factory hospital" chapter, the transitional chapter linking the narrator's baffling and traumatic experiences in the Liberty Paints factory with his equally trying times in Harlem. An "Author's Note" explains that "Out of the Hospital and Under the Bar," published eleven years after the novel (1963), was actually the original version of the chapter. Conceived "during those expansive days of composition before the necessities of publication became a reality," this section, which gives more space to Mary Rambo, would have made *Invisible Man* "a better book," in Ellison's view.[2] For considerations of space, however, Ellison put aside the forty-five page original and composed the novel's present chapter eleven, compressed to fourteen pages.

The author's commentaries notwithstanding, chapter eleven as it appears in the novel has more zestful and more subtly symbolical prose. "Out of the Hospital" becomes snarled, in places, with minute descriptions and conventional symbols conventionally rendered. Nonetheless, in this piece we occasionally see Ellison at his best: the dialogue is spirited, the prose rhythms often captivating. As a short story, "Out of the Hospital" stands on its own, and as a draft of a chapter of *Invisible Man* it is a fascinating piece for study. And it is pleasing to see more of Harlem's Mary Rambo and to discover "that it was Mary, a woman of the folk, who helped release the hero from the machine."[3]

"Out of the Hospital" begins when the narrator awakens in a tight, glass and nickel box where he has been locked up for eight or nine days. His body is strung with electrodes and tubes, his limbs lashed in place. As in the novel, the Invisible Man suffers from some sort of amnesia, remembering neither his name nor anything about his personal history. Mary Rambo, a hospital janitor, refuses to believe he is really sick, so she helps him to escape and offers him a place in her Harlem rooming house. First, though, in this story of symbolic rebirth, the "big ole rusty baby" (the Invisible Man) must find his way out of the strange hospital.

Stark naked, he takes the elevator from the third floor to the basement where he is pursued in the dark by hospital attendants. Underground, he runs in the dark from chamber to chamber like Richard Wright's "man who lived underground," until he fumbles up a ladder and pushes loose a rusty manhole cover. At last, Harlem. The story ends when the Invisible Man runs into a blind man who looks and talks like his grandfather, and who says, "I guess they keep a young fellow like you running." With this statement, ironically all too true and echoing his grandfather's earlier warning, the Invisible Man remembers the college, Bledsoe, the letters—everything. He decides to find Mary's place and hide there until he "could fill in the blank part of my experience."[4]

With its feeding tubes, belts, and electrodes that seem part of the Invisible Man's very flesh, the hospital's glass and nickel box is a kind of grotesque womb where he lies naked "as the day he was born." Mary is the machine's human counterpart; she saves the Invisible Man from the machine by unselfishly playing a maternal role. When she has removed the glass lid, she asks how he feels and, in response to his apparently diffident silence, she says with motherly insistence and chastisement, "Say, son . . . Is you a dummy or something? You look intelligent, so how come you don't say something?" Finally, he tells her he has "forgotten nearly everything" and she responds as if she were family: "Shucks, boy, I ain't one of them doctors. You don't have to tell me that stuff. How long you been from down home?" Since his hands are tied, she feeds him as if he were a baby. "Open your mouth," she says. "Lord, here I is feeding another baby. A big ole rusty baby!" (p. 249). Later she gives him some home-brewed medicine. It tastes bad, but she tells him, "Don't you know ain't no medicine any good unless it's hard to take? . . . That's some good stuff . . . That stuff'll make a baby strong" (p. 261).

Mary insists that the Invisible Man obey certain behavior codes. When she has unlatched the case and the young man stares dumbly at her, she tells him, "Well you could be sociable . . . How come you don't say nothing?" (p. 246). She also requires trust and the simple truth. Interpreting as mistrust his repeated assertion that he does not know his name, Mary threatens to leave him alone in the hospital room: "I got to go," she says, "I can't help nobody who don't trust me." Desperate, the Invisible Man manufactures a story corroborating Mary's belief that he must have done something terrible to cause white folks to lock him in the suffocating box. Ironically, Mary's adamance causes the young man to fabricate a detailed lie. The irony is compounded when, through telling the lie—in which the Invisible Man strikes a racist and sexually aggressive southern white homosexual man who propositions and accosts him—the young narrator edges close to the truth. In the midst of the story he is "suddenly gripped by a feeling that I was relating an actual happening, something that had occurred sometime, somewhere, in my past" (p. 254). Mary seems to know that whatever story he tells will be *his* story, in some sense his truth.

By helping the Invisible Man to escape, Mary not only assists in his ritual rebirth; she also helps to dispel the curse of self-alienation he suffers. As in *Invisible Man* and in several stories, a character steeped in folklore and fully aware of the complexities of black identity helps the young man in "Out of the Hospital" to regain his strength and identity. Again, the mention of bits from folklore restores the protagonist's memory of the

past he has undervalued and forgotten. Mary tells him the doctors have
tied him as if he were a folk champion. "Who they think you is," she
asks, "Jack the Bear, John Henry or somebody like that?" (p. 252). Surely
he is as befuddled as the bear of black folklore, stumbling "into and out of
the hospital, and under the bar." Like the bear of one rhyme, the Invisible
Man "just ain't getting nowhere." But also like Brer Rabbit, John, or any
of several other quick-witted black folk heroes, he does (with help) get
out of the hospital "briarpatch"; and, as it turns out, he knows how to lie
as situations demand. Unlike the novel's Invisible Man, this character
seems to know that to survive he needs to be both trickster and
muscleman: hare and bear. As he strains to lift the box lid, he seems to
recall Mary's words and says a crazy prayer: "Lord, give me the strength
of Jack-the-Bear." He then recalls a childhood rhyme:

> Jack the rabbit
> Jack the bear
> Lift, lift,
> Just a hair.

Lifting the lid, he reflects on folk art and on the task of freeing himself:
"Make poetry of it, sing it — no they might hear. Sing a song in silence in
a strange land, Jack it up, bear it in the dark, it's heavy as the world."
　　In the underground basement of a Harlem bar, the story's Invisible
Man seems to hear Jack-the-Bear growling the "How Long Blues":

> Where had I heard it, what did it mean? Some muted instrument
> sounded for all the world like a muffled voice. Or was it a voice that
> sounded like a muted horn? What was the voice in the juke box
> saying? Another instrument, like a bear growling, took up the
> refrain. It sounds like Jack-the-Bear, I thought for no reason at all
> . . . If only I dare lie down and rest. (p. 277)

As in the novel, the blues themselves — here combined to include the folk
character Jack-the-Bear — seem to "hollar like a mountain jack," calling
the confused Invisible Man back to his senses. Setting him free as his
gradual remembrance and acceptance of the vernacular tradition in which
his identity is rooted.
　　Since the sophisticated doctors do not seem able to help him, Mary also
gives the Invisible Man a dose of her own therapy and folk medicine. She
tells him, first off, that he is not crazy, no matter what the white doctors
and nurses say; to her he is just another "game young scamp" in need of
some home cooking and good company. She sneaks him some bread and

canned pork. Then, for extra strength, she serves him a mixture of herbs brewed by her 104-year-old mother, who learned the recipe from *her* mother's mother. The home remedy seems to act as a kind of magic potion: swallowing the wadded leafy substance, the Invisible Man finds that it seems "to act directly upon my muscles" (p. 263). He raises the lid, with his arms straight above his head. Like Frederick Douglass, who in his 1845 *Narrative* explains how he got power from carrying Sandy Jenkin's *root*, the Invisible Man is restored by Mary's folk remedy.

With her mother-wit, faith, and conjuration, Mary has reaffirmed the Invisible Man's links with his past and with his present reality. He was fast becoming contented in the machine, but Mary remained confident of his readiness for freedom. Back on the street, the Invisible Man finds that suddenly "that which should have been the past had become mixed with the present again, clashing with it, and memory beat upon me like the rain" (p. 289). And though he tries not to think of it, he remembers it all. Mary, and the nightmare she had helped him to endure, restored his memory—most of it anyway—and he is able to assemble many pieces to the puzzle of his identity.

Fortunately, the technical problem of removing the Invisible Man from the hospital to Harlem generated this fine story. Like Faulkner's "That Evening Sun," the piece that forecast *The Sound and the Fury*, "Out of the Hospital" alludes to many themes that are full-blown in the larger work. Here we learn more about the invisibility of the protagonist. Moreover, we see more of one of Ellison's heroic "folk characters," Mary, whose inextinguishable love and faith in the hero's sanity and manhood rescue him from destruction in the tomblike machine.

As noted in the headnote to "Did You Ever Dream Lucky?" (1954), this story, the first published after *Invisible Man*, is a further elaboration of one of the themes of the novel.[5] Like the novel, "Dream Lucky" concerns the naive wishfulness of young black Americans sprung from the South into the tarnished promised land of the North. The narrator is omniscient here, but again the focus is on Mary Rambo, who talks with some of her roomers about the greenness of black youth and about herself when she was "as green as anybody what ever left the farm and came to town." "Dream Lucky" lacks the pace and richness of detail that characterize Ellison's best writing. Nor is it as funny: its humor depends too heavily on the punch line. Yet we do learn still more about one of Ellison's major characters, Mary Rambo, and about his use of folk materials. In this story once again we observe a greenhorn's initiation into modern society.

"Dream Lucky" unfolds on Thanksgiving evening, while Mary Rambo and two of her long-term, senior roomers—Portwood, a retired porter, and Mrs. Garfield, a well-spoken widow and retired cook—lean back from the "tragic wreck of the Thanksgiving turkey" they have consumed. Portwood and Mrs. Garfield sip wine ceremoniously as Mary warms up to recite a tale about her early days in New York. From their window above Harlem, Mary and her daughter Lucy saw an automobile accident, with a bag noisily thrown into the street. The women raced downstairs and secretly retrieved a bulging cloth bag that felt and sounded as if full of money. Nervous and guilty about their good fortune, Mary and Lucy hid the bag, significantly, in the flush box of the toilet. And, Mary tells her roomers, she "got to flushing it just to hear it give out that fine clinking sound . . . Everytime I pulled the chain it was like ringing up money in the cash register!" (p. 142).

Finally, Mary yielded to temptation and pulled the bag, "green with canker," and took a long look inside. What she saw rattled her nerves and she went to bed. When Lucy arrived at home, full of ideas of what to buy first with the money, Mary thought a while and said she really believed they might need a car. "A car!" Lucy replied "We don't want to be like these ole ignorant Negroes who buy cars and don't have anything to go with it and no place to keep it." With pain Mary said she was merely being practical: "How else is we gon' use two sets of auto chains?" Mary had to leap from her bed and catch Lucy before she "swayed dead away in a faint" (p. 145). Yes, Mary tells Mr. Portwood, she had "dreamed lucky," but she "woke up cold in hand," as the blues song says.

As in Ellison's most inspired writing—*Invisible Man*, "Flying Home," and "Mister Toussan"—folklore figures centrally in "Dream Lucky." The title, taken from the blues "Cold in Hand Blues" (also known as "Blues in the Dark"), leads the reader to expect folklore ingredients. In one version of this blues, Genevieve Davis sings:

> Did you ever dream lucky,
> Wake up cold in hand?
> Did you ever dream lucky,
> Wake up cold in hand?
> You didn't have a dollar,
> To pay your house-rent man.[7]

In the story Ellison plays on the lyric. Mary dreams lucky, as she tells Portwood, and when she pulls her dream-bag from the flush box, "it had done got *cooold*! It come up *cooold*" (p. 143). Her luck, too, had run cold.

The story's characters and setting also lead the reader to expect some folklore. Portwood, Mrs. Garfield, and Mary are what George Kent has termed folk characters—not in the sense, of course, that Brers Bear and Fox are folk characters but in that they are closely associated with the oral tradition of black Americans. Portwood has portered on the railroad for twenty-five years; Mrs. Garfield is a retired cook; Mary runs the rooming house. All three places—the train, the kitchen, and the rooming-house parlor—are strongholds of folklore. In the novel the Invisible Man tells the Brotherhood that to learn what blacks are really thinking they should visit such places, along with barbershops, beauty parlors, and drugstores: places where blacks exchange their "lies" apart from white scrutiny. Especially on a holiday like Thanksgiving (the festive holiday celebrating green Americans' endurance in the New World), Mary's diningroom table is just such a place.

Contemporary scholars have observed that folklore is not fully recorded when it is simply transcribed on a page; rather it is the process or performance, the gestures, inflections, enactments, and audience responses, that makes the folklore come alive. Certainly, like Jefferson of "Flying Home," Mary performs her story-within-a-story in "Dream Lucky." And her audience urges her to tell it with verve. Portwood's and Mary's verbal wrangling over who knows the meaning of *green* sets the stage for the performance. When Mary says that Portwood does not even know green when he sees it, Portwood knows a story is brewing: "'Let me get out of here,' Portwood said, getting up. 'Mrs. Garfield, she's just tuning up to lie. I can't understand why we live here with an ole lying woman like her anyhow. And contentious with it too'" (p. 134). Just as this is Portwood's "way of provoking Mary into telling a story, it was Mary's way of introducing the story she would tell." (p. 135) "Look at her," he says, his voice rising indignantly, "sitting there looking like a lady preacher or something." With Portwood maintaining that he already knows all there is to know about green, the stage is set for Mary's tale, which she nearly sings:

> "Hush, Portwood!" Mary said. "What *green*?" She said, singing fullthroatedly now, her voice suddenly folk-toned and deep with echoes of sermons and blue trombones, "Lawd, *I* was green. That's what I'm trying to tell you. Y'all hear me? *I Me, Mary Raaaam-bo,* was green."
>
> "You telling me?" Portwood laughed. "Is you telling *me*?" Nevertheless he leaned forward with Mrs. Garfield now, surrendering once more to Mary's once-upon-a time antiphonal spell, waiting to respond to her stated theme: green. (p. 136)

With the spell cast, Mary pours wine for her guests, and "they drank ceremoniously with lowered eyes, waiting for Mary's old contralto to resume its flight, its tragic-comic ascendance." Mary dramatizes her story. To illustrate the car crash she shifts two knives on the table cloth. In characterizing the hush immediately following the cars' impact, she "rocked forward for emphasis." In the midst of the story, she laughs, she whispers, her eyes become intense.

Mary's tale-within-a-tale cannot be found, word for word, in any compendium of folktales. Yet folk allusions and motifs abound. Mary compares herself and others with animals. The cars that collide are compared with two big bulls that "has done charged and run head-on." The young white policeman is described as a turkey gobbler whose head snaps around when he sees Mary on the curb. Hiding the supposed treasure under her skirts, Mary tries to elude the cop and everybody else, lest someone discover "what kinda egg this is I'm nesting on." Upstairs, both Mary and Lucy sit around nervously "like two ole hens on a nest," guessing the amount of their godsend. Before long the guesswork, fear, and guilt become agonizing; they can neither sleep nor eat. "We was as evil as a coupla lady bears at cubbing time."

Mary's story is much like stories of mysterious treasures which are plentiful in Afro-American folklore and in folklore internationally. Very often in such tales, a treasure is revealed to a person in a dream, by spirits, by persistent thunder, or by beckoning fireballs. Mary and Lucy find their supposed treasure when the usual Harlem street noise is broken by the thunderous "WHAM" of cars colliding. The bag is flung from the wreckage "like a cannon ball."

The discovery and loss of dream treasure has a long history in the annals of folklore.[8] In many American and Afro-American buried-treasure stories good fortune, spirits, or ancestors may lead lucky persons to wealth, but just as often "hants" or taboo infractions cause the values to be lost.[9] For example, talking while a treasure chest is lifted is often considered taboo. When Lucy says the bag is full of money, Mary says "Shhh, fool . . . You don't have to tell ev'y body." To bury the newfound treasure may also be taboo, if not sinful or fatal. The fact that Mary and Lucy hide their money foreshadows their disappointment. It also indicates their greenness.

As Ellison has observed, comic folktales in which high hopes are deflated are typically American. These "lies" reflect the absurdity of the American predicament as well as the likelihood of disappointment in the New World. In Ellison's words:

It was here in a land where we brought our God with us, a land which seemed to frustrate even God, that we found the need for reducing man to practical terms. You knew that if you went out there to those woods, that you were going to die. You knew that if you stepped behind the wrong tree, someone might bury a tomahawk in your head; you knew that if you picked up that piece of gold, it just might turn out to be a turtle.[10]

This kind of humor, in which a bag of gold turns into a turtle or a sack of chains, is "callous" but "it prepares the American for the worst." It reminds the starry-eyed Afro-American that the lofty American dream does not necessarily apply to "the darker brother." The dreamer may, like Mary, *dream* lucky but will probably wake up cold in hand.

In "A Coupla Scalped Indians" (1956), which Ellison called an offshoot of a novel in progress, we return to the red-dirt and oil-rich hills of the Southwest, the turf of two young boys, Buster and his playmate, nameless here. Unlike the Buster-Riley stories of the forties, however, the world of "Scalped Indians" is reminiscent of certain nineteenth-century romances. Complete with darkling lake, bright sliver of a moon, swift and silently flying owls, dancing ghosts, and Aunt Mackie, an herb doctor with snakey hair, "Scalped Indians" is a tightly unified story of suspense and spookiness. The narrator, eleven at the time of the story's dreamlike action, wonders what exactly he went through in the lamplit cabin with strange Aunt Mackie. "The images flowed in my mind, became shadowy, no part was left to fit another."[11] The parts of this youngster's world, shattered when "the air seemed to explode soundlessly," fit together not as figures in a mathematical equation but as elements in a complex initiation ritual, preparing him and his buddy for life as black men in society complicated and mad.

The narrator and Buster race toward the "bright music" of the spring carnival, but they are slowed down by the pain of their recent circumcisions. This operation—having some hygienic value but principally symbolizing a boy's sacrifice for passage into spiritually pure, sexually virile manhood[12]—is the central rite on which the story is based. The surgeon has told the youngsters that the operation would make them men. The narrator, still bandaged and "carrying cat gut stitches," considers with pride, "That's one kind of operation no woman ever gets to brag about" (p. 227).

As in previous Buster-Riley tales, Buster lures his friend into more and more extravagant adventures. As unawed by Aunt Mackie as he is by the truant officer, Buster gives his buddy extra courage as they travel together. To the doctor who says circumcision will make them men, truant officer, Buster gives his buddy extra courage as they travel together. To the doctor who says circumcision will make them men, Buster replies "Hell, I am a man already." What he wants is to be an Indian. To prove it he undertakes to perform the tasks in a Boy Scout handbook he has found, challenging his friend to slip out of his house and perform them too, saying "a real stud Indian could take the tests even right after the doctor had just finished sewing on him." Using the handbook, Buster insists upon test after test: running, swimming, cooking. The bolder boy is both initiator and initiate in his own and his friend's continuing rite of passage into manhood.

The jazz in the background of "Scalped Indians" adds to the story's ritual effect. To begin with, the music helps to transport the reader into the romantic dreamworld of the story's action. "Scalped Indians" begins with these words:

> They had a small, loud-playing hand and as we moved through the trees I could hear the notes of the horns bursting like bright metallic bubbles against the sky. It was a faraway and sparklike sound; shooting through the late afternoon quiet of the hill: very clear now and definitely music, band music. (p. 225)

Somehow the narrator is lured by the brightness of the music: "The horns were blasting brighter now . . . sounding like somebody flipping bright handfuls of new small change against the sky." It is the "bright blare" of the horns that makes the boys forget their weariness and pain as they bound toward the carnival "like young goats in the twilight" (p. 226).

In his essay "Remembering Jimmy" Ellison explains that jazz bandsmen performed a "sacred rite" in the Oklahoma City of his boyhood, where public dances constituted "a third institution" (along with church and school) in the black community. Like a public dance, the spring carnival of "Scalped Indians" provides these youngsters with the chance to hear jazz, to socialize, and to "raise hell." The narrator says he was hurrying to be there "right in the middle of all that confusion and sweating and laughing and all the strange sights to see" (p. 229). Significantly, Buster links his enthusiasm to get there to his being scalped. He says the doctor "scalped so much of my head away I must be crazy as a fool. That's why I'm in such a hurry to get down yonder with the other crazy fools. I want to be right in the middle of 'em when they really start raising hell." To be right in the middle, fully accepted as men, worthy of full participation in the wildness and the ecstatic dancing and courtship associated with the "third institution," is the quest of the boys.

Buster and his buddy interpret the ritual "talk" of the distant bright horns, which speak in stylishly irreverent, masculine tongues. According to the boys' translations, the horns tempt even the devil by starting out proclaiming "Amazing Grace" and ending up mumbling the dirty dozens. The trombone "sounds like he's playing the dozens with the whole wide world." His theme of *drawers* is, according to Buster, typical of the dozens. The trombone says, "Ya'lls mamas don't wear 'em. Is strictly without 'em. Don't know nothing about 'em" (p. 229). The trumpet seems to address the community's church folk—those who do not, of course, play the dozens. He assures the "saved" that, for the jazz-man, sacred and secular merge. The trumpet says:

> So y'all don't play 'em, hey?
> So y'all won't play 'em, hey?
> Well pat your feet and clap your hands,
> 'Cause I'm going to play 'em to the promised land. (p. 230)

The jazzmen speak not only of sex and religion but of the dealings of black men and white. The trumpeter has turned his anger into highly expressive art. "Man," says Buster, "if the white folks knew what that fool is signifying on that horn they'd run him clear on out the world. Trumpet's got a real *nasty* mouth" (p. 230). With his horn he plays the dozens on whites ("slips 'em into the twelves") and offers to fight them at the same time. The clarinet is more subtle: "Clarinet so sweet-talking he just *eases* you into the dozens" (p. 230). As naive as the Invisible Man, the unnamed narrator here says that Buster and he should stop cussing and playing the dozens so much if they want to be Boy Scouts. "Those white boys don't play that mess," he says. With the "nasty mouth" trumpet as his witness, Buster instructs his friend on why white boys do not play the twelves.

> "You doggone right they don't," he said, the turkey feather vibrating above his ear. "Those guys can't take it, man. Besides, who wants to be just like them? Me, *I'm* gon' be a scout and play the twelves too! You have to, with some of these old jokers we know. You don't know what to say when they start easing you, you never have no peace. You have to outtalk 'em, outrun 'em, or outfight 'em and I don't aim to be running and fighting all the time. N'mind those white boys." (p. 230)

Part of being a black man, the nameless boy learns, involves understanding and mastering the sometimes brassy, sometimes "easing" talk of the dozens and jazz. But this does not mean giving up other goals: "Me, I'm gon' be a scout and play the twelves too!" (p. 230).

Rambling toward the music of the spring carnival, the youngsters find themselves in the yard of the dreaded Aunt Mackie. In a marvelously poetical rush of nouns and prepositional phrases, the narrator tells of his fear of this woman whose very name makes him tremble:

> Ho, Aunt Mackie, talker-with-spirits, prophetess of disaster, odd-dweller-alone in a riverside shack surrounded by sunflowers, morning-glories, and strange magical weeds ... Old Aunt Mackie, wizen-faced walker-with-a-stick, shrill-voiced ranter in the night, round-eyed malicious one, given to dramatic trances and firey flights of rage; Aunt Mackie, preacher of wild sermons on the busy streets of the town, hot-voiced chaser of children, snuff-dipper, visionary; wearer of greasy headrags, wrinkled gingham aprons and old men's shoes; Aunt Mackie, nobody's sister but still Aunt Mackie to us all ... teller of fortunes, concocter of powerful body-rending spells ... Aunt Mackie, the remote one though always seen about us; night-consulted adviser to farmers on crops and cattle ... herb-dealer, root-doctor, and town-confounding oracle to wildcat drillers seeking oil in the earth. (p. 228)

As if magically drawn there, the narrator trips over an old stove and sunflower stalks and discovers that, in avoiding Aunt Mackie's watchdog, he has crawled right up to her shack. Buster has gone ahead, and the narrator keeps silent when he hears his friend calling him. "And there," he says, "framed by the window in the lamp-lit room, I saw the woman" (p. 231).

Ellison presents Aunt Mackie awash with moon- and lamplight, and through the dreamy eyes of an eleven-year-old boy. The confusion about her appearance and character is of course intentional. She is at once a dream lady, a harpy from a young boy's fantasy world, and a weird princess from the moonflower garden. This woman in man's clothes is full of contradictions: her face is old and wizened, her body young and supple; she seems enthusiastically "saved" but places spells on people. "Lips that touch wine shall never touch mine," she says—yet her own lips taste greedily of wine. As folklorists tell us, Aunt Mackie is just the sort of woman around whom so many tales cluster.[13] In her encounter with the narrator, we learn more about his consciousness than hers. All we know literally about her is that she is an odd woman and that the narrator fantasizes about her extravagantly.

When the narrator spies the woman dancing in the glow of her cabin—before he sees that it is Aunt Mackie—sexual yearnings and fears are ignited. She appears to him as a "brown naked woman, whose black hair hung beneath her shoulders." With the band music sparkling in the distance, Aunt Mackie sways in a slow dance, "moving as though gathering in something . . . which she drew to her with pleasure." He is paralyzed with fascination at the sight of this dancing woman with the girlish body and slender hips. He is also stilled by guilt and fear of punishment for peeping.

When suddenly she turns to look at him, the shock of seeing Aunt Mackie's hard and wrinkled face makes him want to "laugh wildly and to scream." He feels the "terror of her mystery": how could this lovely body have such an awful face? How could such a mismatched being excite him so? She decides to seduce him, and the prospect of kissing her is terrible. Close up he sees her chin hairs and, he thinks, "It's just like kissing some sweaty woman at church, some friend of Miss Janey's" (p. 234). But she is not to be denied, and, guiltily, he finds himself touching her breast. Ellison suggests here the boy's ambiguous feelings about this maternal figure who is both the seductive angel and the claw-fingered witch.

Aunt Mackie arouses the youngster's fear of castration—a central concern in "Scalped Indians"—which is enflamed by his recent circumcision. "Hell, man," says Buster, hinting at this castration fear, "that damn doctor scalped me last week. Damn near took my whole head off!" (p. 227). In Aunt Mackie's yard, the dog lunges toward the narrator but is yanked backward by his chain. So the animal turns "to mouth savagely on the mangled bird." When Aunt Mackie spots the youngster outside her window, she turns on him fiercely, and again he hears "the growling dog mangling the bird" (p. 231). Aunt Mackie's attempt to seduce the boy makes him more anxious about castration. Suddenly he is crying. "I am hurting in my operation," he says. She insists on examining the wound with "three claw-like fingers." Grinning and cackling, she suggests his inadequacy, if not his castration. "Hmmmmmmm," she says, "a fishing worm with a headache! . . . Boy, you have been pruned. I'm a doctor but no tree surgeon" (p. 235).

Suddenly her eyes become round, and she wants to know his age. The news that he is eleven strikes her like a shot, and she pulls a robe around her body and orders him to leave. If he says anything about her she will "fix" his daddy and mammy too. He runs away through the wisteria and moonflowers, past the dog groaning, (presumably with sage-hen fever) and he wonders where Buster has gone. "Where was that other scalped Indian?"

Aunt Mackie's sneers about the boy's bandaged penis spark his resentment and pride: "*I'm a man*, I said within myself. *Just the same I am a man!*" (p. 232). But how does his encounter with Aunt Mackie contribute to his crossing over into manhood? Above all, this sphinxlike woman personifies the pleasure, anxiety, and pain associated with adult sexuality and reproduction. While lusting for her curvaceous body, the boy notices a long, puckered gash on her stomach. From the young-old, lovely-hideous, seducing-rejecting witchwoman, the young man learns something of the illusiveness and the contradictoriness of human experience. Finally even her nakedness is "no thing more than another veil; much like the baggy dresses she always wore." If the boy's incipient manhood necessitates circumcision and other ritual tests, it also involves confusion, embarrassment, and mystery.

In these three stories of trial and initiation, Ellison reviewed themes he had studied since the thirties. Yet, especially in the case of "A Coupla Scalped Indians," the treatment is fresh and contemporary. After the mid-fifties, however, most of his energy had gone into preparing a new novel about Rev. Hickman and Senator Sunraider. As early as 1953 he had begun devising the structural framework for the Hickman book, which he expected to be much more complex and, he hoped, much better than his first.

7

The Hickman Stories

Since the mid-fifties, when Ellison conceived his second novel, reports of its progress and problems have filtered out to the reading
public. Eight excerpts from this work in progress have appeared in
such journals as *Noble Savage, Iowa Review,* and *New American Review.* It
is as if Ellison were both testing the waters and demonstrating his ability
to stroke like a champion when he chooses to do so. These tantalizing
portions of the novel, some of which he has read on public television and
on college campuses, along with reports from friends who have heard the
writer read privately from the massive manuscript, have made the wait for
the published whole something of a vigil. Interviewers asking about the
book are sometimes quietly rebuffed: that it is still in the making is often
all Ellison will say. At other times, though, Ellison recites the history of a
wayward tome, slow in the initial writing and rewriting, destroyed by
fire, reborn, and very slow in the rerewriting. It seems certain that Ellison
feels the pressure to wrestle what he calls the "damned big book" until it
is as great a work as *Invisible Man*; this ambition is the new book's blessing and its curse.[1]

The design of the novel in progress emerges from the published
fragments. Set in the South during the period from about 1920 to 1960,
its central characters are Rev. Alonzo Zuber Hickman, reformed jazz
trombonist, and the light-skinned (white?) orphan boy Bliss, whom
Hickman adopts and rears to be a revival circuit evangelist. It is Bliss, boy
minister-in-training, who raises the lid of a coffin during Rev. Hickman's

sermon on resurrection, causing wonder (on the boy's part and the reader's) about whether or not the church "performance" debases the sacred ritual with stage tricks. Eventually Bliss (who, like Rineheart in *Invisible Man*, is something of a devilish trickster) disappears into the white community, passing for white. Years later he surfaces as a senator from a New England state. The white/black boy has become Senator Sunraider, bitter and eloquent spokesman for white supremacy who, to compound the mystery, retains certain distinctively Afro-American ways of gesturing and talking.

From several Hickman stories we learn that one spring day a black jazz-man, Lee Willie Minifees, is cruising toward Harlem when he hears Sunraider on the radio ridiculing blacks, especially those who, like Minifees himself, drive Cadillacs. Sunraider announces sarcastically that he wants to draw up a congressional bill renaming the Cadillac the "Coon Cage Eight." Outraged, Minifees drives his white car onto the senator's well-barbered lawn, burns the car, and makes a speech expressing his anger. McIntyre, a white liberal reporter, witnesses the wild scene. A climax is reached when black Severen, whom we first meet as a boy growing up in a southwestern town, stands up during floor debate in the Senate and guns down Sunraider. Hickman has come to Washington to warn the senator of the rumored assassination plan, but the old black preacher is prevented from gaining an audience with Sunraider; powerless, Hickman witnesses the shooting of his "secret son." The senator is delirious on his sickbed when he calls for Hickman, who comes to the hospital to comfort him. Meanwhile (Ellison reports in an interview), Minifees is held in a hospital—not a jail, since any black man who would "flambé" his Cadillac *must* be crazy.[2] McIntyre interviews him there, aided by a black hospital employee who sneaks the white reporter past the barriers. The form of the projected book, Ellison has explained, laughing, is "a realism extended beyond realism."[3]

Like Ellison's earlier protagonists, young Bliss is bright and spunky but inexperienced, naive. Like Riley, Tod, the King of the Bingo, and the Invisible Man, Bliss is a greenhorn who is encouraged, through sometimes brutal confrontations with reality, to discard all illusions and grow up. Bliss is also protected and guided by a strong, folk-wise, loving parent-surrogate, Rev. Hickman—whose counterparts in earlier works include Jefferson, Mary Rambo, and Brother Tarp. But unlike his literary cousins, Bliss recoils from the demanding implications of his life. Instead of "flying home," he flies miles away from home. His decision to become Senator Sunraider is a violent denial of personal history. Moreover, it is a renunciation of the blackness of American experience and culture, a refusal to accept the American past in all its complexity. Somehow he becomes not the hero his upbringing prepares him to become, but a monster, a liar hell-bent toward destruction of blacks and whites and of himself. One critic has observed that Bliss-become-Sunraider emerges as "something of a brutalized metaphor himself of what happened to the baby democracy, tossed from hand to hand and born out of wedlock (à la Fielding's Tom Jones, to say nothing of some of the leading people in the U.S.)"[4]

As we have come to expect, the Hickman stories concern broad questions of identity and history, culture and politics. Also typical is Ellison's fictional use of rituals, secular and sacred: rituals of birth, initiation, purification, death, rebirth. Ellison meditates on the power of language to amuse, to obfuscate, to provoke, and to teach. And again he seeks to unlock the meanings of Afro-American folklore—sermons, spirituals, blues, jokes. Surveying an important area of American history, from just after World War I until the civil rights movement, Ellison looks deeply into the nature of the American way of life. What was dream? What was real? And who, after all, is the American: Sunraider, Hickman, or both?

In the first issues of *Noble Savage*, the London-based literary magazine for which Ellison worked briefly as a contributing editor, he placed "And Hickman Arrives" (1960), the first and, so far, the best of the eight Hickman stories.[5] In this story the white-haired but robust Rev. Hickman and forty-four members of his congregation have journeyed to Washington to tell Senator Sunraider of a rumored plot against his life. Despite their stalwart efforts, the blacks are prevented from leaving a message with the senator and from seeing him until they are seated in the visitors' gallery of the Senate. Suddenly Severen stands as if to leave and then shoots Sunraider. Before going down, the senator cries in his preacher's voice, "Lord, LAWD, WHY HAST THOU . . .?" Watching the "dreamlike world of rushing confusion below him," Rev. Hickman echoes Sunraider's plea, singing, "Oh, Lord . . . why hast thou taken our Bliss, Lord? Why now our awful secret son, Lord? . . . Snatched down our poor bewildered foundling, Lord? LORD, LORD, Why hast thou . . .?"

At the hospital the senator calls for Hickman, and, against doctors' orders, the old preacher sits at Sunraider's bedside. Hickman speaks softly and Sunraider's thoughts sail to the past the two men recall times in the Deep South when they worked together as itinerant ministers. For tent revivals, Rev. Hickman preached about Christ's death and resurrection over a small, closed coffin containing Rev. Bliss. At a particular moment Bliss would open the coffin and sit up. The boy would innocently cry, "LORD WHY HAS THOU FORSAKEN ME?" Then Bliss would preach a short, memorized sermon based on Jesus' words, "I am the resurrection."

One night, in the heat of the ritual, after Bliss has sat up and begun speaking, a white woman rushes forward not, as expected, to praise the Holy Spirit but to grab Bliss whom she claims to be her stolen son Cudworth. Hickman, conscious of the possible repercussions of a southern white woman's screaming and fighting in the midst of blacks at night, tries to calm the crowd, but confusion reigns. The church women refuse to let the white woman remove Bliss; although she holds his body, her red hair is knotted around the fist of Sister Bearmasher. Rev. Hickman conducts the tustling group into a fancy horse-drawn wagon, and, praying and sweating, he drives past a burning barn toward the town. Hickman says that perhaps the fatal error he made that night was that he prayed for every part of the wagon, for himself, the white woman, the man whose barn burned, Sister Bearmasher; and "all that time," he says to the bedridden senator, "I should have been praying for you . . . I left you out Bliss, and I guess right then and there you started to wander." The story closes when the old reverend asks if Bliss is listening and Bliss says he is, but a moment later he has fallen asleep.

In this story the subject is death. At the senator's office, the men who have come with Hickman to warn Sunraider of the assassination are all old; they stand like ushers at a funeral, wearing "neat but old-fashioned black suits" and holding "wide-brimmed, deep crowned panama hats" with a "grave ceremonial air" (p. 693). Like church nurses or usherettes, the women, also old, wear "little white caps and white uniforms." Speaking for the group, Rev. Hickman tells the senator's white secretary, who indignantly refuses to contact the senator, "You're really making a mistake, miss . . . Soon it might be too late." His voice carries no threat; it only echoes "the odd sadness" in the faces of the blacks. Later when they listen to the senator's words from the floor of Congress, their faces are as composed, and their eyes as remote "as though through some mistake they were listening to a funeral oration for a stranger" (p. 696). When he has been shot, the senator and then Hickman scream the dying words of Jesus, "WHY HAS THOU FORSAKEN . . ." And in the hospital, both men recall Bliss's small coffin and their sermons about death and resurrection. They also reflect on the day Bliss died, figuratively, and Sunraider was born. Hickman and the blacks have come north with the hope that Bliss, their "secret son," their "last hope," and "poor bewildered foundling" may somehow be born again.

"And Hickman Arrives" celebrates some of those Afro-American styles and values that historically have provided the means for confronting social chaos and that, in particular, characterized the freedom movement of the fifties. Hickman and the other elderly blacks relentlessly pursue their goal of seeing the senator, but they maintain their serene composure without courting unnecessary white violence, without inviting death. With the senator's secretary, the old blacks are so "solemn, uncommunicative, and quietly insistent" that they violate the woman's sense of the real. Fanning themselves as if "in serene defiance" of the air conditioner, the Afro-Americans block her view of her large abstract paintings and of the framed copies of state documents mounted above the bust of Confederate Vice-President Calhoun. She tells him the senator is out and, accustomed to dismissing bothersome blacks with ease, when these particular blacks do not budge she begins to fluster. "They just stood there, now looking oddly like a delegation of Asians who had lost their interpreter along the way." Having tried every method for getting rid of the blacks, the secretary loses her patience and calls a guard. But the delegation's icy composure prevents physical retaliation.

When Hickman returns the next day, the guard rushes him bodily from the building. But moving the old black man is as infuriating as try-ing to move "the huge stone that resists the bulldozer's power or the chest of drawers that refuses to budge from its spot on the floor." Again Hickman appears to operate on a different plane of reality; he watches the guard "with a kind of tolerance, an understanding which seemed to remove his personal emotions to some far, cool place where the guard's strength could never reach them."

What is the source of this close-mouthed, serene, "Oriental" strength in these blacks? The forty-four blacks here "seemed bound by some secret discipline," born of watchful experience and religious patience. And it is a practical style of life, ritualized in their church. After being thrown out of the senator's office and searched by a zealous guard, one black woman says, "These here folks don't understand nothing . . . If we had been the kind to depend on the sword instead of on the Lord, we'd been in our graves long ago." "You said it," another woman comments. "In the grave and done long finished mold'ing!" (p. 695). These elderly blacks have been disciplined to pursue their lives honestly and robustly in a land where black carelessness serves as an invitation to white violence.

Ellison has pointed out that in the black church one encounters some of the most movingly tragic and some of the most hilariously comic drama in America.[6] A man of many names — Rev. Alonzo Zuber, Brother A. Z.,

God's Trombone, God's Golden Voiced, Black Garrick, Daddy Hickman—this jazz-trombonist-become-preacher leads the church drama with all the ebullience and eloquence of a master showman. At regular church services (recalled in Sunraider's delirious flashback), Hickman raised his old trombone in call and countercall with the choir "when he really felt like signifying on a tune the choir was singing" (p. 704). Hickman is also a master of the spoken word. Preachers must study other word artists, Hickman tells Bliss, in order to speak "good English" and "Good Book English." "Words are your business, boy," he says. "Not just The Word. Words are everything. The key to the Rock. The answer to the Question" (p. 701). Hickman's language is rhythmical and exuberant as he preaches about accepting the call to Christ:

> Yes! Meaning to take up His burden. At first the little baby-sized load that with the first steps we take weighs less than a butter ball; no more than the sugar tit made up for a year-and-a-half-old child. Then, Lord help us, it grows heavier with each step we take along life's way. Until in that moment it weighs upon us like the headstone of the world. Meaning to come bringing it! Come hauling it! Come dragging it! Come even if you have to crawl! Come limping, come lame; come crying in your Jesus' name—but Come! Come with your abuses but come with no excuses. Amen! (p. 705)

As the church services build to a climax, the worshipers "rock in time to the song" delivered by Hickman and the choir, "the rising rhythm of the clapping hands coming to [Bliss] like storming waves from a distance; like waves that struck the boat and flew off into the black sky like silver sparks from the shaking of the shimmering tamborines, showering at the zenith like the tails of skyrockets." Later the women begin to shout and collapse back into their chairs, and Bliss notices one lady in particular "dressed in white leaping into the air with outflung arms, going up then down—over backwards and up and down again, in a swooping motion which made her seem to float in the air stirred by the agitated movement of women's palm leaf fans" (p. 707). The reverends in their thronelike chairs "thundered out deep staccato Amens" and one man in front of the coffin got the spirit. Bliss sees

> an old white-headed man beginning to leap in holy exultation, bounding high into the air, and sailing down; then up again, higher than his own head, moving like a jumping jack with bits of sawdust dropping from his white tennis shoes. A brown old man, whose face was a blank mask, set and mysterious like a picture framed on a

wall, his lips tight, his eyes starry, like those of a blue-eyed china doll—soaring without effort through the hot shadows of the tent. Sailing as you sailed in dreams just before you fell out of bed. A holy jumper, Brother Pegue. (p. 707)

For this holy jumper and for the rest of the black congregation, the church drama is real and sustaining. Jesus, preaches Rev. Hickman, "taught us how to live, yes! And in the sun-drowning awfulness of that moment, he taught us how to die." Man's earthy life is short, says Hickman: it is "but a zoom between the warm womb and the lonely tomb." In the allotted zoom, man must "come unto Jesus" and thereby accept a way of life that brings daily sufferings but everlasting life. Man's challenge is "to help the weak and the downhearted. To stand up to the oppressors. To suffer and hang from the cross for standing up for what you believe." Man is born to suffer and "to surrender with tears and to feel the anguished sense of human loss." Through suffering in human flesh, Jesus, "bemused and confused, mystified and teary-eyed" with pain, realized that "*man was born to suffer and to die for other men!*"

This attitude toward suffering and death is embodied in the "serene new sound" of the black woman who steps forward to discipline the white woman claiming Bliss as her son. The black woman sings: "JUST DIG MY GRAVE . . . AND READY MY SHROUD CAUSE THIS HERE AIN'T HAPPENING! OH, NO, IT AIN'T GOING TO HAPPEN. SO JUST DIG-A MY GRAVE!" (p. 708). Sister Bearmasher takes hold of the white woman and declares her intention to do what is right, even if it means her life. In a passage echoing both T. S. Eliot and Ecclesiastes, Bearmasher says:

Take that child out of this foolish woman's sacrilegious hands. TAKE HIM, I SAY! And if this be the time then this is the time. If it's the time to die, then I'm dead. If it's the time to bleed, then I'm bleeding—but take that child. 'Cause whatever time it is, this is one kind of foolishness that's got to be stopped before it gets any further under way! (p. 710)

This attitude was characteristic of the nonviolent movement of the fifties and sixties. As Martin Luther King said of his threatened death, "It really doesn't matter with me now . . . Mine eyes have seen the glory of the coming of the Lord."

Senator Sunraider turns his back on the difficult black Christian teachings and chooses an easier, cruder set of values. Rather than bear the weighty cross described by Hickman, Sunraider decides to cheat death as long as he can. His goal is not everlasting life—just long, selfishly comfortable, earthly life. Therefore his political philosophy is not shaped by moral considerations but by sheer power. In his role as vicious Sunraider, he transmutes the rhetoric and drama of the black church into bitter, narrow political comedy. "He's almost laughing a devilish laugh in every word," notes Hickman (p. 697).

In this provocative multilayered story, Ellison comes to terms with the white bigot who, especially in the South, often grew up with black children, was nursed and reared by black adults, and who inevitably admired and imitated certain black manners and values. He gives up his black identity, avoiding the dread "narrow way" of blackness and of the black church. In "And Hickman Arrives" the blacks rescue the dreary scene from hopelessness. Like so many slave blacks who nurtured young whites with the hope that they would grow up to treat blacks decently, the blacks here believe in interracial brotherhood and love; they continue to have faith in the ability of the significantly named Bliss to be redeemed. Like the civil rights demonstrators of the fifties and sixties and like generations of American blacks, Hickman and the forty-four other blacks trek to Washington to warn that Sunraider's selfish abandonment of his past and his identity brings death. They who understand death speak their warnings with eyes unblinking, and voices serene.

The second of the Hickman stories, "The Roof, the Steeple and the People" (1960), takes its title from a children's rhyme-game. Here we find Rev. Bliss, the boy-preacher, at about age eight and under the watchful tutelage of Rev. "Daddy" Hickman. As with many Ellison short stories, "Steeple" operates within two distinct time frames. In one, set about 1920, Hickman responds to Bliss's urging by saying yes, he may go *once* to the new silent movies. Previously Hickman has denied his adopted son's requests to see the movies with his friends because it would be unfitting. But, says Hickman, one trip up those "filthy pissy stairs" to the colored section of the movie house will acquaint the boy with the temptations of movie viewing, so they will go as righteous "witnesses." This conversation about going to the movies reminds Bliss of the day when he first heard of the marvelous moving pictures from his friend, Body; and we shift to the story's next scene and time.

The boy-preacher's mind leaps back a year or so when Bliss and Body sit beside the road in a southern town. Sliding occasionally in and out of the dozens and signifying, Bliss and Body talk about race, the Bible, and, especially, the movies. Body has mentioned seeing a small box that contains a hundred people (at least), including whites and Indians (but no "colored") on horseback, and a whole train. Bliss rejects these tales, and he fears the devil must be forcing his buddy to lie. Body wearies of Bliss's upright tone and walks away, leaving his preacher friend intrigued. As the story closes, Bliss thinks that rather than go only once, he prefers never to see a movie. But in the story's last scene, he and Daddy Hickman join the crowd of people ascending the "steep, narrow stairs," into the dark theater "until the roof seemed to rest upon the crowns of our heads."[7]

"Steeple" is concerned with perspective and the role of the artist. Clearly, in telling Bliss about the preacher's responsibilities and craft, Hickman comments on art in general. This comparison of preacher and artist by Ellison, who has written much about the morality of the writer's craft, the rituals upon which all enduring art is erected, and the sacred function of art, is not surprising. The preacher's main task, says Hickman, is the same one Ellison has identified for the novelist, especially in America: it is "to help folks find themselves and to remember who they are." To do this, the preacher must study more than the Word; he must study people and the shifting world they live in. Without losing sight of stable Christian truths, the preacher must be able to escape the prison-house of the single viewpoint and watch the human drama as seen by men themselves, from a variety of perspectives.

Hickman has discouraged Bliss from seeing movies for specific reasons. Church people think of movie theaters as "one of the Devil's hangouts." They may suspect that the preacher who goes there regularly is "going to the devil and backsliding." Movies also present confusing images to Christian people searching for identity "in God's own image." Hickman says:

> Little preacher: too much looking at those pictures is going to have a lot of folks raising a crop of confusion. The show hasn't been here but a short while but I can see it coming already. Because folks are getting themselves mixed up with those shadows spread out against the wall, with people that are no more than some smoke drifting up from hell or pouring out of a bottle. So they lose touch with who they're supposed to be, Bliss . . .
>
> Those pictures can go against our purpose. If they look at those shows too often they'll get all mixed up with so many of those shadows that they'll lose their way. They wont know who they *are* is what I mean. (p. 116)

So, Hickman emphasizes, they are going to see the "shadows" for the first and last time. But why go at all?

Movies are not purely evil, Hickman says; one must find the good in them. "Maybe the Master meant for them to show us some of the many sides of the old good-bad." For the movies are "just like the world"; full of sinners and a few believers. And like the world, movies must be viewed with a perceptively critical eye:

> You see, Bliss, it's not so much a matter of where you are as what you *see* . . . But like old Luke says, "The light of the body is the eye," so you want to be careful that the light your eye lets into you isn't the light of darkness. I mean you have to be sure that you *see* what you're looking at. (p. 115)

Many times the preacher (like the artist) is called upon to use his insight to see the bright side of a dreary predicament: "Many times you will have to preach goodness out of badness . . . Yes, and hope out of hopelessness." To do so the preacher must know what temptations the people face, including those in the marvelous darkness of the movie theater. Hickman wants the little preacher to see movies, and all the world's evils, from the proper perspective.

Attending the theater only once and viewing the action with an evaluating, skeptical eye will give Bliss the discipline necessary in his (and the artist's) profession. "*Self-control's* the word," says Hickman. "That's right, you develop discipline, and you live so you can feel the grain of things and you learn to taste the sweet that's in the bitter and you live more deeply and earnestly" (p. 117). A man lives more time than a cat, but he forgets his previous lives because they were so painful. Viewed from the "old good-bad" perspective, man's life can be fuller and richer.

In Bliss's conversation with Body, perspective is also a central concern. Body, says Bliss, is "of my right hand," but—as their names suggest—the two youngsters look at the world through quite different eyes. Bliss strains to bring into focus a world he sees from his sometimes perplexing position as a preacher who at the same time is a curious if inexperienced youngster. When Body asks Bliss for a bit of scriptural exegesis —specifically, if the boy who led Samson to Gaza knew what the strong man had in mind—the boy preacher gives a less than candid reply:

> Look, Body, I said, I truly dont feel like working today. Because, you see, while you're out playing cowboy and acting the fool and going on cotton picks and chunking rocks at the other guys and things like that, *I* have to always be preaching and praying and studying my Bible. (p. 122)

The fact is that he cannot reconcile Daddy Hickman's heroic portraits of Samson with Body's suggestion that the boy who accompanied him was an ignorant fool. Bliss has trouble reconciling these conflicting perspectives.

Bliss suspects that his "right hand" is lying about the people moving against a wall "like a gang of ghosts." He gently reminds his friend that lying is a sin and says he will pray for him, will even get Hickman to have the whole church pray for him. But Body warns Bliss not to carry his self-righteousness too far or to forget that on a weekday Bliss is just another boy, subject to be booted by Body:

> Dont come preaching me no sermon. Cause you know I can kick your butt. I dont have to take no stuff off you. This here aint no Sunday, no how. Cant nobody make me go to church on no Friday, cause on a Friday I'm liable to boot a preacher's behind until his nose bleeds . . . That's the truth, Rev, and the truth is what the Lord loves. I'll give a doggone preacher *hell* on a Friday. Let him catch me on Sunday if he wants to, that's all right providing he aint too long-winded. And even on Wednesday ain't so bad, but please, *please*, dont let him fool with me on no Friday. (pp. 123-124)

The problem of perspective comes to bear on the boys' discussion of race. Body has heard whites talking about the box with moving pictures in it, but he would not inquire about it directly. "I rather be ignorant than ask them anything," he says. Body would not even ask Sammy, even though "he aint white . . . he a Jew," because he looks white and around his white friends he often acts white. When Bliss defends Sammy, saying he always calls him rabbi, which "means preacher in Jewish talk," Body suggests further complexity: maybe Sammy speaks to Bliss because Bliss looks white too. Cavorting with a white-looking Jew then brings suspicion on the head of the white-looking black boy, Bliss; Body accuses Bliss of wanting to be white. The young reverend flatly denies it, but the joke — seen in the context of the complete line of Hickman stories — is that Bliss eventually does "become" white — and, indeed, a surly white bigot.

In trying to convince Body that Jews are not white, Bliss unveils further racial conundrums. On revival tour in Tulsa, Rev. Hickman has introduced Bliss to a "colored" man who could "talk Jewish." This man learned Hebrew while portering in a Jewish store that the owners let him run on Saturdays. He quit because "he couldn't stand pushing that broom on Monday after handling all that cash on Saturday" (p. 120). The minute this man stepped into a certain store in Tulsa, the Jewish owners rushed forward to hear him "talk their talk." They liked him so much that when they heard his friend Hickman needed money to get back home, they gave him fifty dollars.

Somewhat like Langston Hughes's Semple, who almost always looks at circumstances from a racial standpoint, Body says the black porter sure was smart, beating the Jews out of their cash. "He must know something bad on them," he says. Later in the story Bliss asks if any colored people are in these new-fangled movies. "Naw, just white," says Body. "You know they gon' keep all the new things for theyselves. They put us in there about the time it's fixing to wear out" (p. 125).

In "The Roof, the Steeple, and the People," we see Rev. Bliss on the threshold of the age of the moving picture and of the adult world of shadows and complexities. Holding Hickman's large hand, he ascends the theater stairs to the colored section. Experiences and exchanges with Hickman and Body have taught him the inescapability of the world of contradictions: sometimes black is white, white is Jewish, black is Jewish, sacred is profane. A preacher plays the dozens, a biblical hero plays the fool, a porter plays boss on Saturdays. Even the church steeple has dirt under its fingernails. Insofar as movies are "just like the world" — full of puzzles — Bliss must view movies with the same critical eye that he turns on everyday experience. Like any preacher and, in a sense, like any artist, he must perceive the sweet and the bitter, translating what he perceives into forms usable in his work. But Bliss must also learn that the movie theater is a place where profane may be quite meaningful, even sacred.

The little preacher appears here as an apprentice artist learning the rigorous discipline of his calling and the vital need to evaluate the world in all its forms. The training and its contradictions ultimately overwhelm Bliss who, we learn in other Hickman stories, eschews vigorous, hard-won artistic truth and craft in favor of white racial arrogance and the slick, sentimental, and brutal outlook on experience fostered by Hollywood. He suffers a loss of perspective so dizzying that he loses his ability to unthread right and wrong or to know who he is.

"It Always Breaks Out" (1963) is a humorous story told mainly in conversation among a group of Washington journalists, relaxing over drinks after work. Though the narrator goes unnamed, we presume the northern liberal reporter to be McIntyre, witness to the car-burning incident on Senator Sunraider's lawn. This "weird, flamboyant sacrifice," which provides the white reporters with this week's discussion topic, is treated here in jest. One reporter says, "The senator's a joker, the Negro is a joker, this is a nation of jokers . . . Welcome to the United States of Jokeocracy."[8]

But behind the racial wisecracking—especially by the southern McGowan, whose hyperbolic explanation of his statement "Everything the Nigra *does* is political" drives to the heart of the story—is something that McIntyre finds horribly unsettling. "Even as I laughed," says McIntyre, "I . . . became agitated. My laughter—it was really hysteria—was painful" (p. 27).

The sustained humor of "It Always Breaks Out" springs from a variety of techniques. Facetious descriptions, startlingly apt in their imagery, produce a comical effect typical in Ellison's prose. McIntyre refuses to explain to his editor, Vannec, the contradictory implications of the car burning because of Vannec's passion for reducing all phenomena to "formulae—intricate ones—that can be displayed in the hard sparkling center of a crystal paperweight" (p. 13). Whence came the Negro "wildman?" "He rose," says one reporter, "like a wave of heat from the Jeff Davis highway" (p. 15). The juxtaposition of pithy, direct statement of fact and absurd metaphor is also comic: "Yeah," McGowan said, "ole senator was up there cooking up a barbeque and here comes a Nigra straight out of nowhere to prepare the hot sauce!"

Also humorous are the outrageous exaggerations, the droll vernacular turns of phrase, and the overall mock-serious tone of McGowan's minute catalogue of political "Nigra" behavior. In general, he observes, blacks who fail to conform to the cultural stereotype are engaging in subtle politics. "You all can smile if you want to," he says, but "there are few things in this world as political as a black Nigra woman owning her own washing machine" (p. 20). And watch for the black rascal who "starts to baking his pigs feet in cheese cloth instead of boiling them naked in Southern Nigra fashion—right there you have a potentially bad Nigra on your hands" (pp. 22-23). The reader laughs with the reporters at McGowan's rashness in daring to indulge in taboo racial ribaldry. "One simply didn't laugh at the unfortunates—within their hearing," notes McIntyre. But McGowan roars on: "One of the meanest, lowdownest forms of Nigra politics I have observed [occurs] when a sneaky, onery, smart-alecky Nigra stands up in a crowd of peaceful, well-meaning white folks, who's gathered together in a public place to see justice done, and that Nigra breaks wind!" (p. 23). One such subversive black man passed gas in the heat of a murder trial and so flabbergasted the judge and everybody present that the black killer on trial was allowed to go scot free. Right in Washington one sees more subtle evidence of black political behavior: Be careful, McGowan says, of "Nigras . . . carrying brief cases with real papers in them."

Beneath their banter and japery there lurks something that mystifies and terrifies these white reporters. If the black man's burning of his car is a consciously political gesture—rather than mere madness as the newspapermen have reported—then it is an incredibly bold, self-sacrificing, and violent one. Perhaps other such acts will follow: "Have we ever had a Negro assassin?" asks one reporter, "frowning, looking like a man remembering a bad dream" (pp. 16-17). McGowan turns the question into jest, but it is clear that he "was obsessed by history to the point of nightmare. He had the dark man confined in a package and this was the way he carried him everywhere, saw him in everything" (p. 27). McGowan's strained humor ("It looked as though he wanted desperately to grin but like a postage stamp which had become too wet, the grin kept sliding in and out of position") guards him from the moral implications of America's history of racism and prejudice. His ideal is a romanticized past, which he hates to see go with the wind. "And was it possible," McIntyre asks, "that the main object of McGowan's passion was really an idea, the idea of a non-existent past rather than a living people?" (p. 27).

For McIntyre there is also horror in realizing that McGowan is in some ways freer than himself. At least the southerner's coarse racist humor provides a medium for expressing (and to that extent expelling) his fears concerning Afro-American history and politics. Moreover, McGowan's honest expression of his feelings leads him closer to the truth concerning the car-burning incident than does McIntyre's apparent willingness to dismiss it as mere madness, or to forget the complicated scene altogether:

> Laughing, I realized that I envied McGowan and admitted to myself with a twinge of embarrassment, that some of the things he said were not only amusing but true. And perhaps the truth lay precisely in their being seen humorously. For McGowan said things about Negroes with absolute conviction which I dared not even think. Could it be that he was more honest than I, that his free expression of his feelings, his prejudices, made him freer than I? Could it be that his freedom to say what he felt about all that Sam the waiter symbolized actually made him freer than I? (p. 27)

Surely it is true that black freedom is often won on a secret or symbolic level. Surely, too, Minifees' burning of his Cadillac *is* a political act: "That doggone Nigra was trying to politicalize the Cadillac! . . . You . . . have to watch the Nigra who doesn't want a Cadillac, because he can stand a heap of political analysis" (p. 26). By speaking of the varied lifestyles and values of blacks, McGowan seems to have a fuller sense of the forms of Afro-American humanity than McIntyre, who discreetly chooses to ignore the subject.

"It Always Breaks Out" deals with the "innocent" McIntyre and with McGowan, who is haunted by the idea that thwarted black political activity can, like repressed sexuality, "break out in a thousand forms." Ironically, the southerner's comic monologue, designed to teach and delight its listeners with its Jim Crow wisdom, actually shocks McIntyre into realizing his own more subtle racism. As the story closes, McIntyre considers the humanity of blacks as he sees something that even McGowan has missed: racial humor cuts both ways. Watching the Negro waiter Sam, he wonders:

> Were there Negroes like McGowan . . . And what would they say about me? . . . How completely did I . . . dominate Sam's sense of life, his idea of politics? Absolutely, or not at all? Was he, Sam, prevented by some piety from confronting me in a humorous manner, as my habit of mind, formed during the radical thirties, prevented me from confronting him; or did he, as some of my friends suspected, regard all whites through the streaming eyes and aching muscles of one continuous, though imperceptible and inaudible, belly laugh? (p. 28)

He realizes that in the United States of Jokeocracy, blacks like the arsonist on the senator's lawn might be thumbing their noses at white people. He realizes, too, that Minifees' act is a political one designed to rattle the cages of hardened racists and well-meaning liberals alike. Both McGowan's and Minifees' "jokes" serve to jolt McIntyre into a higher plane of consciousness. "*What the hell*, he wonders, *is Sam's last name?*" (p. 28).

When "Juneteenth" appeared in 1965, Ellison had been publishing fragments of the new novel for five years. This dazzling piece of the Hickman puzzle is evidently one of the author's own favorites. He read part of it for a short movie, "Works in Progress," in which he discusses his new fiction and demonstrates how he uses a tape recorder to test the sound of his prose.[9] Like the Trueblood and Barbee sections of *Invisible Man*, where the spoken word achieves an almost poetic eloquence, "Juneteenth" is made to be read aloud. In fact, this story—taking up the Hickman saga somewhat after the action of "And Hickman Arrives" and "Night-Talk"—consists primarily of a sermon recollected from his boy preacher days by Bliss-become-Sunraider. The senator winces to recall his part in Juneteenth, the annual black celebration commemorating Emancipation Day, June 19, 1865.

As usual in Ellison's fictional world, folklore and ritual play important roles in "Juneteenth." The dialogue sermon, preached antiphonally by Revs. Hickman and Bliss, is distinctively Afro-American in its form, its idiom, and its allusions to folklore. References are also made to spirituals ("I Want to Be Ready," "Many Thousand Gone," "Keep Inchin' Along") and to biblical tales that recur in black lore (Jonah and the Whale, Samson in Gaza). Moreover, the sermon comprises a wonderfully elaborated rendering of the "Valley of Dry Bones" folk sermon.[10] In one version, printed as a poem, the folk preacher speaks of

> Dry bones, dry bones
> Well, them bones, dry bones, that are
> Laid in the valley.
> Well, them bones, dry bones, that are
> Laid in the valley,
> You can hear the word of the Lord.
> Or from my toe bone to my
> Foot bone, or from my
> Foot bone to my
> Ankle bone, or from my
> Ankle bone to my
> Leg bone, or from my
> Leg bone to my
> Knee bone.
> Well, them bones, dry bones, that are
> Laid in the valley,
> You can hear the word of the Lord.

In "Juneteenth," Hickman and Bliss revive this folk sermon, declaring that blacks in the New World were "Like the Valley of Dry Bones." "We were dead," Hickman says,

Except . . . Except
. . . Except what, Rev. Hickman? [asks Rev. Bliss]
Except for one nerve left from our ear . . .
Listen to him!
And one nerve in the soles of our feet . . .
. . . Just watch me point it out, brothers and sisters . . .
Amen, Bliss, you point it out . . . and one nerve left from the throat . . .
. . . From our throat—right *here*!
. . . Teeth . . .
. . . From our teeth, one from all thirty-two of them . . .

. . . Tongue . . .
. . . Tongueless . . .
. . . And another nerve left from our heart . . .
. . . Yes, from our heart . . .
. . . And another left from our eyes and from our hands and arms
and legs and another from our stones.[12]

Rev. Hickman tells his young cohort to "hold it right there." He reports that God spoke to blacks as he did to the Israelites, crying
"Doooo—These dry bones live?" In the tradition of the black folk
preacher, Hickman and Bliss transform the Bible story into a vision of
black resurrection in a strange land.

Indeed, against this folkloric and mythic backdrop, Hickman and Bliss
recite a version of Afro-American history in which two prime movers are
language and music. African languages were discouraged in the New
World. Whites "divided and divided and divided us again like a gambler
shuffling and cutting a deck of cards," says Hickman, until the memory
of Africa was "ground down into powder and blown on the winds of
foggy forgetfulness." They cut out our tongues, he says, "left us without
words." And "they took away our talking drums." "Drums that talked,
Daddy Hickman?" asks Rev. Bliss. "Tell us about those talking drums."
Hickman responds:

> Drums that talked like a telegraph. Drums that could reach across
> the country like a church bell sound. Drums that told the news
> almost before it happened! Drums that spoke with big voices like
> big men! Drums like a conscience and a deep heart beat that knew
> right from wrong. Drums that told glad tidings! Drums that sent
> the news of trouble speeding home! Drums that told us *our* time
> and told us where we were. (p. 268)

Without language and music (and thus without the traditional means of
communication, celebration, and ritual) Africans in America did not
know who they were. "We were made into nobody and not even *mister*
nobody either, just nobody. They left us without names" (p. 267).

According to "Juneteenth," Africans in America were dead, culturally,
like the valley of dry bones. But despite being "divided and scattered,
ground down and battered," Africans found that even in America "the
earth was red and black like the earth of Africa." Dead in the earth like
the valley of dry bones, the Africans were reborn as Afro-Americans. As
in the folk sermon, "Valley of Dry Bones," one nerve at a time, "we
began to stir."

Blacks heard the Word from God and woke up speaking (and singing and shouting) a new language. Punning on the phrase "the Word," Hickman proclaims this rebirth as he testifies to the saving power of God and of language. When called from the Dry Bones Valley, blacks took the Word as a life source:

> We were rebirthed from the earth of this land and revivified by the Word. So now we had a new language and a brand new song to put flesh on our bones . . . We had to take the Word for bread and meat. We had to take the Word for food and shelter. We had to use the Word as a rock to build up a whole new nation, cause to tell it true, we were born again in chains of steel. (p. 273)

The word, says Hickman, is "a rock to build up a whole nation." Through the power of language, American blacks have clung to a sense of tradition. Rev. Hickman opens his sermon:

> Let's us begin this week of worship by taking a look at the ledger. Let us, on this day of deliverance, take a look at the figures writ on our bodies and on the living tablet of the heart. The Hebrew children have their Passover so that they can keep their history alive in their memories—so let us take one more page from their book and, on this great day of deliverance, on this day of emancipation, let's us tell ourselves our story . . . We have got to know our story before we can truly understand God's blessings and how far we have still got to go. (p. 263)

Blacks also arose from the valley of dry bones clapping, singing, and dancing. "They had us bound," says Hickman, "but we had our kind of time, Rev. Bliss. They were on a merry-go-round that they couldn't control but we learned to beat time from the seasons." This ability to carve rhythms from nature kept blacks from being divided:

> They couldn't divide us now. Because anywhere they dragged us we throbbed in time together. If we got a chance to sing, we sang the same song. If we got a chance to dance, we beat back hard times and tribulations with a clap of our hands and the beat of our feet, and it was the same dance. (p. 275)

The rhythm continues to give blacks a secure sense of identity and strength:

We know who we are because we hear a different tune in our minds and in our hearts. We know who we are because when we make the beat of our rhythm to shape our day the whole land says, Amen! It smiles, Rev. Bliss, and it moves to our time! Don't be ashamed, my brothern! Don't be cowed! Don't throw what you have away! Continue! Remember! Believe! Trust the inner beat that tells us who we are. (p. 276)

The music not only lifts the spirits, but it gives blacks a saving perspective from which to view racial oppression as well as life's hardship in general:

Learn from what we've lived. Remember that when the labor's back-breaking and the boss man's mean our singing can lift us up. That it can strengthen us and make his meanness but the flyspeck ir-ritation of an empty man. Roll with the blow like ole Jack Johnson. Dance on out of his way like Williams and Walker. Keep to the rhythm and you'll keep to life. God's time is long; and all short-haul horses shall be like horses on a merry-go-round. Keep, keep, keep to the rhythm and you won't get weary. Keep to the rhythm and you won't get lost. (p. 274)

In his ritual recitation of Afro-American history, how does Hickman explain the hardships that blacks have endured in America? Here we see Ellison's philosophy as reflected in his essays transmuted into fiction. The tribulation to which black Americans were subjected has built in them a saving discipline:

Oh God hasn't been easy with us because he always plans for the loooong haul. He's looking far ahead and this time He wants a well-tested people to work his will. He wants some sharp-eyed, quick-minded, generous-hearted people to give names to the things of the world and to its values. He's tired of untempered tools and half-blind masons! Therefore, He's going to keep on testing us against the rocks and in the fires. He's going to heat us till we almost melt and then He's going to plunge us into ice-cold water. And each time we come out we'll be blue and as tough as cold-blue steel! (p. 273)

Hardened by a mean life, blacks also developed the resiliency of a willow switch, knowing that "life is a streak-a-lean — a — streak-a-fat." Hardship has made blacks dependent on basic life sources — the rhythm of the seasons and the power of the Word. They are God's people, chosen to work his art on the world, to name, to evaluate, to lead.

"Juneteenth" is a powerful story, rich in folklore and vivid in language. Here we find a mythic and folkloric version of Afro-American history, answering the "simple" questions: Where do black Americans come from? How did they become Afro-Americans? What does their suffering mean? How do they know who they are? Hickman focuses on music and language and, like an African griot, he pronounces his rhythmical answers in his trombone voice: "We know who we are by the way we walk. We know who we are by the way we talk. We know who we are by the way we sing. We know who we are by the way we dance. We know who we are by the way we praise the Lord on high." (p. 276). Thus blacks will be able to lead their countrymen, when "time comes round." Lying half-conscious, shot down by an assassin's bullet, Bliss-become-Sunraider recalls the promise made in an old Juneteenth sermon: "Let those who will despise you . . . Time will come round when we'll have to be their eyes; time will swing and turn back around. I tell you, time shall swing and spiral back around" (p. 276).

"Night-Talk" (1969), the most demanding of the Hickman pieces, was published with the following author's headnote:

> This excerpt from a novel-in-progress (very long in progress) is set in a hospital room located in Washington, D.C., circa 1955, the year the novel was conceived. In it the Senator is passing through alternate periods of lucidity and delirium attending wounds resulting from a gunman's attempt on his life. Hickman, in turn, is weary from the long hours of sleeplessness and emotional strain which have accumulated while he has sought to see the Senator through his ordeal. The men have been separated for many years, and time, conflicts of value, the desire of one to remember nothing and the tendency of the other to remember too much, have rendered communication between them difficult.
>
> Sometimes they actually converse, sometimes the dialogue is illusory and occurs in the isolation of their individual minds, but through it all it is antiphonal in form and an anguished attempt to arrive at the true shape and substance of a sundered past and its meaning.[13]

The action in this "excerpt" follows in sequence the events described in "And Hickman Arrives." As in that story, the two men's conversation and Senator Sunraider's interior monologue (presented in italics) raise the question: Why did the white-looking, culturally black preacher abandon his calling to become the hysterically anti-black Sunraider, stern repressor of his black past?

Tired and distraught, Hickman and Sunraider/Bliss talk about the moment the boy preacher began passing for white. He started by playing hookey from church and hiding from everyone he knew, including Hickman. The old preacher recalls discovering the youngster coming from a white-only movie theater, "face all screwed up with crying."[14] This image triggers the senator's painful recollection of the day he first tested his ability to pass. This modern passing story—reminiscent of certain of Ernest J. Gaines's contemporary stories on an old theme—is unique in that it is narrated principally by Bliss, an intelligent boy whose language is flavored by the Bible, Shakespeare, Homer, Whitman, Freud, the movies, as well as by white and black talk and folklore.

Led by a confused youngster in search of a secure place in a world torn into black and white sections, we meander through white Atlanta. In secrecy and bewilderment, Bliss seeks his actual parents, whom he never knew. On this desperate day, he takes a giant step away from his black adopted family—Rev. Hickman and the congregation—in favor of the illusory, glittering realm of whiteness. "Night-Talk" is a complexly organized study of black and white mother and father images as seen by a boy living on the sharp edge of the tracks.

The black women Bliss has known as a boy were righteous women of church and tent meeting. He was, in a sense, born "in the womb of wild women's arms," black women seen week after week before, during, and after church services. Sister Georgia with the soft-looking but "sanctified" breasts and with fervent and red fire in her green eyes was one such black maternal figure. Such women are among the three hundred church folk who scour the playgrounds, alleys, stores—even church steeples—looking for Bliss when he disappears into white Atlanta. In "And Hickman Arrives," it is made clear that these black women claim Bliss—whatever his race—as their "secret son." The trembling boy, seated in the white-only movie theater, thinks of these black mamas as he waits for the next Mary Pickford movie: "So I waited . . . yearning for one more sight . . . even if seventy outraged deaconesses tore through the screen to tear down the house around us" (p. 326). These rejected black women are associated with the discipline and responsibility involved in being black and being servants of a severe and scrutinizing Lord.

What about the black men? Sauntering through downtown Atlanta, Bliss passes a large restaurant and spots a "jolly fat black man cutting slices from a juicy ham." This black chef winks knowingly at Bliss, who is practicing his passing act, and the boy feels discovered and runs off through the crowd. When Bliss is finally located by his church "family," Deacon Wilhite turns to Hickman, saying "Well . . . it looks like Rev. Bliss has gone and made himself an outlaw, but at least we can be thankful that he wasn't stolen into Egypt" (p. 318). If this reference to the biblical Joseph suggests the favored-son status accorded Bliss by the black men of the church, it also recalls that Hickman, like Joseph's father Jacob, lost his favorite child to hostile neighbors. The black father figure whom Bliss agonizes over and rejects is Big Daddy Hickman.

Hickman is a man who has reconciled himself to an upside-down world. The wayward son of a black preacher, as a youth Hickman became a gambler and musician who enjoyed the fast secular life. He "rejoiced in the sounds of our triumph in this world of deceitful triumphs." Converted to the Word, Hickman knew how to read God's plans in many forms. Half-awake, Hickman mumbles this prayer:

> Down there in the craziness of the Southland, in the madhouse of down home, the old motherland where I in all my ignorance and desperation was taught to deal with the complications of Thy plan, yes, and at a time when I was learning to live and to glean some sense of how Thy voice could sing through the blues and even speak through the dirty dozens if only the players were rich-spirited and resourceful enough, comical enough, vital enough and enough aware of the disciplines of life. In the zest and richness Thou were there, yes! (p. 329)

Despite his wisdom, though, Hickman wonders why, like Jacob, Abraham, and God himself, he has to give up the son he worked so hard to rear as a righteous man.

Ironically and tragically, Hickman's complexity of vision costs him Bliss. When the boy asks about his white skin and his parentage, Hickman gives him a spiritual answer that sounds to the youngster like sheer evasion. "Bliss," Hickman tells him, "thy likeness is in the likeness of God, the Father, Because, Reverend Bliss, God's likeness is that of *all* babes." God is his *true* father, says Hickman. And where shall man find God?: "I say, let him who seeks into his own *heart*. I say, let him search his own *loins*" (p. 318). A man must, then, become his own father and accept this inner parent as the true Father, God.

And who is his true mother? Hickman says that she's "most likely a Mary even though she be a Magdelene": a pure woman chosen to bear God's child, even if the woman be a sinner. This complicated answer is designed to make Bliss feel confident and even called by God for special service. Like Jesus, his father is God and his mother Mary—or at worst Mary Magdelene, the penitent sinner forgiven by the Son of Man. Every man, says Hickman, is an individual and yet part of the glorious oneness of God the Father. Hickman explains this intricate concept in terms obliquely political: "There's always the mystery of the one in the many and the many in one." Every American is a child of God and of America as well. Despite Hickman's fatherly reassurances, however, Bliss feels not proud and secure, but frightened, confused, and orphaned. He rejects the theology, the political perspective, and, indeed, the black man who has taught them to him.

In "And Hickman Arrives" Sunraider/Bliss recalls the nighttime disruption of a tent revival by a white woman who charges forward claiming to be his mother. The vigorous church sisters prevent the intruder from taking Bliss, but inevitably the boy begins to wonder about his race and his past. Was the hysterical lady his true mother? But she was white! Was *he* white? In "Night-Talk" Bliss remembers that when she disrupted the church service with her claims, the woman "broke the structure of ritual and the world erupted . . . A blast of time flooded in upon me, knocking me . . . into a different time" (p. 327). When the boy plays hookey from church and cannot be found, Hickman fears he has been kidnapped—perhaps by the hysterical white woman. And indeed Bliss has ambled into white Atlanta, lured by an image he fantasizes to be his mother's. "I saw her picture moving past all serene and soulful in the sunlight."

Several white females in "Night-Talk" excite young Bliss: the "smiling, sharpnosed women in summer dresses" he sees on the streets; the "kindly blueyed cotton-headed Georgia grinder" who smiles at him from a theater ticket window; the girls in "white silk stockings and pastel dresses" who giggle at the billboards outside the theaters; the Hollywood bathing beauties, "big-eyed and pretty in their headbands and bathing suits and beaded gowns but bland with soft-looking breasts." Yet it is a billboard image of the actress Mary Pickford that triggers Bliss's fantasy that she is his real mother. "Alright kid," says the theater ticket taker, unwittingly raising the question that haunts Bliss, "where's your maw?" "Her name's 'Mamma'—I mean Miz Pickford," says the nervous preacher. Along with a generation of Americans, Bliss chooses as his idol Miz Pickford, the roguish, fearless blonde of "Rebecca of Sunnybrook Farm" and "My Best Girl." Mary Pickford was cast in film after film in the twenties as the tomboy comedienne who, with her innocently wide eyes and dimples, managed to remain enchantingly feminine. No femme fatale, she was the perpetually adolescent dream girl, America's Sweetheart. (Part of the Ellisonian twist here is that the teenaged Rebecca was actually a thirty-year-old Pickford who had been married three times. Also, the "sweetheart" played not only in such charming movies as "Rebecca," but in "The Taming of the Shrew," "Coquette," and "Heart of the Hills," a Ku Klux Klan film.) Still, Bliss (whose mother, Hickman told him, is "most likely a Mary") feels he has found *his* Mary—Mary Pickford.

Once in the theater, seated in the white-only seats, Bliss lives through a fantasy that is escapist as well as oedipal: "The blossoms were falling where the hill hung below the afternoon and we sprawled and out of time that never entered into future time except as one nerve cell, tooth, hair and tongue and drop of heart's blood into the bucket" (p. 325). Like the mythic black man of the Valley of Dry Bones sermon in "Juneteenth," Bliss is anesthetized, lulled into the sleep of death—all except for one nerve, one hair, one blood drop. And this Oedipus daydreams about his mother as an alluring woman-child, thus ironically fulfilling Hickman's suggestion that his mother is the Virgin Mary and that every man must be his own father. The movie Mary, the reader is told, seems to invite Bliss to "go in." The invitation suggests sexual entrance, entrance into the pastel dream realm of popular culture and into the white world. So Bliss decides to "reject circumstance, live illusion." Walking out of the movie, torn with feelings of longing and guilt, Bliss is spotted by Hickman and the deacon. The boy runs and is caught; but he realizes that at another time he could run behind the "white curtain" and not be found. He could retreat forever into his world of fantasies.

How does Bliss view white fathers? How does he imagine his own father (if white) to act? Reared among blacks, Bliss at first shares Hickman's view of white men as harsh authority figures. Hickman says he did not call the police to help find Bliss, "considering they'd probably have made things worse." Several of the white men cited in "Night-Talk" wear uniforms and are bigots. As he debates whether or not to enter the movie, Bliss walks to a corner drugstore and listens to white Eskimo piemen in white shoes and white pants—a sterling uniform of authority to a child's eyes—who tell lies about blacks and Yankees. A white boy, taking Bliss for white, speaks of his grandfather, skilled teller of racial jokes. The old man mocked black rights and ceremonies: "The colored don't need rights," he says, "they only need rites . . . Just give niggers a baptism or a parade or a dance and they're happy" (p. 327). Aside from these white males—and the keystone cops, cowboys, and hoboes of the movies—the white man who dominates "Night-Talk" is the ambiguous figure who goes unnamed, the annoying ticket taker.

Dressed, ironically, in patriotic colors (like so many minor characters in the fictional world of Ellison), this immature young man whose job offers admission to the dream world of the movies is complexly symbolical. A latter-day Uncle Sam who flaunts his petty power, he is cross-eyed (again, this inability to see well is characteristically Ellisonian) but has a certain clairvoyance. He harps on the question of Bliss's identity, not only asking about the boy's "maw," but calling him by a variety of names, trying to bully the little preacher. He calls Bliss, "kid," "Ezra," "Snot," "Clyde," even "Son." When Bliss tells him Mary Pickford is his mother, the ticket man calls Bliss a "lying little peckerwood." Bliss becomes especially nervous when the uniformed man doubles the irony by addressing Bliss by names often given to minstrel men—whites in blackface: "Mister Bones," "Mister Tambo." As Bliss scurries off, the man even imitates a black speaker, saying: "Y'all be quiet, y'all heah-uh? An' Rastus, Ah mean it!" (p. 324).

Defensively, Bliss remembers a racial taunt that spins through his mind and eases his fear of the noisy ticket man:

> Peckerwood, peckerwood,
> You can't see me!
> You're just a red head gingerbread
> Five cents a cabbage head— (p. 322)

The typically Ellisonian irony, here, is that this peckerwood, like Bliss himself, is as much black as he is white, at least culturally. Seeing some giggling girls outside the movie house, the ticket taker speaks to Bliss and to the girls in language tingling with black tones:

> Hush, son, he said and pray you'll understand it better bye'n bye. Cause right now I got me some other fish to fry. You'all come on in, gals, he said in a low, signifying voice. Come on in, You sweet misstreaters, you fluffy teasers. I got me a special show for ever one of you lilly-white dewy-delled mama's gals. Yes, sir! You chickens come to pappa, cause I got the cawn right here on the evuh-lovin' cob! (p. 323)

If Bliss decides to pass for white to escape complexity, the cross-eyed, white-black ticket taker should have been warning enough: whites are mixed up too. Even as Senator Sunraider he would still have to deal with his own confusions and with such contradictory figures as Karp, whose name is a homonym for the verb "carp." Karp is a white businessman who speaks out against Sunraider's racism. Yet Karp himself inflicts outrageous and degrading fashions as well as hair-straightening products upon black consumers. And as a stockholder in porkers, beans, and corn, Karp seems to bank on the continued poverty of at least some part of the American community. Karp makes money on exploitation and racism. Then he "steps with the fetch" to a bank in Switzerland where he pays no taxes. "Who's Karp kidding?" wonders Sunraider. "Who's kidding Karp?"

Dreamily considering the hypocrisy of American businessmen, Sunraider considers the automobile industry that, in its appeal to the Afro-American market, converts knowledge of black psychology into money: "Them making black bucks into millejungs and fraud pieces in spectacularmythics on assembly lines?" This cluster of images brings the senator back to the question of his mother's identity, as he thinks of black men "detroiting my mother who called me Goodrich Hugh Cuddyear in the light of tent flares" (p. 321). He wonders if his mother is a whore, exploited for money, and if he is a detroit product, Goodrich Hugh Cuddyear. Who, he asks, will "speak the complicated truth?"

Partially to avoid the complicated truth, which he associates with bastardy, exploitation, and hypocrisy, Bliss decides to become a white boy. And once having escaped into this dream world, metaphors for which are the Hollywood movie and the local movie theater, he finds it impossible to emerge into the searing light of reality. Failing to find his real white parents, he takes Hickman's advice and becomes his own militantly white parent—indeed, as a senator, he becomes a public parent figure: "I told myself: man and woman are a baby's device for achieving governments—ergo I'm a politician" (p. 327).

Backing away from the contradictoriness of his person history—and, by extension, American history—Bliss fails to accept the mysterious truth that his true father, in terms of shared experience, love, and culture, is Hickman, "the dark daddy of flesh and Word." Reflecting on his failure, Sunraider says: "Later I thought many times that I should have faced them down—faced me down and said, Look, this is where I'll make my standing place" (p. 325). In this fine scene in the Hickman drama, Bliss comes close to tragic awareness. All he need do now is to accept his guilt, along with both his blackness and his whiteness, and be saved. Yet both his spirit and flesh remain weak.

Like several other Hickman tales, "A Song of Innocence" (1970) consists of a series of flashbacks.[15] In this case the remembrances are those of a new character, Cliofus, who is a childhood crony of Severen, the assassin of Bliss/Sunraider. Taking its title and, to an extent, its themes from William Blake, this "song" relates incidents from the innocent (vulnerable, stupid, clumsy, and destructive, as well as pure and unspoiled) youth of Cliofus. As a youngster Cliofus is haunted by a variety of ailments: obesity, epilepsy, stuttering. These physical problems cause him to begin school late; thus as a first-grader he is too large for the first-grade desks and his head presents "the biggest target in the class." Getting teased or smacked in the head with grapes brings on his nervous stuttering and then an epileptic spell may follow. Like a number of other Ellison figures, this boy is an orphan, raised by Miss Janey whom we hear of briefly in "And Hickman Arrives."

But, also typical of Ellison, this is no song of complaint—unless it is a vigorous blues. Rather, it is a portrait of a potential writer as a young man. Cliofus, who narrates the story, is plunged into solitude and anguish by his diseases, but he transcends his physical conditions as he grapples with language. In addition to the portrait of artist-in-the-making, in "A Song of Innocence" Ellison gives us a meditation on the powers and vagaries of the slippery medium of the word.

This story is presented as Cliofus's rambling, dreamlike monologue to McIntyre, presumably the white reporter of "It Always Breaks Out." (It appears that McIntyre is interviewing Cliofus among others to uncover the meanings of the car burning and the assassination.) In his twisting yarn Cliofus recalls for McIntyre a day in the first grade when language got him into trouble, and the day when Severen, his close friend from childhood, returned to the town Cliofus never left. The remembered conversation with Severen fires Cliofus's excellent memory, and more incidents—each concerning language and problems—surface into Cliofus's consciousness. Though deft in selecting if not in pronouncing words, language has spelled trouble all his life.

In the first grade Cliofus, self-conscious because of his size, age, and sicknesses, is publicly shamed because of his misunderstanding of words. Miss Kindly, the first-grade teacher, tells Cliofus, who has confessed he does not know the father of our country, that he "must know history." Thinking Miss Kindly has made reference to someone named "*Mister* History," Cliofus replies in courteous innocence: "Yes mam . . . I be pleased to meet him, mam." The class begins to titter and hurl dozens at Cliofus ("He a bad granny-dodger this morning!") and the ever mannerly Cliofus inquires, "But do you think Mr. History would have time to be bothered with somebody like me, mam?" This comment he makes not because he is smart-alecky, "but because I already felt despised and so unnecessary." Rapidly "the words had betrayed me twice over" (p. 33).

Then words, sharpened into weapons, turn upon Cliofus. "Boy, what do you mean," demands the outraged Miss Kindly. Jack imitates Cliofus's voice, saying loudly, "Why shucks, Miss Kindly, I'm plumb full of history; even the dogs know that." Buster (again making an appearance from the Buster-Riley stories of the thirties and forties) leads a series of chants and yells:

> Well, if at first you don't succeed
> Well a-keep on a-sucking
> Till you sucka seed . . .
>
> Cliofus ripped it, he ripped it, he ripped it, he
> really ripped it
> like a fool! . . .
>
> Friends, Romans, Country women, Cliofus
> Is an ape-sweat with too much mustard on his
> Bun! (p. 33)

Tyree flaps his arms like a rooster: "Cliofus is a soft horse-apple and a ripe goose egg." Cliofus is pelted with rotten grapes and begins to tremble after Miss Kindly (whose name is beyond irony) demands an apology from Cliofus.

Small wonder that Cliofus feels victimized by double-edged words. As an adult, he echoes Lewis Carroll:

> They say that folks misuse words but I see it the other way around, words misuse people. Usually when you think you're saying what you mean you're really saying what the words want you to say . . . Words are tricky, they keep a thumb stuck in their noses and wave their fingers at you all the time . . . No matter what you try to do, words can never mean meaning. (p. 32)

Gestures are less ambiguous:

> Now you just wave your hand at somebody and it means bye-bye. Throw a kiss or hold out your arms and even a baby can understand you. But just try to say it in words and you raise up Babel and the grapes of wrath. If you nod your head and smile even folks who don't speak your language will get the idea, but you just whisper *peace* somebody will claim you declared war and will insist on trying to kill you. (p. 32)

Words, abused by people and abusing people, cause wars. And history, according to Cliofus, whose name alludes to the Greek muse of history, is rife with abuses of language. "No wonder," he says, "History is a bitch on wheels with wings traveling inside a submarine. Words are behind it all" (p. 32).

If gestures are clearer than words, poor Cliofus, an epileptic, is still at a loss. "Even my gestures make me out a fool," he says. When the first-grade class boils over with derisive songs and dances aimed at Cliofus, the youngster feels an epileptic spell coming on. His simple gesture, a hand raised to request to leave class, is misunderstood: his fingers will not open and his hand looks like a fist clenched in rage. Miss Kindly then turns green and bellows "ORDER." "Which," says Cliofus as he remembers falling to the floor, blacking out, "she did not get" (p. 34).

To the proper Miss Kindly, who rolls her *r*'s as she does her small eyes, and who calls each first-grade girl a "lay-di," the most innocuous language can be horrifyingly dirty. Jack, the deep-voiced first-grader who can throw his voice, sometimes calls out to Miss Kindly when he sees her "walking sedately down the street as though she was carrying a thin-shelled egg between her knees" (p. 36). Jack would yell, "Cherries are ripe! Cherries are ripe!" and whistle loudly to make Miss Kindly pull down her dress, pat her chest and neck, quicken her pace. And "dark as she was," like the good-loving woman in the blues "Hollywood Bed," Miss Kindly's face turned "cherry red."

Even when the children try to cooperate politely with Miss Kindly, their words come out "obscene." She takes them to the train station to see a whale displayed atop a freight car. She tells them this great "animule" gives good rich milk to her whale babies and then asks if anyone has a question. "A bowlegged, knock-kneed, pigeontoed, mariney son-of-gun named Bernard" says he has a question, and Miss Kindly sets up the boy as an example to his mates: "That's how we learn chilldreen, by asking questions . . . Bernard is *highly* intelligent." But his innocent question turns Miss Kindly "boxcar red." "Miss Kindly," says Bernard, "if that there whale is an animule, what gives rich milk, where do she carry her tits?" (p. 37).

Given the ambiguity and explosiveness of words, it is not surprising that Cliofus recalls that other forms of expression better described the misery and inanity of his childhood situation. "A Song of Innocence" begins with a marvelous description of Cliofus lying on his pallet listening to someone walking in the middle of the street below and whooping plaintively. Somehow this "ole long, slow-winding whoop that's neither a word or a song," answered by another walker who whoops in reply, expresses something beyond mere words. Cliofus tells McIntyre:

> You know they've (the whoops) got to be saying something because all that lonesome rising and falling of sound like singing has you by the short hair . . . I roll over on the pallet and listen to those whoops rising and falling and dying and you try to understand

what they're saying and even though you will never in this world
quite make it before sleep comes down, you know just the same
that it means beyond anything the straight words could ever say.
(p. 30)

This statement of the meaning of the nighttime whoops (serving also as
an explanation for this story's experimental nature) suggests the direction
of one of this story's themes: "the unsayable meaning of mankind's
outrageous condition in the world." It also suggests the inadequacy of
"the straight words."

"A Song of Innocence" is not, to be sure, a shrill diatribe against the
power of the writer's medium. Part of the irony here is that, in the very
process of decrying the weakness of words to say the unsayable, Ellison
uses words to present images, such as those of the night walkers and
whoopers, that *do* express the mysterious, shadowy world that is his setting and his subject. Also, even as Cliofus expresses (in words) the
unspeakable misery of man's fate, he is still yakking away, living proof
that he has managed to forge the word manacles into tools for survival.
What, then, are some of the saving qualities of language?

To begin with, Cliofus' identity is wrapped up in his language. His
talk, he says, is "what makes me *me.*" Cliofus' mind and senses collect
ideas and impressions faster than they can be sorted out; when aroused,
the words stream forth without conscious regulation. In this sense he
seems to have the gift of automatic writing (William Blake said he took
dictation from spirits). Thus when Severen, his boyhood friend, arrives
after many years abroad and sits on Cliofus' front porch, Cliofus does not
recognize him but "the words" do: "the *words* started talking to him"
(pp. 34-35).

The words, like muses, are a disembodied force speaking to and
through Cliofus. They seem independent and highly perceptive:

It was as though he's asked a question and they [the words] were
out to answer before I had a chance to stop them. They didn't need
me anyway, they were in there waiting to get out and didn't care
how they got started. Because they had recognized him long before
I did; smelled him or heard him coming from a long way off like
dogs do. (pp. 34-35)

Cliofus "can't help but say" certain things; the words take over. But he
listens, remembers what they say, and learns about himself in the process.

"All things considered, I got built-in feed back." "Do you mean that you always tell the truth?" asks Severen. "No," he replies, "but the truth gets into it." Words mirror the depths of Cliofus' consciousness and, "talking breakneck" as he has to do, he brings into focus complexities of his past and his soul. "Oh I see me, Mr. McIntyre, do you see you?" (p. 35).

Straight, unpretentious talk can often best preserve the spirit of truth—even though it may be laced with a lie. Miss Kindly is unable to explain, without becoming embarrassed, that the whale at the freight yard is a mammal. But a red-haired railroad man at the same yard actually teaches the children some facts about whales and whaling. Charging the children a nickel each "just to listen to him lie," the man claims to have caught the whale as easily as "digging a crawdad out of a hole." Further-more, like Ahab, he claims to have lost one of his legs in the struggle. He tells them about Jonah and about unlikely products that come from whales—such as hairpins and perfume. "Lissen here, y'all," whispered one second-grader, looking at the ambergris from which perfume is made, "That there is whale hockey; I don't care what that white man says" (p. 40).

The children's language here is used as an antidote to the pale talk of Miss Kindly and the other school officials. Behind her straight-laced back, the "big bad gals" in her class sing about the proper Miss Mable Kindly:

> Oh Rust Mop Mable
> She swears she would if she could
> But she a-just aint able—Mable! (p. 36)

Deftly, too, the children name Reverend Samson "Blue Goose" and honk at his church when they ride by on their bicycles: "Dam' his soul," says Cliofus, "dam' his ball-headed soul to hell. Blue Goose, your nickname was our small revenge" for totally unearned and brutal beatings.

The real heroes of Cliofus' childhood were not the preachers and teachers—the heroes projected by society—but Jack, who could count the dozens and talk like Louis Armstrong; China Jackson, who tried to murder Blue Goose; and quiet Severen, who always accepted the misfit Cliofus without condescension or meanness. "A Song of Innocence" is a patchwork of scenes in which these outlaws fight off the respectable role models with pointed words and with action. Severen, the romanticist who weeps for the whale at the end of this story, later stands up in "And Hickman Arrives" and guns down racist Senator Sunraider.

Cliofus is a man with the agonizing blues, a man driven into isolation and tragic awareness of mankind's outrageous condition. And he is a man with a bluesman's itch to ramble: "I'm a yearning man who has to sit still." Even as a child he was fascinated by trains, so important in blues imagery. His playmate Severen would draw him pictures of trains because "he knew how trains eased me." Severen would also take him to watch the trains racing past. Miss Janey, who also took him to see trains, used to say, "Cliofus, you really must have been born with a truly aching heart to need a whole big engine and line of cars to soothe your agitation." He never had spells while watching the trains—seeing them seemed to help him deal with being an orphan child; he yearned to ride atop the engine car "like it was the daddy and I was the baby riding high on his shoulders." Late at night, hearing the train whistles "talking" in the distance, Cliofus knew he had "all the world I'll ever need—mama and papa and jelly-roll" (p. 31).

The point about language made most compellingly in "A Song of Innocence" is that, despite everything, it can be a vehicle for transcendence: words can drive the blues away. When the trains huff and storm by, Cliofus talks to them and feels purged of some evil: "All those words go jumping out to them like the swine in the Bible that leaped off the cliff into the sea" (p. 31). Trains and language, and the dreams of escape and familial completeness they inspire, help Cliofus to cast out his demons. "They hop on the Katy, the Rock Island and the Sante Fe," train names that appear in many blues songs. "Maybe those trains need those words to help them find their way across this here wide land in the dark," says Cliofus. "I don't know." All he knows is that for him the trains and the words they inspire are, for him, a blessing. Having come to blues terms with his predicament, sometimes late at night he hears the train whistling to him, and "all those things that I've been tumbling and running and bouncing through my mind all day have got quiet as a ship in a bottle on a shelf" (p. 31).

"A Song of Innocence" is a splendid story about a boy who, like Ellison, is fatherless; who, like young Ellison, stutters badly; and who, like Ellison, feels compelled to verbal expression. Obvious differences exist between author and character: Ellison never weighed three hundred pounds or was socially awkward or epileptic. And as a boy Ellison wanted to express himself through music, not literature. When we meet him, Cliofus has not, in fact, become a writer at all; he simply possesses some of the drives and talents of a writer. Nonetheless Cliofus is one of Ellison's several fictional personae: a curious black youngster who deals with his private demons—the least hurtful of which seem to involve race—by using the bluesman's and the writer's magic of the well-turned word.

According to Ellison, "Cadillac Flambé (1973) will appear in the

Hickman novel "in somewhat different form."[16] Told from the dubious perspective of a naive white reporter (whom we assume to be McIntyre), this story is topfull of irony. *Invisible Man* uses invisibility as its central metaphor; "King of the Bingo Game," the wild game of chance; "Flying Home," the trip to heaven on the wings of myth and folklore. In this story we meet the black musician who drives his white Cadillac onto the lawn of Senator Sunraider and ceremoniously sets it ablaze: "Cadillac Flambé." Turning this bizarre incident over and over and inside out, Ellison creates a vibrant metaphor armed with references to literature, folklore, myth, and history. Still, the metaphor of the burning car is very special in literature; with the same excited curiousity that we ask, "Who is Urizen?" in Blake's epic poetry, we ask, "What is the Cadillac Flambé?" We find that the burning car has political significance as well as meanings that are broadly ritualistic.

Like the motives of the black rioters of the 1960s, Minifees' reasons for torching his car are mixed. As the narrator tells us, the immolation is "an extreme gesture springing from the frustration of having no adequate means of replying, or making himself heard above the majestic roar of the Senator."[17] But Minifees visits the senator not merely to "bark at the big gate," to shout empty threats for the sake of mere personal release. As flames engulf the car, he tells the crowd to ignore the railing senator for a moment: "Never mind that joker up there on top of the hill . . . You can listen to him when I get through. He's had too much free speech anyway. Now it's my turn" (p. 257). The sacrificial car provides him an audience with the senator and with the public at large.

Like Jefferson in "Flying Home" and like Trueblood and Mary in *Invisible Man*, Minifees is a seasoned man of the people, a jazz musician who lives in Harlem. He minds his own business. He is not a professional politician, but when the occasion demands, he rises to a certain eloquence, stating the case for simple respect and freedom. In burning his Cadillac, Minifees burns in effigy a revered symbol of American greed, materialism, and vanity. As he does so, he tells the crowd on Sunraider's lawn:

I know that it's very, very hard for you folks to look at what I'm doing and not be disturbed, because for you it's a crime and a sin . . . That's because you know that most folks can't afford to own one of these Caddies. Not even good, hardworking folks, no matter what the pictures in the papers and magazines say. So deep down it makes you feel some larceny. You feel that it's unfair that everybody who's willing to work hard can't have one for himself. That's right! And you feel that in order to get one it's o.k. for a *man to lie and cheat and steal—yeah, even swindle his own mother if she's got the cash. That's the difference between what you say you believe and the way you act if you get the chance. Oh yes, because words is words, but life is hard and earnest and these here Caddies is way, way out of this world!* (p. 257)

In what observers term his "crude and portentous" statement, this "crazy nigger" cuts to what, in his essays, Ellison has called the heart of America's political dilemma: Americans do not begin to live up to their lofty national principles. Ellison speaks through Minifees to point out again that, for Americans, this disjuncture between theory and practice most involves the black man. Like the ambiguous Uncle Sam of minstrelsy (Mister Coon), at once personifying American freedom as well as its denial to blacks, Minifees sings a chorus of "God Bless America."

Other political meanings emerge from the story's imagery. In rejecting his Cadillac, Minifees rejects American idolatry of machines. He also celebrates human emotions over cold mechanical efficiency. To highlight this point, throughout the story cars are contrasted with slower, more natural means of travel. Approaching the senator's estate, the narrator notices that parading on the boulevard are "lovers, dogs and leash, old men on canes, and laughing children, all enjoying the fine weather." Meanwhile, the noisy boulevard is "heavy with cars." And the heavy car Minifees sacrifices is the embodiment of decadent display: this eight-valved white Cadillac is an air-conditioned, leather-upholstered convertible with whitewall tires, automatic dimmers, power brakes, and the thrust of three hundred and fifty horses.

Slow travelers are apt to be the wise men (and women) in the world of Ellison. Like Tod in "Flying Home," who crashes his plane and learns certain crucial facts of life from Jefferson, an old black man who travels on foot, Minifees encounters an old man who travels as Jesus did, on a mule. When Minifees shoots by in his luxury "dreamboat" and the man says "Go on, fool!" Minifees realizes that the senator has, in a profound sense, made a fool of him. The old man's words help the jazzman reach the conclusion that, rather than drive a Cadillac, "I, me, Lee Willie Minifees, am prepared to WALK. I'm ordering me some club-footed pigeontoed SPACE SHOES. I'd rather crawl or FLY. I'd rather save my money and wait until the A-Rabs make a car. The Zulus even. Even the ESKIMOS! Oh, I'll walk and wait. I'll grab me a GREYHOUND or a FREIGHT" (p. 264).

The immolation occurs in front of the senator's "dream castle," a house seeming to float from the sky like the Bellevedere palace in Vienna, from which the architectural trick was copied. Thus the flames consume not only Minifees' Cadillac; they mock the senator's "beautiful-to-see" Bellevedere, the architectural imitation and hoax. Symbolically, too, the fire destroys the original Bellevedere palace, stately symbol of the Hapsburgs, the once grand monarchs whose viciousness and decadence destroyed the House. Furthermore, Minifees' fire on the carpetlike lawn of a mid-twentieth-century despot represents the hope that a modern era of political cruelty and decay will go up in smoke.

Minifees' act is also one of ritual drama. His attire and disposition alert the reader to his ceremonial role: he wears an all-white suit, blue and white tie, blue handkerchief, and expensive black alligator shoes. His hair is conked, and he drives onto the senator's lawn with the "engrossed, yet relaxed, almost ceremonial attention" of a grand sportsman. He steps from the car and salutes the senatorial terrace in the grand fashion of one skilled in protocol. He douses the car with gas and fires a flaming arrow at the white car with ceremonial delicacy. He makes his speech, sings a chorus of "God Bless America," and then holds his wrists limply to be handcuffed as if this too were part of the ritual. As a professional musician Minifees knows about communal rites and forms: jazz musicians are more than role models in terms of dress, language, and style. As Ellison points out in "Remembering Jimmy," jazzmen lead a community institution, the Saturday night dance being as important an institution as Sunday morning church services.

Minifees is not only a secular ritual leader; in a sense he is a preacher too. He borrows forms from the church, even if ironically it is not Jesus but the senator who has shown him the light. In language ringing with lines from "Amazing Grace," he says,

> I had me a rolling revelation. The *scales* dropped from my eyes. I had been BLIND, but the Senator up there on that hill was making me SEE . . . Yes, sir and yes, mam, and it's Sunday and I'm told that *confession* is good for the soul. "So Mister Senator," he said, turning toward the terrace above, "this is my public testimony to my coming over to your way of thinking. This is my surrender of the Coon Cage Eight! You have unconverted me from the convertible. (pp. 261, 263)

Then the black jazzman proclaims that his "unconversion" covers more than the convertible Cadillac. Like a black Baptist preacher, he shakes his head, stamps his foot, and chants:

"Listen to me, Senator: I don't want no JET!
(stamp!) But thank you kindly.
"I don't want no FORD! (stamp!)

"Neither do I want a RAMBLER! (stamp!)

"Ditto to THUNDERBIRD! (stamp-stamp!)

"Yes, and keep those CHEVYS and CHRYSLERS away from me—
do you (stamp!) *hear* me, Senator?" (p. 264)

Including in his sermonette a fractured line from a popular song, Minifees
booms, "You have taken the best . . . So dammit, take all the rest! Take
all the rest!" And he concludes his sermonette with an allusion to a
spiritual: "Because before I'd be in a CAGE, I'll be buried in my
GRAVE" (p. 264). Minifees seems to emerge from fire and smoke like the
Old Testament God; furthermore, in his conscious sacrifice, he is identified with Jesus whose birth and resurrection significantly come to the
narrator's mind as he watches Minifees.

Despite the sacred allusions, however, this jazz musician leads a rite
that is essentially secular in nature. On one level, he is simply playing the
dozens with that "NO GOOD, NOWHERE SENATOR SUN-
RAIDER." Ritually, too, the burning is an act of purification, an offering to the gods imploring them to lift an old curse and to allow a new
birth. The Phoenix and Icarus myths are clearly analogues to "Flambé,"
but—as always in Ellison—no facile equations are possible. For not only
are Minifees and his car high-flying and flaming birds, but birds appear on
virtually every page of the story. One function they serve is to announce
the spring. When "Cadillac" begins, just outside Washington, it is
cherryblossom time, and McIntyre has gone birdwatching with some
married friends and their children. To toast the occasion, the host im-
provises an appetizer of chicken broth and vodka, proclaiming it the
"chicken-shot." Like Hawthorne's moonstruck narrators, McIntyre
prepares us for his strange tale, saying that these chicken-shots have him,
if not drunk, a little hazy of vision. He is a bit "spring-feverish" from the
heady experience of drinking the brew made from bird juices.

Several times in the story, Minifees refers to himself as a bird. He thinks
he is free as a bird—"even though a black bird"—flying home to Harlem
in his Cadillac. Suddenly, however, the senator makes him feel caged.
Minifees also thinks he is dressed "real FINE" in his white suit and
alligator shoes, but the senator makes him see that he is "as naked as a
jaybird sitting on a limb in the drifting snow" (p. 261). This harsh-
voiced, chattering bird often shows up in blues lyrics to suggest that the
blues singer is truly down and out: "I'm just as raggedy," Joe Turner
shouts, "as a jaybird at whistling time!"

Other references to Minifees as a bird are oblique and as ambiguous as
the birdmen of folklore, myth, and literature, which include harpies,
furies, and sphinxes: winged creatures with the bodies of lions. Minifees,

flying high like Icarus in his "slow, graceful bird" of a Cadillac, is brought to earth by the words of a grandfatherly black man (and, as Minifees imagines, his mule, Afro-American folk figure of fun and, sometimes, of wisdom). He is also grounded by the flaming words of Senator Sunraider. Hearing Sunraider on his radio, Minifees begins speeding, trying to fly above the trouble:

> I couldn't *help* myself. What I was hearing was going against my whole heart and soul, but I was listening *anyway*. And what I heard was beginning to make me see things in a new light. Yes, and that new light was making my eyeballs ache . . . The air was biting my face and the *sun* was on my head and I was feeling that good old familiar feeling of *flying*—but ladies and gentlemen, it was no longer the same! Oh, no—because I could still hear that Senator playing the *dozens* with my Cadillac! (p. 260)

To increase the irony, this black Icarus burns his own "wings," preferring to "walk . . . crawl, or FLY" without them!"

The use of fire and the omnipresence of birds and other images associated with birth, death, and rebirth suggest that the rite is one of fertility and celebration. The flaming Cadillac, like "a huge fowl being flambéed in cognac," inevitably summons up the phoenix, dying only to be reborn in fire. Minifees sings as the bird-car groans and dies, with its short-circuited horn "wailing like some great prehistoric animal heard in the throes of its dying." But then of course, phoenixlike, the flaming bird gives birth to new life. In a passage filled with Freudian imagery, the narrator reports the strange birth:

> It was unbelievably wild. Some continued to shout threats in their outrage and frustration, while others, both men and women, filled the air with a strangely brokenhearted and forlorn sound of weeping, and the officers found it difficult to disperse them. In fact, they continued to mill angrily about even as firemen in asbestos suits broke through, dragging hoses from a roaring pumper truck and sprayed the flaming car with a foamy chemical, which left it looking like the offspring of some strange animal brought so traumatically and precipitantly to life that it wailed and sputtered in protest, both against the circumstance of its debut into the world and the foaming presence of its still clinging afterbirth. (p. 266)

Minifees' act is one of political outrage and protest. "I never stop thinking about the difference between what it is, and what it's supposed to be." But the torching of the Cadillac is more than a plea for American justice. It is a ceremony designed to lift the spell from American government: "Somebody put the *Indian* sign on this town a long, long time ago," says Minifees. Perhaps above all it is a tragic statement about man's yearning for redemption. And it expresses the hope that, in the place of the winged Cadillac flambé, new life will take, brilliantly, to the skies.

The latest of the Hickman stories is the slight but fascinating "Backwacking: A Plea to the Senator" (1977). The "Plea" is framed as a letter to Senator Hickman from Norm A. Mauler,[18] a white supremacist Alabamian who, like McGowan (the storyteller in "It Always Breaks Out"), is obsessed by the black American, his past and his politics. "Everything the Nigra *does* is political," insists McGowan in the earlier story—even, Mauler chimes in, the black man's sex life. Nowadays Southern blacks have abandoned having sex "in the old fashion way they was taught by the WHITE man back there in slavery" in favor of backwacking, declares Mauler. Are whites losing control? What is backwacking? Mauler explains:

The nigger . . . and his woman have taken to getting undressed and standing back to back and heel to heel, shoulderblade to shoulderblade, and tale to tale with his against her's and her's against his, and then after they have horsed around and maneuvered like cats in heat and worked as tight together as a tick to a cow's tit, HE ups and starts in to HAVING AFTER HER BACK-WARDS![19]

Mauler warns the senator that backwacking is sinful, unnatural, and "no less than RADICAL!" He asks for a congressional committee to investigate and bring this backwacking to a "teeth-rattling halt."

This is a humorous tale about the silliness of taking too seriously an American stereotype or folk motif—black sexual deviancy, promiscuity, and supremacy. The driven Mauler accepts backwacking as plain fact. "The most reliable authority," says he, confirms that watching black backwackers reach a climax is "like watching somebody being struck down by greased lightening . . . like seeing somebody being knocked down and dragged by an L & N freight train that has been doing a high-ball on a down-hill grade with its brakeshoes busted and with no red light ahead!" (p. 413). The backwacker is blasted "as close to dying as any normal human being can come and still not die." But instead of dying, "the nigger just lets out a big ole hoop-and-a-holler and leaps back to his position and commences this 'BACKWACKING' again!" More than mere racist lunacy provides the humor and the meaning in the "Plea." Indeed, like the bemused narrator of "It Always Breaks Out," the reader of this story wonders if Mauler is not to some degree correct in his analysis. Dated April 4, 1953 (fifteen years before the day of Martin Luther King's assassination; a matter of months before the pivotal Birmingham bus boycott and the Supreme Court decision outlawing segregated schools; the year the Korean War ended), the letter does correctly predict the "tradition-busting," radical social change that spread throughout America from the civil rights movement. Perhaps he is correct, too, in linking the incipient change in civil rights law to the end of the Asian war. "We are confronted," says Mauler, "by a crisis the likes of which we haven't had to face since back in 1918 when the nigger come home trying to talk and act like French men" (p. 415).

Moreover, as Ellison points out in an early essay, political truths are revealed in folklore. What explains the enduring cycle of tales about black sexual gymnastics? Surely one social function served by these tales, as told by white men, has been to justify the oppression of blacks, who are deemed more physical than intellectual or emotional in nature, more animals than men. But blacks also create their own yarns and songs alleging sexual supereminance. These serve to disarm white man equipped with stereotypes, and—within the group—to celebrate blacks' capacity to endure even if the stereotypes were true. In the blues, black sexual prowess is a frequent theme; here the assertions of amorous powers comprise a lusty celebration of the self, the couple, and the racial group. Memphis Slim sounds jubilant as he sings:

> I want you to rock me baby,
> Rock me all night long.
> Rock me baby,
> Rock me all night long
> I need you to roll me baby
> Like my back didn't have no bone.

Jimmy Rushing shouts, "When I start to lovin', I holler 'Ooooh, god-dog!'" Whereas the white lore about black sex denied black humanity, the black lore celebrates it with great exuberance.

Norm A. Mauler is agitated about black sexual prowess not as a sign of bestiality (as white racist lore would claim) but as a source of power (as black folklore would have it). Backwacking, warns Mauler, seems to unleash "raw naked POWER." He tells Sunraider that "what we actually have down here is not only a serious threat to our orderly society, but we are in the middle of something that can best be described as a 'clear and present danger.'" (p. 415)

Writing about Leslie Fiedler's labeling as homosexual the relationship between Huck and Jim in *Huckleberry Finn*, Ellison says:

> Fiedler was accused of mere sensationalism when he named the friendship homosexual, yet I believe him so profoundly disturbed by the manner in which the deep dichotomies symbolized by blackness and whiteness are resolved that . . . he leaped squarely into the middle of that tangle of symbolism which he is dedicated to unsnarling, and yelled out his most terrifying name for chaos. Other things being equal, he might have called it "rape," "incest," "parricide" or—"miscegenation."[20]

So, Mauler yells out his most terrifying name for the black political advances he sensed are brewing: "BACKWACKING!"

Beyond this, by considering the political meanings of rumored black sexual doings, Mauler raises the larger question of the social functions, for blacks and whites, of an American folk motif: black sexual superiority. The question here also is one that Ellison has pondered throughout his career as a writer: How does folklore predict and inform social change? And how might a writer unleash the great power of folklore in a short story or, harder still, a novel?

At this point it is not possible to know exactly what Ellison will do with the Hickman puzzle pieces. Each stands on its own as a complete short story, some, like "It Always Breaks Out," simple and straightforward; others, like "Cadillac Flambé," so complex they seem overwrought. In fact, the main problem facing Ellison appears to be one that slowed down *Invisible Man*: providing effective transitions from chapter to chapter. Perhaps with additional sections or interchapters, the stories could be ordered as a compendium like Faulkner's *Go Down, Moses* or Hemingway's *In Our Time*. Or, as Ellison has said all along, they could turn up in a novel or in a series of novels. Preceding the first novel by five years was a short story that later became the novel's "battle royal" chapter. And its prologue was published a few months before *Invisible Man*.

Whatever their ultimate shape and placement, however, these related Hickman stories describe a topsy-turvy world in which Bliss loses his grasp on reality; in which Hickman holds fast to personal and political goals and values. The tone and the narrative angles shift from story to story, but not much more so than the sections of *Invisible Man*, where one also finds letters, remembered events, speeches, dreams. And as with the first novel, Ellison tries here to bring into focus a huge teeming area of Americana.

8

Shadow Actor:
Ellison's Aesthetics

The initial appeal of *Shadow and Act* seemed to be that here, at last, the "invisible man" would emerge from underground; that here, as one reviewer proclaimed, was Ralph Ellison's "real autobiography." It is true that *Shadow and Act* has autobiographical overtones. Two pieces, the Introduction and "Hidden Name and Complex Fate," are explicitly autobiographical in design. And in the book's reviews and interviews the author draws extensively upon his own experience. Furthermore, by including essays (none retouched) written over a span of twenty-two years, Ellison reveals certain aspects of his development from the twenty-eight-year-old, Marxist-oriented WPA worker of "The Way It Is" (1942) to the seasoned writer of 1964: now he was "not primarily concerned with injustice, but with art."

In his Introduction Ellison offers a sort of apologia, explaining that the essays "represent, in all their modesty, some of the necessary effort which a writer of my background must make in order to possess the meaning of his experience."[1] When the first of the essays appeared, he regarded himself "in my most secret heart at least—a musician," not a writer. "With these thin essays for wings," he notes, "I was launched full flight into the dark." Looking at the publication date printed at the end of each text, we may trace the growth of a young intellectual's consciousness. Thus "their basic significance, whatever their value as information or speculation, is autobiographical" (p. xviii). Nonetheless, the book has thematic unities that are even more compelling. A good deal of the cumulative power of *Shadow and Act* derives from its basic contrast of black American life as seen through the lenses of politics, sociology, and popular culture with black American life as observed and lived by one sensitive, questioning black man.

Shadow and Act, a compilation, has enduring validity as a unified work of art because of its author's single-minded intention to define Afro-American life. Sometimes Ellison gently punctures, sometimes wields an ax, against inadequate definitions of black experience. In place of what he detects as false prophesies, usually uttered by social scientists, Ellison chooses as broad a frame of reference as possible to interpret black experience in richly optimistic terms. "Who wills to be a Negro?" he asks, rhetorically. "*I* do!"

In a number of essays Ellison points out that all too often the white critic treats black art as if it had appeared miraculously, without tradition, as if the black artist just grew like Topsy. To correct for this kind of condescension, Ellison is very careful in his criticism to discuss black music, literature, and the visual arts in the context of tradition: black, American, Western, Eastern, universal. Ellison's warnings notwithstanding, *Shadow and Act* is a singular achievement. It is not possible to point out another work that deals as fully with Afro-American and American literature and music and politics; and that is varied enough to include tightly drawn literary essays and a formal address alongside breezy interviews and autobiographical reflections. That it all comes together as a well-unified whole is a tribute to its author's power as editor/philosopher/artist.

This is not to suggest that *Shadow and Act* is without precursors. With its emphasis on ritual and folk forms in art, it recalls the writings of Kenneth Burke, Audré Malraux, and Stanley Edgar Hyman. The political persuasion, which Arthur P. Davis terms "integrationist," as well as the rhetoric remind us of Ellison's support for the freedom movement. As a study of Americana from the expansive perspective of a writer, *Shadow and Act* falls within the tradition of Henry James's *The American Scene* (1907). James Baldwin's *Notes of a Native Son* (1955), which includes book and movie reviews and political commentary as well as documents for an autobiography, provides another context for *Shadow and Act*.

Ellison's book of essays has also inspired others, including Imamu Amiri Baraka's *Home* (1966). Although the perspectives of Ellison and Baraka, who in *Home* professes his strident black nationalism, clash dramatically, their books are very similar in form. Both consist of essays on Afro-American art and politics; both have autobiographical underpinnings. Then too, in that he painstakingly stresses the particular contributions of blacks to American society, Ellison is in his way undoubtedly a black cultural nationalist.

The central theme of "The Seer and the Seen" (the first of the three sections of *Shadow and Act*) is "segregation of the word." White Americans, says Ellison, because of their "Manichean fascination with the symbolism of blackness and whiteness," tend to see the world in black (bad) and white (good). When whites contemplate a "profoundly personal problem involving guilt," the conjured images and characters appear, as it were, darkly. Thus:

> It is practically impossible for the white American to think of sex, of economics, his children or womenfolk, or of sweeping socio-political changes, without summoning into consciousness fear-flecked images of black men. Indeed, it seems that the Negro has become identified with those unpleasant aspects of conscience and consciousness which it is part of the American's character to avoid. Thus when the literary artist attempts to tap the charged springs is-suing from his inner world, up float his misshapen and bloated im-ages of the Negro, like the fetid bodies of the drowned, and he turns away, discarding an ambiguous substance which the artists of other cultures would confront boldly and humanize into the stuff of a tragic art. (p. 100)

According to Ellison, certain nineteenth-century writers, notably Her-man Melville, Mark Twain, and Stephen Crane, produced classic Amer-ican fiction because they were able eloquently to confront the "blackness of darkness" on the guilt-shadowed edges of their minds. For them, the black man, even when portrayed in the garb of minstrelsy, represented America's moral concern and quest for freedom. Much of the vitality of *Moby Dick*, *Huckleberry Finn*, and Crane's short stories derives from the blackness of these works. When other writers left out black characters (or reduced them to the dimensions of badmen, angels, and clowns), these writers presented black characters whose humanity was great and whose principles provided the fiction with a moral context. When other writers ignored or excused Americans' "blackest" political and moral transgres-sions, these writers faced them directly. "Mark Twain knew that in his America humanity masked its face with blackness" (p. 44).

Ellison writes that, with the Hayes-Tilden Compromise, this moral concern slipped underground. Blacks disappeared almost completely from American fiction; and with them the "deep-probing doubt and a sense of evil" that had immortalized certain nineteenth-century writers. Muck-rakers, proletarian writers, and "lost generation" writers raised some doubt about morality. "But it is a shallow doubt, which seldom turns in-ward upon the writer's own values; almost always it focuses outward,

upon some scapegoat with which he is seldom able to identify himself . . .
This particular naturalism explored everything except the nature of man"
(pp. 35-36).

Even Hemingway's stories, which the young Ellison loved for their
descriptions of nature and human emotions, and which he once imitated
for their technical excellence, also failed to explore deeply the nature of
man. Hemingway authored "the trend toward technique for the sake of
technique and production for the sake of the market to the neglect of the
human need out of which [these techniques] spring." The understated,
hard-boiled novel, "with its dedication to physical violence, social cynicism and understatement," performs on the social level "a function similar
to that of the stereotype: it conditions the reader to accept the less worthy
values of society, and it serves to absolve our sins of social
irresponsibility" (p. 35).

Ellison goes on to consider William Faulkner and Richard Wright,
who present a variety of black characters in their fiction. Both recall
nineteenth-century writers in their outward and unrelenting concern
with America's moral climate. Faulkner's characters, like Mark Twain's,
have stereotypical outlines, but Faulkner is willing to "start with the
stereotype, accept it as true, and then seek out the human truth which it
hides" (p. 43). Wright's characters also verge on the stereotypic: often
they are either the usual "bad niggers" of white folklore or the evil,
broken blacks of what one critic has called "filthlore" of social-science fiction. Nonetheless, Wright pulls from underground the black character
and, with him, the disturbing moral questions that cluster around the
black as "seen" by whites. Armed, says Ellison, with the insights of Freud
and Marx, Wright sought "to discover and depict the meaning of Negro
experience; and to reveal to both Negroes and whites those problems of a
psychological and emotional nature which arise between them when they
strive for mutual understanding" (p. 77).

Aside from his comments on Wright, Ellison says very little in *Shadow
and Act* about Afro-American writing per se. As a boy he was introduced
to New Negro poets, and their works inspired pride and excitement over
the glamor of Harlem. "And it was good to know that there were Negro
writers." But after reading T. S. Eliot, black poetry faded in Ellison's
eyes: "The Waste Land" gripped his mind. "Somehow its rhythms were
often closer to those of jazz than were those of the Negro poets, and even
though I could not understand them, its range of allusion was as mixed
and varied as Louis Armstrong." Ellison says that white writers like Eliot,
and later Malraux, Dostoevsky, and others, helped to free him from
segregation of the mind. Black writers' portraits of blacks were often un-

satisfactory, but certain white writers, dealing "darkly" with the complex human condition, led Ellison to realize some of the possibilities for black characters *he* would create. The Invisible Man, of course, is as much Candide and Stephen Daedalus as he is Richard (of *Black Boy*) or Big Boy (of Sterling Brown's poem, "The Odyssey of Big Boy").

In *Shadow and Act* Ellison spars openly with two literary historians, Irving Howe and Stanley Edgar Hyman. Both "The World and the Jug" and "Change the Joke and Slip the Yoke" began as informal, if heated, rebuttals to articles on *Invisible Man*. "The World and the Jug" germinated through a telephone conversation with Myron Kolatch of the *New Leader*; "Change the Joke and Slip the Yoke" through a letter to Hyman. Irritated by the condescending reductionism he felt to be implicit in their approaches, Ellison took aim with both barrels. In fact, in his attempts to correct what he saw as these critics' distortions of the Afro-American image, he scatters the form and substance of certain of their literary theories, twisting them, sometimes unfairly, to serve his own purposes.

In "The World and the Jug" Ellison takes issue with Howe's essay "Black Boys and Native Sons," which deals what it means to be a black American writer. Ellison objects to the notion that, while Richard Wright kept the faith by maintaining his militant stance, Ellison and Baldwin became overrefined, "literary to a fault." Making Howe a strawman, Ellison labels this critic a sociology-oriented writer who values ideology over art and who is blind to works that are not explicitly political. Howe is also stung for his statement that Wright's release of anger allowed Baldwin and Ellison to express their own anger. "What does Howe know of my acquaintance with violence," writes Ellison, "or the shape of my courage or the intensity of my anger? I suggest that my credentials are at least as valid as Wright's . . . and it is possible that I have lived through and committed even more violence than he" (p. 115). Furthermore, Wright, though a hero and friend, was not as great a literary influence as were Malraux and Hemingway.[2] To say that blacks are influenced only by other blacks assumes that blacks live in a "colored-only" jug with a tight cork. We must remember, however, that the jug is not opaque, but transparent: blacks influence and are influenced by whites and others outside the jug.

Too often, Ellison warns, a writer like Howe, who believes that good art must be overtly *engagé*, shrinks the image of the black man he is purporting to defend. "One unfamiliar with what Howe stands for would get the impression that when he looks at a Negro he sees not a human being but an abstract embodiment of living hell." Thus the raging Bigger Thomas is preferred to the bemused Invisible Man. Overlooked here is the belief that blacks are unquestionably human and that

Their resistance to provocation, their coolness under pressure, their sense of timing and their tenacious hold on the ideal of their ultimate freedom are indispensable values in the struggle, and are at least as characteristic of American Negroes as the hatred, fear and vindictiveness which Wright chose to emphasize. (p. 114)

Ellison states succinctly where he differs with Wright (and Howe) regarding the purpose of art:

Wright believed in the much abused notion that novels are "weapons" — the counterpart of the dreary notion, common among most minority groups, that novels are instruments of good social relations. But I believe that true novels, even when most pessimistic and bitter, arise out of an impulse to celebrate human life and therefore are ritualistic and ceremonial at their core. Thus they would preserve as they destroy, affirm as they reject. (p. 114)

Ellison says that just as he, and most blacks, have disciplined themselves to live sanely in a hostile America, his novel is a product not of political struggle alone but of disciplined literary struggle. The writer's job is not to deny but to transmute the loadstone of anger and injustice into art.

With its comment on folklore and art, Stanley Edgar Hyman's chapter on *Invisible Man*, published in *The Promised End*, could be seen as derivative of Ellison's own critical work. Yet Ellison takes sharp issue with Hyman in "Change the Joke." In a typical preface he puts his essay in context, explaining that it originated as a letter to "an old friend and intellectual sparring partner." Their two articles, he adds, "are apt to yield their maximum return when read together." Despite this gentle beginning, Ellison is quick to point out that Hyman's conception of how literature draws on folk sources is so much at variance from his own that he "must disagree with him all along the way" (p. 46).

Ellison finds fault with the "racially pure" aspects of Hyman's discussion. Hyman identifies the "darky entertainer" as a figure from black American folklore and as one related to the "archetypal trickster figure, originating from Africa." This minstrel man, a professional entertainer who plays dumb, metamorphoses in Afro-American literature into such characters as the wiley grandfather of *Invisible Man*. This argument offends Ellison by veering toward the claim that black Americans possess idiosyncratic forms directly traceable to an African homeland.

Ellison responds that the black American writer draws on literature of any and all kinds to create character and circumstance. If he uses folklore, it is not because of his ethnic heritage but because he is a student of *Ulysses* and "The Waste Land" where folk and myth sources provide structure and resonance. The black writer should not be backed into a corner where the oddments and exotica of folklore are said to preside over the true source of good writing, which is *good writing*.

Ellison adds that when black writers do tap folk sources, they do not use the "darky" figures of minstrelsy. Such characters are by no means black folk types but white ones, born of the white American's need to exorcise the true black man and to drape in black certain troubling behavioral patterns and attitudes. When these entertainers show up in American literature they are repulsive to Afro-Americans. Furthermore, masking and "playing dumb" are American games, not just black ones. Black characters in novels by American blacks are, Ellison says, as homegrown as their authors. Trace them to Africa, and the critic takes a political position not a literary one.

This hyperbolic statement seems to contradict Ellison's belief that folklore provides a secure base for great literature. But, troubled by the "segregated" idea that black writers strictly depend on black sources, and angered by even the dimmest suggestion that as a black writer he himself performed the obscene function of a blackface minstrel man, Ellison threw Hyman a hyperbole. Afro-American folklore provides riches, Ellison says, "but for the novelist, of any cultural or racial identity, his form is his greatest freedom and his insights are where he finds them."

So where does the writer find true portraits of Afro-Americans? In black folklore, yes. In churches, barbershops, workgangs, and playgrounds where the lore abounds. But that kind of study can never replace the needed study of images and modes of characterization in literature. And this does appear in the works of Toni Morrison, Ernest J. Gaines, Ishmael Reed, Al Young, Alice Walker, and James A. McPherson — all of whom also use folklore in their fiction — whose characters spring from the Bible, James Fenimore Cooper, Jonathan Swift, Henry James, Zora Neale Hurston, from Ralph Ellison.

When jazz saxophonist Marion Brown taught at the University of Massachusetts, he required his students to read the second section of *Shadow and Act,* "Sound and the Mainstream." There, he said, you get an idea of the milieu in which the black musician operates. There, too, are several portraits of Afro-Americans at their eloquent best: as musicians, as artists.

"Blues People," a review of Imamu Amiri Baraka's study of black music, is the theoretical cornerstone of *Shadow and Act's* middle section. Baraka, another strawman, is said to strain for militancy and to falsify the meaning of the blues and the background of the bluesman. Afro-Americans of any kind are likely to produce genuine art, notes Ellison, not just dark-skinned, country, lower-class, or militant blacks. Furthermore, Afro-American music may not correctly be considered in isolation from mainstream American music. "The most authoritative rendering of America in music is that of American Negroes." One of Ellison's major points here is that black American musicians, throughout their history in the New World, have functioned not as politicians but as artists, leaders of transcending ritual. "Any effective study of the blues would treat them first as poetry and ritual." To white society, Bessie Smith may have been purely an entertainer, a "blues queen"; but "within the tighter Negro community where the blues were part of a total way of life, and a major expression of an attitude toward life, she was a priestess, a celebrant who affirmed the values of the group and man's ability to deal with chaos" (p. 257). The same is true of other black musicians too, as Ellison carries out the theme in his portraits of Mahalia Jackson, Charlie Parker, Charlie Christian, and Jimmy Rushing.

The piece on Mahalia Jackson, "As the Spirit Moves Mahalia," contains a fine thumbnail sketch of the renowned gospel singer, whose ebullience brought her international fame. Also, though untrained in a formal sense, she is portrayed as a highly conscious artist who extended the gospel form. Disciplined by her experiences in a black southern rural and then black northern urban setting, she was influenced not only by blues and jazz, but by the European classics, flamenco, and certain Eastern forms.

Ellison gives an excellent discussion of black sacred music as the music of ritual. He advises those who would truly understand this singer to hear her in the Afro-American church, where she reigns as "a high priestess in the religious ceremony."

> It is in the setting of the church that the full timbre of her sincerity sounds most distinctly . . . Here it could be seen that the true function of her singing is not simply to entertain, but to prepare the congregation for the minister's message, to make it receptive to the spirit and, with effects of voice and rhythm, to evoke a shared community of experience. (pp. 218-219)

The recordings are wonderful, but only in church may she sing truly "until the Lord comes." Only in the music's ritual context may the full mystery and meaning of her songs be comprehended.

"Remembering Jimmy" is Ellison's eloquent appreciation of Jimmy Rushing who, like Mahalia Jackson, is portrayed as the leader of a ritual, in this case a secular one: the public dance. The combination of blues, dancers, musicians, and singers "formed the vital whole of jazz as an institutional form, and even today neither part is quite complete without the rest." Rushing's blues and ballads must be experienced in ritual context. So, too, his music is a product of the black neighborhood, his voice seeming to echo something wondrous about the east side of Oklahoma City where he like Ellison got his start. And Rushing's music has political, social, and national implications, reminding Americans of "rock-bottom reality" along with "our sense of the possibility of rising about it." Herein lies the force of the blues, "our most vital popular art form," and the universal appeal of an artist/interpreter, Rushing.

Ellison's tribute to another childhood acquaintance in "The Charlie Christian Story" focuses on the jazz musician in American society. In a country where high art is viewed as entertainment, and where the complexities of history are reduced to the clichés of legend, the meanings of jazz are dimly understood. Charlie Christian was exposed to many kinds of music as he grew up. Oklahoma City was a bustling, energetic blues and jazz center where Second Street was comparable to Kansas City's famous Twelfth. Moreover, at school, on the radio, at the movies, and, in Christian's case, at home, classical music as well as popular and folk songs were heard. Many jazz performers, including Christian before he reached New York City, remain local heroes inside the narrow radius of their traveling circuit. But the tradition from which their art springs is a rich and diverse one, tapping blues and classics, folk and high art.

As with Rushing and Jackson, Christian and other jazz artists can be most fully understood in the context of ritual. For jazzmen the public dance is a vital institution. But the "academy"—the principal ritual and testing ground—is the jam session. Here the artists exchange ideas (which then, imitated, drift into the vocabulary of mainstream jazz, leaving their creators anonymous); they also participate in a rite wherein the musician's identity is discovered and asserted. In Ellison's words, "Each true jazz moment . . . springs from a contest in which each artist challenges all the rest; each solo flight, or improvisation, represents (like the successive canvases of a painter) a definition of his identity: as individual, as member of the collectivity and as a link in the chain of tradition." For Ellison, black musicians are tough, astute artists and ritual leaders who teach, purge, destroy, mourn, initiate, delight—and, above all, celebrate.

And black music that is unconnected to these life-sustaining rituals—the church, the dance, the jam session—is liable to be sterile. Such seems the case even with the eloquent saxophone virtuoso, Charlie "Bird" Parker, portrayed in "On Bird, Bird-Watching, and Jazz" as an artist without roots. Though Parker studied and jammed with Kansas City musicians, he (and a generation of imitators) threw off the mask of the dance-hall entertainer only, Ellison says, to become a "white hero" and, ironically, "entertainment for a ravenous, sensation-starved, culturally disoriented public," mostly white. To Ellison, Parker's music reflected the triumph of technique over real feeling (as expressed in sacred and secular ritual) and, finally, adolescent impotence. Of Parker's style, Ellison writes: "For all its velocity, brilliance and imagination there is in it a great deal of loneliness, self-deprecation and self-pity. With this there is a quality which seems to issue from its vibratoless tone: a sound of amateurish ineffectuality, as though he could never quite make it" (p. 230). "Bird lives," in Ellison's view, because he transforms postwar discord and yearning into "a haunting art." Ellison, who obviously is deaf to virtually all jazz beyond Basie and Ellington, says that if Bird could be said to reign as a ritual leader, his was a cult of sad-eyed, self-destructive whites, trying desperately, decadently, to be "hip."

The third and final "movement" of *Shadow and Act*, the one that gives the book its title, is its least focused section. This "eldest" division (containing essays dated 1942, 1944, 1948, 1949, and 1958) comprises two topical essays, a piece on black Hollywood images, a book review, and a self-interview on politics, race, and culture. This mixed section is not, however, a mere grab bag stuffed with old essays unfitted to the rest of the book. Dealing primarily with culture and politics—rather than literature and music—it provides the reader a background against which to evaluate Ellison's discussions of specific art forms and artists.

Also, the essays in this final section are the book's most radical in analysis. In "The Way It Is," published in *New Masses* (1942) Ellison coolly defines the misery and near despair of Harlemites on the home front of the world war fought by a Jim Crow army. In "Harlem Is Nowhere" (unpublished, 1948) he discusses the wretched conditions in Harlem and their effects on the minds of desperate "folk" residents. And in "An American Dilemma: A Review" (unpublished, 1944) he delineates the invidious relation of "philanthropic" big business, social science, and black politics. Here we seem to be in the presence of a Young Turk who hurls elaborate curses from the sidelines of American culture. That two of these essays were not previously published (because of their radical bent?) suggests that Ellison may have yet more gems filed away.

As in the first two thirds of *Shadow and Act*, in this section Ellison deals with the image and role of the Afro-American in the United States. Here again he observes that in terms of culture Afro-Americans are more American than purely African. What binds people of African ancestry throughout the world is "not culture . . . but an identity of passions." "We share a hatred for the alienation forced upon us by Europeans during the process of colonialization and empire are bound by our common suffering more than by our pigmentation" (p. 263). Thus blacks around the world share what one anthropologist has termed a common "culture of oppression" rather than language and other cultural forms and rites.[3] Now we meet Ellison at his stubborn and limiting worse, blindly ignoring the multiplicity of cultural forms shared by peoples of African descent. According to the Ellison of "Some Questions and Some Ancestors," all that blacks in America have in common with blacks in Ghana or South Africa is white oppression.

This is not to say that Afro-Americans do not constitute a distinctive group; nor, as Ellison makes clear elsewhere, does it mean that Afro-Americans are defined simply by their relation to white Americans. In an often-quoted passage from his review of Gunnar Myrdal's *An American Dilemma*, Ellison bristles:

> Can a people (its faith in an idealized American Creed not withstanding) live and develop for over three hundred years simply by *reacting*? Are American Negroes simply the creation of white men, or have they at least helped to create themselves out of what they found around them? Men have made a way of life in caves and upon cliffs, why cannot Negroes have made a way of life upon the horns of the white man's dilemma? (pp. 315-316)

In fact, black Americans *have* made a way of life which they do not wish to sacrifice entirely, even in their drive for full freedom in America. Ellison accuses Myrdal of presuming that blacks do not participate in "white" culture because they are kept away from it. Ellison offers an important corrective here:

> It does not occur to Myrdal that many of the Negro cultural manifestations which he considers merely reflective might also embody a *rejection* of what he considers "higher values." There is a dualism at work here. It is only partially true that Negroes turn away from white patterns because they are refused participation. There is nothing like distance to create objectivity, and exclusion gives rise to counter values. Men, as Dostoevsky observed, cannot live in revolt. (p. 316)

Men tend to prefer the styles and values of their particular cultural group. Sounding somewhat more like Imamu Amiri Baraka than the moderate integrationist, Ellison comments on the effect of integration on black culture:

I see a period when Negroes are going to be wandering around because, you see, we have had this thing thrown at us for so long that we haven't had a chance to discover what in our own background is really worth preserving. For the first time we are given a choice, we are making a choice . . . Most Negroes could not be nourished by the life white Southerners live. It is too hag-ridden, it is too obsessed, it is too concerned with attitudes which could change everything that Negroes have been conditioned to expect from life. (p. 22)

Shadow and Act presents explicit and compelling definitions of Afro-American life. The most comprehensive of these appears in "The World and the Jug" (which I talked about earlier in terms of its literary argument):

It is not skin color which makes a Negro American but cultural heritage as shaped by the American experience, the social and political predicament; a sharing of that "concord of sensibilities" which the group expresses through historical circumstance . . . Being a Negro American has to do with the memory of slavery and the hope of emancipation and the betrayal by allies and the revenge and contempt inflicted by our former masters after the Reconstruction, and the myths, both Northern and Southern, which are propagated in justification of that betrayal . . . It has to do with a special perspective on the national ideals and the national conduct, and with a tragicomic attitude toward the universe. It has to do with special emotions evoked by the details of cities and countrysides, with forms of labor and with forms of pleasure; with sex and with love, with food and with drink, with machines and with animals; with climates and with dwellings, with places of worship and places of entertainment; with garments and dreams and idioms of speech; with manners and customs, with religion and art, with life styles and hoping, and with that special sense of predicament and fate which gives direction and resonance to the Freedom Movement. (p. 131)

Ellison closes this lyrical definition with: "Most important, perhaps, being a Negro American involves a *willed* affirmation of self against all outside pressure—an identification with the group as extended through the individual self which rejects all possibilities of escape that do not involve a basic resuscitation of original American ideals of social and political justice" (pp. 131-132).

As seen by Ellison, the Afro-American's life has been torturous and tragic, but it has also been heroic and rich in form and spirit. Sociologists and sociological critics, indeed critics of all kinds, and writers, black and white, have failed for the most part to focus on black American men and women of flesh and blood. A few writers have seen through the greasepaint stereotypes. In *Shadow and Act* Ellison recommends that those who would truly "know the Negro" study certain nineteenth- and twentieth-century writers (including the Russians) and to learn about black folklore. Moreover, in this abstracted autobiography Ellison surveys his own experience and recommends that blacks be seen (and, especially, that they see themselves) as a group with a special perspective, with beautiful and useful cultural forms, and with a flaming desire for freedom.

9

More Shadows, More Actors

I n the years since the appearance of *Shadow and Act*, Ralph Ellison has published only a few essays and reviews—very little, when one considers that in 1940 he contributed about an essay per month to the radical literary magazines. Several interviews have come out, usually carefully edited by Ellison. These often redundant exercises reveal the author's desire to remain in communication with the public. Also, he often alludes to works yet unpublished, suggesting that another book of essays is brewing. He has mentioned, for instance, a review of Stanley Dance's book, *The World of Duke Ellington*, and a long piece—based in part on his New York University course—on the relation of vernacular style to fine art in American culture. Ellison has also published some of his lectures, again usually painstakingly reworded, in a wide variety of places: from the *Wilson Library Bulletin* (June 1967) to the *Harvard Advocate* (Spring 1973). Some of these, like private interviews, remain as unpublished sections of master's theses or doctoral dissertations.

Since *Shadow and Act* Ellison has often been asked which Afro-American fiction writers he reads with enjoyment. He usually shies away from general pronouncements on this subject. It is perhaps clutching at straws to cite promotional comments on other books as an index to Ellison's current views. But what he praises now, in print, carries a connection with his own work, and I shall risk charges of straw-clutching to mention these brief statements: his book-jacket comments for Albert Murray's *The Omni-Americans* (1970), James Alan McPherson's *Hue and*

Cry (1969), and *Elbow Room* (1977), and his foreword to Leon Forrest's *There Is a Tree More Ancient than Eden* (1973). Furthermore, his only essay on a painter, "Romare Bearden: Paintings and Projections" (1968), throws light on Ellison's view of current Afro-American art and iconography. In that essay he grapples once again with the issue of how the black American has been depicted in art.

Of these statements, the Bearden piece is the only comprehensive one. Originally published as the introduction to a catalogue for a Bearden exhibition at the State University of New York at Albany, it deals with the development of Bearden's work from the thirties to the sixties. But the broader subject is the role of the Afro-American artist (including the writer and the musician). Perhaps because Ellison writes here not specifically of black writers but of black painters, and is thus less vulnerable to the question of his *own* creative output, he crashes the boom down on black artists. In "Paintings and Projections," Ellison portrays Bearden as the heroic black artist of social consciousness who slays the dragons that haunt and cripple other black artists.

What shapes do these dragons take? The ugliest of all is racial prejudice. Not only does white racism impede the black artist's development and recognition; even worse, it has created black *self*-segregation. Excluded for so long from white Americana, the black artist, in despair, has surrendered to the belief that mainstream American culture is unavailable to him. Forgetting that blacks have helped to shape America's art and iconography, this black artist has considered himself an outcast in his native land and has excluded himself from the traditions and techniques (always key words for Ellison) of American and world art, choosing instead to limit himself to those materials and methods that are "purely black." To Ellison, this self-imposed exile is defensive and "lachrymose"; fearful of competing with whites—with the best artists in the world, whatever their ethnic background—the black artist has too often been comfortable in his provincialism. "Turn Picasso into a Negro and *then* let me see how far he can go," such artists complain.[1]

Lacking in a deeply rooted Afro-American tradition in the visual arts, and cut off from white traditions, the black artist is cast upon the hard rock of artistic "realism." He decides to "tell it like it is." This results, says Ellison, in weakly sentimental black propaganda paintings, aimed at social reform. And, as artists, these "realists" err in adopting the methods of the photographer and the cartoonist. The power of their works fades with the issues they defend, and the public, whose perceptions are already dulled by the mass media, is cheated of true art.

In this forest of delusion and decline, Bearden stands out mightily. A black man "whose social consciousness is no less intense than his dedication to art," Bearden recognized early that if black protest would be projected as art, it must undergo a metamorphosis. When painting scenes from the Harlem of the Depression, Bearden clearly captured the wretchedness of the people's condition. But by borrowing methods from the Mexican muralists, he caught something of both the universality of Harlem life and the "harlemness of the human predicament." Significantly Bearden fell under the influence of Federico Garcia Lorca and Ernest Hemingway, and became interested in ritual and myth as forms for structuring the human drama. Also using ideas from African, Dutch, and Italian schools of painting, Bearden was able to transform Afro-American patterns of birth, death, and rebirth in his work. His is an ambiguous and tragic vision, like that of the blues, peopled by conjure women and strange figures standing by roaring freight trains. By learning from and competing against artists from any time and place, Bearden projected powerful images of blacks "without violating his passionate dedication to art as a fundamental and transcendent agency for confronting and revealing the world."

In his published commentary since *Shadow and Act*, Ellison has unequivocally praised only three black writers, Murray, McPherson, and Forrest. McPherson's first book of short stories, *Hue and Cry* (1969), carries on its back jacket this comment by Ellison:

> With this collection of stories, McPherson promises to move right past those talented but misguided writers of Negro American cultural background who take being black as a privilege for being obscenely second-rate and who regard their social predicament as Negroes as exempting them from the necessity of mastering the craft and forms of fiction. Indeed, as he makes his "hue and cry" over the dead-ends, the confusions of value and failures of sympathy and insight of those who inhabit his fictional world, McPherson's stories are in themselves a hue and cry against the dead, publicity-stained writing which has come increasingly to stand for what is called "black writing" . . . [McPherson] is a writer of insight, sympathy, and humor and one of the most gifted young Americans I've had the privilege to read.[2]

Like Bearden, McPherson is depicted as a craftsman with a jazz saxophonist's urge to challenge (or to "jam" with and against) the best artists in his field. As in the Bearden article, other black artists are dismissed (all too quickly) as second-rate craftsmen. In Ellison's view these other black writers merely capitalized on their color during the arts explosion of the sixties.

In his note on the back of McPherson's second collection of stories, *Elbow Room*, Ellison uses a milder tone. He is careful, however, to place McPherson in the context not merely of black writers but of "our" American writers:

> *Elbow Room* is the most rewarding collection of short stories to come my way in quite some time. In them James Alan McPherson reveals a maturing ability to convert the ironies, the contradictions of American experience into sophisticated works of literature. To my mind McPherson ranks with the most talented and original of our younger writers. The title story alone reveals more about the spiritual condition of Americans during the 1960s than is to be found in most novels.[3]

A Tree More Ancient than Eden, a first novel by former editor of *Muhammad Speaks*, Leon Forrest, is the most recent black novel singled out for praise by Ellison. "How furiously eloquent is this man Forrest's prose," writes Ellison, "how zestful his jazz-like invention, his parody, his reference to the classics and commonplace of literature, folklore, tall-tale and slum street jive!" Here is a craftsman who has "rejected the stance of cultural self-segregation" and who pits "his talents against the achievements of the great masters of the form." And he touches on "the great themes of life," revealing mysteries not only of his characters' blackness but of their "black-white, white-black Americanness." *A Tree More Ancient than Eden* uses forms beyond realism and beyond those of any "neat, minor slice of life." Instead, Forrest's book is experimental in design and "cathedral-high and cloaca-low" in scope.[4]

In 1970 Ellison wrote a laudatory note for *The Omni-Americans*, a collection of essays by his old friend and intellectual sparring partner, Albert Murray. This comment, appearing on the cover of the paperback edition, reads: "For all who would deal creatively with the problem of who we Americans are, what we are, and where we are; it is indispensable."[5] Murray's essential thesis that black Americans are not just Afro-Americans but Omni-Americans, shaped by the many cultural patterns endemic to this country, is one to which Ellison could only utter a hearty Amen. Also, Ellison must have been delighted to read a book that values black art resonant in allusion and finely shaped by tradition over black art written for the sake of the political moment. That Murray defines black-American life as affirmative and rich could only win his Tuskegee schoolmate's endorsement. The similarity in perspective recalls Ellison's acknowledgement of Murray in *Shadow and Act*. There Ellison says that his angle of vision is very strongly influenced by Murray. Men of quite different styles of writing, Murray and Ellison, in a steady flow of letters and manuscripts, in countless conversations about black art and culture, have influenced and inspired one another for years. There was no need for a long Ellison introduction to *The Omni-Americans*; in the text Murray himself speaks, eloquently at times, for the two of them.

Ellison has not written about such excellent young Afro-American writers as Michael Harper, Alice Walker, Ernest J. Gaines, Ishmael Reed, Jay Wright, Al Young, or Toni Morrison.[6] Nor does he seem to have separated the facile painters of the sixties from such artists as James Phillips, Alfred J. Smith, Edgar Sorrells-Adewale, Charles Searles, Wendy Wilson and Richard Yarde—whose work is influenced not so much by realism or the impulse to protest as by African iconography and philosophy, black music, decorative art, and by scores of other artists near and far, including Romare Bearden. And if black writers and painters of the sixties did consider themselves a group apart, why is this necessarily limiting? Were they not all struggling to give expression to a shared black experience? Ellison seems too impatient with new developments in Afro-American literature, painting, and—as we saw in *Shadow and Act*—in music.

Still, in his criticism of black American expression Ellison has been fairly consistent—from the thirties through the seventies. His overriding thesis is a simple and straightforward one, but it has got him into great trouble with black artists—especially the writers. Good art, he says, must be conscious of sociopolitical realities but, for its forms and techniques, it must turn to other art. Good novels reflect their authors' awareness of previous achievements by novelists. Good novels comment implicitly on other novels and explore new possibilities in the form. Bearden, McPherson, Forrest, and Murray—all black artists struggling to communicate the functions and forms of American life—have succeeded, according to Ellison, because blackness for them was not an excuse to be "obscenely second rate," but the cultural designation of a complex, tragic, zestful group of people, stubbornly determined to endure.

Epilogue

In June 1975 the Ralph Ellison Public Library in Oklahoma City was formally opened. Ellison, along with his wife, brother, and many other family members and friends, attended the heady dedication ceremony. He spoke of the historical significance of the erection of a library to replace the hastily assembled one that he and his peers had used in old Deep Second's Slaughter's Hall. The new library represented, he said, a communal victory. No doubt, too, it was a personal victory for Ellison who on this day was lionized as a local hero and a symbol of Afro-American accomplishment. He was a favorite son come home.

At the ceremony, a large sculpture by Ed Wilson was unveiled. The piece contained two bronze images of Ellison: one showing him engrossed at work at his writing table; the other, a bust portrait. In the bust, Ellison's head appears behind a bronze surface in which an oval opening has been cut. The shadowed figure of Ellison seems to be standing in another room, staring intensely through a hole in the wall. In the first image, we see Ellison performing his professional and public role as a writer. In the second image, Ellison the private man steadily scrutinizes life outside while staunchly retaining his own privacy.

Throughout his life, Ellison has played this dual role of the private man making occasional and well-calculated public gestures. At the library dedication ceremony, several of Ellison's high school classmates said frankly that teenage Ralph had seemed the least likely to push his way to the top. Yet through the power of his language and his ideas, Ellison has succeeded as a shaper of public opinion. "On the lower frequencies," as it turns out, he does speak for many of us.

178

Before *Invisible Man*, Ellison was a struggling writer, publishing when possible, performing odd jobs to make ends meet. Beyond the circle of his family, friends, and the relatively few readers of academic, literary, and radical journals, Ellison's name was unknown prior to 1952. Suddenly the novel was a bestseller. The media interviewed Ellison regularly, and he began receiving more lecture invitations than he could accept. Most reviewers praised the book highly; some termed it a truly great American novel in the tradition of *Huckleberry Finn* and *Moby Dick.*

In 1953, *Invisible Man* won the National Book Award, the National Newspaper Publishers' Russworm Award, and the Chicago Defender's Award for "symbolizing the best in American Democracy." The novel proved to have lasting power. In 1965, a *Book Week* poll of two hundred authors, critics, and editors named *Invisible Man* as the "most distinguished work" published in the last twenty years. In 1969, Lyndon B. Johnson awarded Ellison the Medal of Freedom, and in 1970, the Minister of Cultural Affairs in France, André Malraux, Ellison's hero from the thirties, awarded him the Chevalier de l'Ordre des Artes et Lettres.

More accolades showered in. Honorary doctorates came to the "drop out" from Tuskegee, Rutgers, Michigan, Williams, Harvard, and Wesleyan. He was awarded fellowships by the National Academy of Arts and Letters and Yale.

Ellison's influence on the American intellectual community may be measured, to an extent, by his professional affiliations. He has served as an honorary consultant to the Library of Congress and a member of the Carnegie Commission on Educational Television and the National Council of the Arts. He has belonged to the American Academy of Arts and Sciences and the National Institute of Arts and Letters. Also, he has served on advisory and trustee boards for several institutions, including the John F. Kennedy Center for the Performing Arts, the Museum of the City of New York, Bennington College, and the Educational Broadcasting Corporation.

Quietly, persistently, Ellison has made his influence felt in the upper echelons of the American intellectual and artistic world. He is now in a position from which he can give a respected opinion on which writers' work will be published.

Critics often wonder why the author of *Invisible Man* "disappeared" after the one big book. He operates, in a sense, invisibly. But transcripts of the meetings of the American Academy of Arts and Letters reveal his effectiveness: they throw light upon a tough, cagey Ellison, insisting in any company upon cultural pluralism and artistic integrity. At times one even finds the sophisticate Ellison gently slipping his colleagues into the murky depths of the dozens.

Ellison's life has been one of vigor, change, and fruition. He set out early to become a musician who, like Wagner, would compose a symphony by age twenty-six. In 1940, when Ellison turned twenty-six, he had given up music and had been publishing reviews and stories for three years. He had started and abandoned a novel, *Slick Gonna Learn*, but his stories "The Birthmark" and "Afternoon" showed that he was beginning to discover a personal style beyond that of his models Hemingway and Wright. Moreover, his critical essays (of which he published ten in 1940 alone) were brimming with insights. He was developing the foundations of a theory of art and society which would sustain him for decades to come.

Since 1940, Ellison has been sympathetic to the Communist Party, then a black nationalist, then a staunch defender of the integrationist freedom movement. In the sixties, Ellison fell out of step with the advocates of black power and the black aesthetic. For one thing, he could not see that the political and cultural nationalists' emphasis on Africa was more than mere escapism or reactionary neo-Garveyism. Nor could he admit that their straightforward militancy was more than foolhardy "barking at the big gate." Through it all, however, as a writer Ellison consistently has argued for the integrity of art and for the distinctive richness and beauty of Afro-American life and culture.

Ellison's political and critical positions have won him considerable animosity from whites and blacks alike. He maintains that art has functions that embrace the political but that differ from the rhetoric and cant of most political testimony. Ellison's truth is that of the artist; he insists upon the variety, ambiguity, comedy, tragedy, and terror of human life—beyond all considerations of political platforms. As a writer, Ellison's challenge is to charge one's work with as much life and truth as possible. Art, he says, is fundamentally a celebration of human life; it is not a wailing complaint about social wrongs.

This loftiness has not meant that Ellison has lost sight of his beginnings. Quite the contrary. Since his first review was printed in 1937, he has called for precise, sympathetic writing about the true nature of Afro-American experience. Never having written any fiction in which blacks do not figure centrally, Ellison has sought to capture in fiction the language and lore, the rites and the values, the laughter and the sufferings, as well as the downright craziness, which characterize black life in America. Ellison knows that the only way to grasp universal values and patterns is by holding fast to particularities of time, place, culture, and race. The Invisible Man is an identifiably Afro-American creature whose experience, nonetheless, is so deeply *human* that readers throughout the world identify and sympathise with him.

Like the figures in Ed Wilson's sculpture, Ellison is a very private man. Quiet, stubborn, intensely proud, he looks out on the world with eyes disciplined to the perspective of irony. Fortunately, too, Ellison, like one of Wilson's bronzes, has done his work. *Invisible Man* and *Shadow and Act* abide. The collected stories and essays will someday make fine editions. And, as Jervis Anderson has said, if anyone can pull together the pieces of the new novel, Ellison is just the man to do it. The book is actively in the making.

Ralph Ellison is a progressive and accomplished writer and intellectual, an American "man of good hope" in the tradition of Emerson, Mark Twain, Du Bois, and James Weldon Johnson. His importance lies in his unsinkable optimism concerning his race, his nation, man's fate. Moreover, it lies in his insistence on literary craft under the pressure of inspiration as the best means of transforming everyday experience, talk, and lore into literature.

Bibliography
Notes
Index

Bibliography

Works by Ralph Ellison (listed chronologically)

Fiction

"Slick Gonna Learn." *Direction*, 2 (September 1939), pp. 10-11, 14, 16.

"The Birthmark." *New Masses*, 36 (2 July 1940), pp. 16-17.

"Afternoon." *American Writing*, ed. Otto Storm et al. Prairie City, Illinois: J. A. Decker, 1940, pp. 28-37.

"Mister Toussan." *New Masses*, 41 (4 November 1941), pp. 19-20.

"That I Had the Wings." *Common Ground*, 3 (Summer 1943), pp. 30-37.

"In a Strange Country." *Tomorrow*, 3 (July 1944), pp. 41-44.

"King of the Bingo Game." *Tomorrow*, 4 (November 1944), pp. 29-33.

"Flying Home." *Cross Section*, ed. Edwin Seaver. New York: L. B. Fischer, 1944, pp. 469-485.

"Invisible Man." *Horizon*, 23 (October 1947), pp. 104-107; later published as the "battle royal" chapter of *Invisible Man*.

"Invisible Man: Prologue to a Novel." *Partisan Review*, 19 (January-February 1952), pp. 31-40.

Invisible Man. New York: Random House, 1952.

"Did You Ever Dream Lucky?" *New World Writing*, 5 (April 1954), pp. 134-145.

"February." *Saturday Review*, 1 January 1955, p. 25.

"A Coupla Scalped Indians." *New World Writing*, 9 (1956), pp. 225-236.

"And Hickman Arrives." *Noble Savage*, 1 (1960), pp. 5-49.

"The Roof, the Steeple and the People." *Quarterly Review of Literature*, 10 (1960), pp. 115-128.

185

"Out of the Hospital and Under the Bar." *Soon, One Morning*, ed. Herbert Hill. New York: Knopf, 1963, pp. 242-290.

"It Always Breaks Out." *Partisan Review*, 30 (Spring 1963), pp. 13-28.

"Juneteenth." *Quarterly Review of Literature*, 4 (1969), pp. 317-329.

"A Song of Innocence." *Iowa Review*, 1 (Spring 1970), pp. 30-40.

"Cadillac Flambé." *American Review*, 16 (February 1973), pp. 249-269.

"Backwacking: A Plea to the Senator." *Massachusetts Review*, 18 (Autumn 1977), pp. 411-416.

Literary Essays and Reviews

"Creative and Cultural Lag." *New Challenge*, 2 (Fall 1937), pp. 90-91.

"Practical Mystic." *New Masses*, 28 (16 August 1938), pp. 25-26.

"Ruling-class Southerner." *New Masses*, 30 (5 December 1939), p. 27.

"Javanese Folklore." *New Masses*, 34 (26 December 1939), pp. 25-26.

"The Good Life." *New Masses*, 34 (20 February 1940), p. 27.

"TAC Negro Show." *New Masses*, 34 (27 February 1940), pp. 29-30.

"Hunters and Pioneers." *New Masses*, 34 (19 March 1940), p. 26.

"Romance in the Slave Era." *New Masses*, 35 (29 May 1940), pp. 27-28.

"Anti-War Novel." *New Masses*, 35 (18 June 1940), pp. 29-30.

"Stormy Weather." *New Masses*, 37 (24 September 1940), pp. 20-21.

"Southern Folklore." *New Masses*, 37 (5 November 1940), p. 4.

"Big White Fog." *New Masses*, 37 (12 November 1940), pp. 22-23.

"Argosy Across the USA." *New Masses*, 37 (26 November 1940), p. 24.

"Negro Prize Fighter." *New Masses*, 37 (17 December 1940), pp. 26-27.

"Richard Wright and Recent Negro Fiction." *Direction*, 4 (Summer 1941), pp. 12-13.

"Recent Negro Fiction." *New Masses*, 40 (5 August 1941), pp. 22-26.

"The Great Migration." *New Masses*, 51 (2 December 1941), pp. 23-24.

"Transition." *Negro Quarterly*, 1 (Spring 1942), pp. 87-92.

"Native Land." *New Masses*, 42 (2 June 1942), p. 29.

"The Darker Brother." *Tomorrow*, 4 (September 1943), pp. 67-68.

"Boston Adventure." *Tomorrow*, 4 (December 1944), p. 120.

"The Magic of Limping John." *Tomorrow*, 4 (December 1944), p. 121.

"New World A-Coming." *Tomorrow*, 4 (December 1944), pp. 67-68.

"Escape the Thunder." *Tomorrow*, 5 (March 1945), pp. 91-92.

"Richard Wright's Blues." *Antioch Review*, 5 (Summer 1945), pp. 198-211.

"Beating That Boy." *New Republic*, 113 (22 October 1945), pp. 535-536.

"Stepchild Fantasy." *Saturday Review*, 29 (8 June 1946), pp. 25-26.

"The Shadow and the Act." *Reporter*, 1 (6 December 1949), pp. 17-19.

"Collaborator with His Own Enemy." *New York Times Book Review*, 1 February 1950, p. 4.

"Twentieth-Century Fiction and the Black Mask of Humanity." *Confluence* (December 1953), pp. 3-21.

"Society, Morality, and the Novel." *The Living Novel: A Symposium*, ed. Granville Hicks. New York: McMillan, 1957, pp. 58-91.

"Change the Yoke and Slip the Yoke." *Partisan Review*, 25 (Spring 1958), pp. 212-222.

"Resourceful Human." *Saturday Review*, 41 (12 July 1958), pp. 33-34.

"Stephen Crane and the Mainstream of American Fiction." Introduction to Crane's *The Red Badge of Courage and Four Great Stories*. New York: Dell, 1960, pp. 7-24.

"The World and the Jug." *New Leader*, 46 (9 December 1963), pp. 22-26.

"A Rejoinder." *New Leader*, 47 (3 February 1964), pp. 15-63.

"If the Twain Shall Meet." *Washington Post Book Week* 8 November 1964, pp. 1, 20-25.

"Hidden Name and Complex Fate." *The Writer's Experience*, ed. Ellison and Karl Shapiro. Washington, D.C.: Library of Congress, 1964, pp. 1-15.

"The Blues." *New York Review of Books*, 1 (6 February 1964), pp. 5-7.

"On Becoming a Writer." *Commentary*, 38 (October 1964), pp. 57-60.

Shadow and Act. New York: Random House, 1964.

"The Novel as a Function of American Democracy." *Wilson Library Bulletin*, June 1967, pp. 1022-1027.

Book-jacket comment. *Culture and Poverty* by Charles A. Valentine. Chicago: University of Chicago Press, 1968.

Book-jacket comment. *Hue and Cry* by James A. McPherson. Boston: Atlantic Monthly Press, 1969.

"American Humor." "Comic Elements in Selected Prose of James Baldwin, Ralph Ellison and Langston Hughes, unpublished thesis by Elwyn E. Breaux. Fisk University, 1971, pp. 146-157.

Book-jacket comment. *The Omni-Americans* by Albert Murray. New York: Outerbridge, 1970.

Advertisement comment. *The Unwritten War* by Daniel Aaron. *New York Review of Books*, Fall 1973.

Foreword. *There Is a Tree More Ancient Than Eden* by Leon Forrest. New York: Random House, 1973, pp. i-ii.

"On Initiation Rites and Power: Ralph Ellison Speaks at West Point." *Contemporary Literature*, 15 (Spring 1974), pp. 165-186.

"The Alain Locke Symposium." *Harvard Advocate*, Spring 1974, pp. 9-28.

"Perspectives of Literature." *American Law: The Third Century, the Law Bicentennial Volume*, ed. Bernard Schwartz. Hackensack, New Jersey: Rothman, 1976, pp. 391-406.

Book-jacket comment. *Elbow Room* by James A. McPherson. Boston: Atlantic Monthly Press, 1977.

"The Little Man at Chehaw Station." *American Scholar*, Winter 1977-1978, pp. 25-48.

Essays and Speeches on Politics and Culture

"Anti-Semitism Among Negroes." *Jewish People's Voice*, 3 (April 1939), pp. 3, 8.

"Judge Lynch in New York." *New Masses*, 33 (15 August 1939), pp. 15-16. A shortened version, "They Found Terror in Harlem," in *Negro World Digest*, July 1940, pp. 43-45.

"Camp Lost Colony." *New Masses*, 34 (6 February 1940), pp. 18-19.

"A Congress Jim Crow Didn't Attend." *New Masses*, 35 (14 May 1940), pp. 5-8.

"Phillipine Report." *Direction*, 4 (Summer 1941), p. 13.

"The Way It Is." *New Masses*, 44 (20 October 1942), pp. 9-11.

"Editorial Comment." *Negro Quarterly*, 1 (Winter 1943), pp. 294-303.

"Eyewitness Story of Riot." *New York Post*, 2 August 1943, p. 4.

"Address at Tuskegee Institute." Press release issued by Division of Public Relations, Tuskegee Institute, July 1954.

"Nôtre lutte nous proclame à la fois negres et américains." *Preuves*, 87 (May 1958), pp. 33-38.

"What These Children Are Like." *Education of the Deprived and Segregated.* Dedham, Massachusetts: Bank St. College, 1965, pp. 44-51.

"Tell It Like It Is, Baby." *Nation*, 201 (20 September 1965), pp. 129-136.

"Harlem's America." *New Leader*, 49 (26 September 1966), pp. 22-35.

"What America Would Be Like Without Blacks." *Time*, 6 April 1970, pp. 32-33.

Speech Honoring William A. Dawson. Philadelphia, Tuskegee Alumni Club, 1971.

"Ralph Ellison." *Attacks of Taste*, ed. Evelyn B. Byrne and Otto M. Penzler. New York: Gotham, 1971, pp. 20-22.

"Address at Harvard's Alumni Meeting." Press release issued by Harvard University News Office, 12 June 1974.

"Middle-Income Blacks Need To Find Cultural Awareness." *Los Angeles Times*, February 2, 1975, p. 37.

Speech at the Opening of the Ralph Ellison Public Library. Oklahoma City, 21 June 1975.

Interviews

"The Art of Fiction: An Interview." Alfred Chester and Vilma Howard. *Paris Review*, 8 (Spring 1955), pp. 55-71.

"An Interview with Ralph Ellison." Ted Cohen and N. A. Samstag. *Phoenix*, 22 (Fall 1961), pp. 4-10.

"That Same Pain, That Same Pleasure: An Interview." R. G. Stern. *December*, 3 (Winter 1961), pp. 30-32, 37-46.

"An Interview with Ralph Ellison." Allen Geller. *Tamarack Review*, 25 October 1963, pp. 3-24.

Under Pressure, ed. A. Alvarez. Baltimore: Penguin, 1965, pp. 120-121, 136-137, 148-149, 160-163, 172-173, 178-179.

"Dialogue." *Who Speaks for the Negro?* Robert Penn Warren. New York: Random House, 1965, pp. 325-354.

"Ralph Ellison." Center for Cassette Studies, no. 7508, ca. 1965.

"A Very Stern Discipline." Steve Cannon, Lennox Raphael, and James Thompson. *Harper's*, 234 (March 1967), pp. 76-95.

"An Interview with Ralph Ellison." Mike McGrady, *Newsday*, 28 October 1967, pp. 7-15.

"A Dialogue with His Audience." *Barat Review*, 3 (January 1968), pp. 51-53.

"Indivisible Man." James A. McPherson. *Atlantic Monthly*, 206 (December 1970), pp. 45-60.

"A Conversation with Ralph Ellison." Leon Forrest. *Muhammad Speaks*, 15 December 1972, pp. 29-31.

"Ralph Ellison: Twenty Years After." David L. Carson. *Studies in American Fiction*, 1 (Spring 1973), pp. 1-23.

"Through a Writer's Eyes." Hollie West. *Washington Post*, 19, 20, 21 August 1973.

"Ralph Ellison." *The Writer's Voice*. George Garrett. New York: Morrow, 1973, pp. 221-227.

"Ralph Ellison." *Interviews with Ten Black Writers*. John O'Brien. New York: Liveright, 1973, pp. 63-77.

Appendix. "Invisibility: A Study of the Works of Toomer, Wright, and Ellison," unpublished thesis by Arlene Joan Crewdson, University of Chicago, 1974.

Interview with Ralph Ellison. WGBH-TV, Boston, 12 April 1974.

"Introduction: A Completion of Personality." John Hersey. *Ralph Ellison, a Collection of Critical Essays*, ed. Hersey. Englewood, New Jersey: Prentice-Hall, 1974, pp. 1-19.

News Report. KVTV-TV, Oklahoma City, 15 June 1975.

A Talk with Ralph Ellison. KVTV-TV, Oklahoma City, 19 June 1975.

Unpublished Interview. Robert G. O'Meally. New York, 8 May 1976.

"Study and Experience, an Interview With Ralph Ellison." Michael S. Harper and Robert B. Stepto. *Massachusetts Review*, 18 (Autumn 1977), pp. 417-435. Reprinted in *Chant of Saints*, ed. Harper and Stepto. Urbana: University of Illinois Press, 1979).

"The Essential Ellison." Steve Cannon, Ishmael Reed, and Quincy Troupe. *Y-Bird Reader*, Autumn 1977, pp. 126-159.

"Ralph Ellison's Territorial Vantage." Ron Welburn. *The Grackle*, 4 (1977-78), pp. 5-15.

Essays on Music and Art

"Modern Negro Art." *Tomorrow*, 4 (November 1944), pp. 92-93.

"Introduction to Flamenco." *Saturday Review*, 37 (11 December 1954), pp. 38-39.

"Living with Music." *High Fidelity*, 4 (December 1955), pp. 60 ff.

"The Swing to Stereo." *Saturday Review*, 41 (26 April 1958), pp. 37, 39, 40, 60.

"The Charlie Christian Story." *Saturday Review*, 41 (17 May 1958), pp. 42-43, 46.

"Remembering Jimmy." *Saturday Review*, 41 (12 July 1958), pp. 36-37.

"As the Spirit Moves Mahalia." *Saturday Review*, 41 (27 September 1958), pp. 41, 43, 69-70.

"The Golden Age Time Past." *Esquire Magazine*, 51 (January 1959), pp. 107-110.

"On Birds, Bird Watching, and Jazz." *Saturday Review*, 45 (28 July 1962), pp. 47-49, 62.

"Romare Bearden: Paintings and Projections." *Crisis*, March 1970, pp. 81-86.

Editorial Work

The Negro in New York, ed. with Roi Ottley et al. New York: Arno Press, 1966; originally written and edited during the 1930s by the New York Federal Writers' Project.

Negro Quarterly. Ellison was Managing Editor, 1942-43.

Noble Savage. Ellison was Contributing Editor, 1960.

The Writer's Experience, ed. with Karl Shapiro. Washington, D.C.: Library of Congress, 1964.

Transcribed Conferences, Group Discussions

"What's Wrong with the American Novel?" *American Scholar*, 24 (Autumn 1955), pp. 464-503.

Proceedings, American Academy of Arts and Letters and the National Institute of Arts and Letters, 2nd series, 15 (1965), pp. 452-454; 17 (1967), pp. 178-182, 192.

"Conference Transcript." *Daedalus*, 95 (Winter 1966), pp. 408-441.

"Literature and the Human Sciences on the Nature of Contemporary Man." *The Writer as Independent Spirit*. New York, 1968, pp. 37-44.

"The Uses of History in Fiction." *Southern Literary Journal*, 1 (Spring 1969), pp. 57-90.

Profiles with Extensive Quotes from Ellison

"Inside a Dark Shell." Harvey Curtis Webster. *Saturday Review*, 35 (12 April 1952), pp. 22-23.

"Talk with Ralph Ellison." Harvey Breit. *New York Times Book Review*, 4 May 1952, pp. 26-27.

"Light on *Invisible Man*." *Crisis*, 60 (March 1953), pp. 154-156.

"Sidelights on Invisibility." Rochelle Gibson. *Saturday Review*, 36 (14 March 1953), pp. 20, 49.

"A Best-Seller Starts Here." Jim Simpson. *Daily Oklahoman*, 23 August 1953, p. 3.

"Five Writers and Their African Ancestors." Harold Isaacs. *Phylon*, 21 (Winter 1960), pp. 317-322.

"The Visible Man." *Newsweek*, 12 August 1963, pp. 81-82.

"An American Novelist Who Sometimes Teaches." John Corry. *New York Times Sunday Magazine*, 20 November 1966, pp. 55, 179-185, 196.

"Ralph Ellison: Novelist as Brown Skinned Aristocrat." Richard Kostelanetz. *Shenandoah*, 4 (Summer 1969), pp. 56-77.

"Going to the Territory." Jervis Anderson. *New Yorker*, November 22, 1976, pp. 55-108.

"Alfred Ellison of Abbeville." Stewart Lillard. Unpublished monograph, 1976.

Miscellaneous

"Ralph Ellison Explains." *'48 Magazine of the Year*, 2 (May 1948), p. 145.

"At Home: Letter to the Editor." *Time*, February 9, 1959, p. 2.

"No Apologies." *Harper's*, 205 (July 1967), pp. 4 ff.

Writer's Project Interviews, Essays. Unpublished; available at Library of Congress, Folklore Archives.

Writer's Project Interviews, Essays. Unpublished; available at New York Public Library, 135th Street branch.

"A Page in Ralph Ellison's Life." *Brown Alumni Monthly*, 80 (November 1979), pp. 40-41.

Selected Works by Others

Aaron, Daniel. "The Hyphenate Writer and American Letters." *Smith Alumnae Quarterly*, July 1964, pp. 213-17.

Baker, Houston. *Long Black Song: Essays in Black American Literature and Culture.* Charlottesville: University of Virginia Press, 1972.

Baumbach, Jonathan. "Nightmare of a Native Son." *The Landscape of Nightmare.* New York: New York University Press, 1965, pp. 68-86.

Benston, Kimberly. "Ellison, Baraka, and the Faces of Tradition." *Boundary 2*, 6 (Winter 1978), pp. 333-354.

Black World, 20 (December, 1970); special Ellison issue.

Blake, Susan L. "Ritual and Rationalization: Black Folklore in the Works of Ralph Ellison." *PMLA*, 94 (January 1979), pp. 121-136.

Bluestein, Gene. *The Voice of the Folk.* Amherst: University of Massachusetts Press, 1972.

Bone, Robert A. *The Negro Novel in America.* New Haven: Yale University Press, 1958, 1965, pp. 196-212.

Bryant, Jerry H. "Wright, Ellison, Baldwin—Exorcising the Demon." *Phylon,* 37 (June 1977), pp. 174-188.

Cambon, Glauco. "Ralph Ellison dell' invisibilità." *Aut, Aut,* 3 (March 1953), pp. 135-144.

Chaffee, Patricia. "Slippery Ground: Ralph Ellison's Bingo Player." *Negro American Literature Forum,* 10 (Spring 1977), pp. 23-24.

Cheshire, Ardner R. *Invisible Man* and the Life of Dialogue." *CLA Journal,* 20 (September 1977), pp. 19-34.

CLA [College Language Association] *Journal,* 13 (1970); special Ellison issue.

Covo, Jacqueline. *The Blinking Eye: Ralph Waldo Ellison and His American, French, German and Italian Critics, 1952-1971.* Metuchen, New Jersey: Scarecrow Press, 1974.

Cruse, Harold. *The Crisis of the Negro Intellectual.* New York: Morrow, 1967.

Davis, Arthur P. *From the Dark Tower.* Washington, D.C.: Howard University, 1974.

Feuser, Willfried. "The Men Who Lived Underground: Richard Wright and Ralph Ellison." *A Celebration of Black and African Writing,* ed. Bruce King (Kolawale Ogungbesan). Zaria, Nigeria: Âhmadu Bello University Press, 1976, pp. 81-101.

Guerard, Albert. "Ralph Ellison et le delemme noir." *Revue général belge.* 97 (October 1960), pp. 89-104.

Harding, Vincent. "Black Reflections on the Cultural Ramifications of Black Identity." *Black Books Bulletin,* Winter 1972, pp. 4-10.

Heermance, J. N. "The Modern Negro Novel." *Negro Digest,* 13 (May 1964), pp. 66-76.

Hersey, John, ed. *Ralph Ellison, a Collection of Critical Essays.* Englewood Cliffs, New Jersey: Prentice-Hall, 1970.

Horowitz, Floyd R. "Enigma of Ellison's Intellectual Man." *CLA Journal,* 7 (December 1963), pp. 126-132.

Kazin, Alfred. *Bright Book of Life.* New York: Dell, 1971.

Kent, George. *Blackness and the Adventure of American Culture.* Chicago: Third World, 1972.

Kirst, E. M. "A Langian Analysis of Blackness in Ralph Ellison's *Invisible Man.*" *Studies in Black American Literature,* 7 (Spring 1976), pp. 19-34.

Lewis, R. W. B. "Ellison's Essays." *New York Review of Books,* 28 January 1964, pp. 19-20.

Murray, Albert. *The Omni-Americans.* New York: Outerbridge, 1970.

Nash, R. W. "Stereotypes and Social Types in Ellison's *Invisible Man.*" *Sociological Quarterly,* 6 (Autumn 1965), pp. 349-360.

O'Daniel, Thermon B. "Image of Man as Portrayed by Ralph Ellison's *Invisible Man.*" *CLA Journal,* 10 (June 1967), pp. 277-284.

Olderman, Raymond M. "Ralph Ellison's Blues and *Invisible Man.*" *Wisconsin Studies in Literature,* 7 (1966), pp. 142-157.

Overmyer, Janet. "The Invisible Man and White Women." *Notes on Contemporary Literature,* 6 (May 1971), pp. 13-15.

Reilly, John M., ed. *Twentieth Century Interpretations of Invisible Man.* Englewood Cliffs, New Jersey: Prentice-Hall, 1970.

Saunders, Pearl I. "Symbolism in Ralph Ellison's 'King of the Bingo Game.'" *CLA Journal,* 20 (September 1976), pp. 19-34.

Tischler, N. M. "Negro Literature and Classic Form." *Contemporary Literature,* Summer 1969, pp. 352-365.

Williams, Phillip G. "A Comparative Approach to Afro-American and Neo-African Novels: Ellison and Achebe." *Studies in Black Literature,* 7 (Winter 1976), pp. 15-18.

Notes

Introduction

1. Ralph Ellison, interview on WGBH-TV, Boston, 12 April 1974.
2. Ralph Ellison, interview with Michael S. Harper and Robert B. Stepto, "Study and Experience," *Massachusetts Review*, Autumn 1977; reprinted in *Chant of Saints*, ed. Harper and Stepto (Urbana: University of Illinois Press, 1979), p. 462.

1. Beginnings

1. Jervis Anderson, "Going to the Territory," *New Yorker*, 22 November 1976, p. 74; Stewart Lilliard, "Alfred Ellison of Abbeville," 1977, unpublished monograph; see also *Black History in Oklahoma*, ed. Kay M. Teall (Oklahoma City: Public City Schools, 1971), and Ralph Ellison and Hollie West, interview, "Growing Up Black in Frontier Oklahoma," *Washington Post*, 21 August 1973.
2. Ralph Ellison, from a speech (unpublished) at the ceremonies dedicating Oklahoma City's Ralph Ellison Public Library, 16 June 1975.
3. Ralph Ellison, "Tell It Like It Is, Baby," *Nation*, 20 September 1965; reprinted in *Writers and Issues*, ed. Theodore Solataroff (Englewood Cliffs: Prentice-Hall, 1965), p. 196; see also Anderson, p. 82.
4. Ellison, library speech.
5. Ralph Ellison and John Hersey, "Introduction: 'A Completion of Personality,'" in Hersey, ed., *Ralph Ellison, a Collection of Critical Essays* (Englewood Cliffs: Prentice-Hall, 1974), p. 4.
6. Ralph Ellison, *Shadow and Act* (New York: Random House, 1964), p. 158.

7. Ibid., p. 19.

8. Ibid., p. 157.

9. Interview with J. L. Randolph, 16 July 1976.

10. Ellison and West, *Washington Post,* p. G3.

11. *Shadow and Act,* p. 122.

12. Ibid., p. 136.

13. Ibid., p. 122.

14. Ralph Ellison, "Harlem's America," *New Leader,* 26 September 1966, p. 23.

15. *Shadow and Act,* p. 90.

16. Ralph Ellison, "What These Children Are Like," *Education of the Deprived and Segregated* (Dedham, Mass.: Bank Street College, 1965), pp. 44-45; see also Henry A. Bullock, *A History of Negro Education in the South* (Cambridge: Harvard University Press, 1967).

17. See, for example, *Tuskegee Messenger,* May 1934; April-May 1935.

18. Ralph Ellison, *Invisible Man* (New York: Random House, 1964), p. 107.

19. Ibid., p. 105.

20. Musician Bobby Short speaks of this in his autobiography, *Black and White Baby* (New York: Dodd, Mead, 1971), p. 26. These forced black contests were also staged by slaveholders in the antebellum South. See, for example, *Puttin' On Ole Massa,* ed. Gilbert Osofsky (New York: Harper and Row, 1969), p. 68.

21. Booker T. Washington, *Up from Slavery* (New York: Dell, 1901), p. 93.

22. Ibid.

23. Ibid., pp. 92-93.

24. Louis R. Harlan, *The Making of a Black Leader, 1856-1901* (New York: Oxford University Press, 1972), pp. 275-276.

25. Ibid., pp. 279-280.

26. Washington, *Up from Slavery,* p. 155.

27. Louis Lomax, introduction to the Dell edition of *Up from Slavery,* pp. 12-13.

28. W. E. B. Du Bois, *The Autobiography of W. E. B. Du Bois* (New York: International Publishers, 1968), p. 243.

29. Washington, *Up from Slavery,* p. 123.

30. Ibid., p. 64.

31. Ibid., pp. 131-132.

32. William H. Hughes and Frederick D. Patterson, *Robert Russa Moton of Hampton and Tuskegee* (Chapel Hill: University of North Carolina Press, 1956), pp. 128-143.

33. *Invisible Man,* p. 96.

34. Ibid., 103-104.

35. Ibid., pp. 127, 128.

36. Ibid., p. 93,

37. Louis R. Harlan, et al., eds., *The Booker T. Washington Papers* (Urbana: University of Illinois Press, 1972), I, xxv.

38. Ibid.

39. Harlan, *Making of a Black Leader*, pp. 157-158.

40. *Tuskegee Messenger*, November 1933, p. 4.

41. Robert Russa Moton, *What the Negro Thinks* (New York: Doubleday, 1929), p. 228.

42. Ibid., p. 71.

43. Unpublished transcript of Ralph Ellison's speech honoring William L. Dawson; given at the fiftieth anniversary of the Philadelphia Tuskegee Alumni Club, 1971.

44. Ibid.

45. Harlan, *Making of a Black Leader*, p. 285.

46. Bullock, *Negro Education in the South*, p. 165.

47. *Tuskegee Institute Bulletin*, May 1934, p. 154.

48. Ibid., pp. 154-155.

49. Ralph Ellison et al., "The Arts and the National Commitment," *American Academy of Arts and Letters, Proceedings*, 2nd series (1967), p. 181.

50. Alain Locke, *The New Negro* (New York: Boni and Liveright, 1925).

51. Ralph Ellison, "Alain Locke Symposium," *Harvard Advocate* Spring 1974, pp. 165-186.

52. Alain Locke, "Jingo, Counter-Jingo and the U.S.," *Opportunity*, January 1938, pp. 4-5.

53. Ellison and West, an unpublished portion of their *Washington Post* interview.

54. Ellison, "Locke Symposium."

55. Interview with Albert L. Murray, 4 April 1974.

56. Ellison dedicated *Shadow and Act* to Sprague, "Dedicated Dreamer in a Land Most Strange."

57. Albert Murray, *South to a Very Old Place* (New York: McGraw-Hill, 1971), p. 126.

58. *Tuskegee Institute Bulletin*, May 1934, p. 158.

59. Locke, *The New Negro*.

60. Ellison, "Locke Symposium;" see also Ellison, "The Little Man at Chehaw Station," *American Scholar*, Winter 1977-78, pp. 25-26.

61. *Shadow and Act*, p. 160.

62. Ellison and West, p. B3.

63. T. S. Eliot, "Tradition and the Individual Talent" (1919).

64. Ellison, Locke symposium address.

65. *Invisible Man*, p. 38.

66. *Shadow and Act*, pp. xi-xii.

67. *Shadow and Act*, p. xx.

68. Robert Park and Ernest W. Burgess, *Introduction to the Science of Sociology* (Chicago: University of Chicago Press, 1919), p. 136.

69. *Shadow and Act*, p. 306.

70. Ibid., p. 308.

71. Ibid., p. 307.

72. Ibid., p. 123.

73. Ellison and West, *Washington Post* interview, unpublished portion; letter from Ellison to O'Meally, 28 September 1979.

2. Up North

1. Ralph Ellison, "Harlem's America," *New Leader,* 26 September 1966, p. 2.

2. Ibid.

3. Ralph Ellison, *Invisible Man* (New York: Random House, 1952), p. 136.

4. Ralph Ellison, *Shadow and Act* (New York: Random House, 1964), pp. 295-296.

5. Ibid., pp. 298-299.

6. "Harlem's America," p. 28.

7. Ibid., p. 23.

8. Ralph Ellison and Ron Welburn, "Ralph Ellison's Territorial Vantage," *The Grackle: Improvised Music in Transition* (1977-78), p. 15.

9. *Shadow and Act,* p. 199.

10. Ralph Ellison, "Big White Fog," *New Masses,* 12 November 1940, p. 22.

11. Ralph Ellison and Robert G. O'Meally, unpublished interview, 8 May 1976.

12. Ralph Ellison and Hollie West, interview, "Through a Writer's Eyes: A Ralph Ellison of Life and Literature," *Washington Post,* 21 October 1973, p. B3.

13. From an unpublished interview by Arlene Joan Crewdson, included in her *"Invisibility: A Study of the Works of Toomer, Wright, and Ellison,"* unpublished Ph.D. dissertation, University of Chicago, Loyola, 1974, p. 493.

14. "Harlem's America," p. 23; see also Susan Edmiston and Linda D. Cirino, *Literary New York: A History and Guide* (Boston: Houghton Mifflin, 1976), pp. 298-99.

15. Ellison and West, *Washington Post* interview, unpublished portion; see also Ellison, "Alain Locke Symposium Remarks," *Harvard Advocate,* Spring 1974, p. 21; letter from Ellison to O'Meally, 28 September 1979.

16. Michel Fabre, *The Unfinished Quest of Richard Wright* (New York: Morrow, 1973), pp. 219-220; see also Ralph Ellison, Steve Cannon, Ishmael Reed, and Quincy Troupe, "The Essential Ellison," *Y-Bird Reader,* Autumn 1977, p. 146.

17. Fabre, *Unfinished Quest,* pp. 145-146.

18. Ibid., p. 146.

19. Ralph Ellison, "February," *Saturday Review,* 1 January 1955, p. 25.

20. Ibid.

21. Ralph Ellison and Robert Penn Warren, *Who Speaks for the Negro?* (New York: Vintage, 1966), p. 325.

22. Ralph Ellison, "Paris Interview—Headnote," in *The Black Experience,* ed. Francis Kearns (New York: Viking, 1970) p. 554.

23. Interview with Sterling A. Brown, 1 October 1974.

24. Jerre Mangione, *The Dream and the Deal* (Boston: Little, Brown, 1972), p. 256.

25. Ibid., pp. 155, 193, 257.

26. Ibid., p. 153.

27. New York Public Library, Schomberg Collection.

28. From the Library of Congress Folklore Archives.

29. Ellison and West, *Washington Post* interview, p. B1.

30. Ralph Ellison and James A. McPherson, interview, "Indivisible Man," *Atlantic Monthly*, December 1970, p. 59.

31. Library of Congress Folklore Archives.

32. Ellison and McPherson, "Indivisible Man," p. 155.

3. Lure of the Left

1. Ralph Ellison, "A Very Stern Discipline," *Harper's*, March 1967, p. 86.

2. Langston Hughes, *Good Morning Revolution* (New York: Lawrence Hill, 1973).

3. Jerre Mangione, *The Dream and the Deal* (Boston: Little, Brown, 1972), p. 187.

4. "Stern Discipline," p. 86.

5. Ralph Ellison, "Twentieth-Century Fiction and the Black Mask of Humanity," *Confluence*, ed. Henry Kissinger (Cambridge: Harvard University Press, 1953), p. 14.

6. Ralph Ellison, "Recent Negro Fiction," *New Masses*, 5 August 1941, pp. 22-23.

7. Ibid., p. 22.

8. Ibid., pp. 22-23.

9. Ibid., p. 26.

10. Ralph Ellison, "Creative and Cultural Lag," *New Challenge*, Fall 1937, p. 90.

11. Ralph Ellison, "Stormy Weather," *New Masses*, 24 September 1940, p. 20.

12. See Ralph Ellison, "Ralph Ellison Explains," *'48 Magazine of the Year*, (1948), p. 145.

13. Ralph Ellison, "Transition," *Negro Quarterly*, Spring 1942, pp. 90-91.

14. Wright, "Blueprint," p. 60.

15. Ibid.

16. "Recent Negro Fiction," p. 41.

17. Ibid., p. 22.

18. Ibid., p. 25.

19. See Ralph Ellison, interview with Michael S. Harper and Robert B. Stepto, "Study and Experience," *Massachusetts Review*, Autumn 1977, pp. 417-435.

20. Ralph Ellison, *Shadow and Act* (New York: Random House, 1964), p. 114.

21. Ibid., pp. 78-79, 246.

22. Ibid., p. 82.

23. Ibid., p. 87.

24. Richard Wright, *Black Boy* (New York: Harper, 1945), p. 45.

25. *Shadow and Act*, p. 103.

26. Wright, *Black Boy*, p. 45.

27. *Shadow and Act*, p. 126.

28. Ibid., p. 140.

29. Ibid., p. 86.

30. Ibid., p. 84.

31. Ralph Ellison, "Judge Lynch in New York," *New Masses*, 15 August 1939, p. 15.

32. Ralph Ellison and David L. Carson, "Ralph Ellison: Twenty Years After," *Studies in American Fiction*, Spring 1973, p. 8.

33. Ralph Ellison, "A Congress Jim Crow Didn't Attend," *New Masses*, 4 May 1940, p. 8.

34. "Stern Discipline," p. 88.

35. *Shadow and Act*, p. 310.

36. Ralph Ellison, "Editorial Comment," *Negro Quarterly*, Winter 1934, p. 298.

4. Apprenticeship

1. Ralph Ellison, "Slick Gonna Learn," *Direction*, 1939, p. 10.

2. Ralph Ellison, "The Birthmark," *Negro World Digest*, November 1940; reprinted from *New Masses*, 2 July 1940, p. 65.

3. Ralph Ellison and David L. Carson, "Ralph Ellison: Twenty Years After," *Studies in American Fiction*, Spring 1973, p. 5.

4. Ralph Ellison, "Afternoon," *American Writing*, ed. Otto Storm et al. (Prairie City, Illinois: J. A. Decker, 1940), p. 34.

5. Lawrence Levine discusses Johnson's folk heroism in *Black Culture and Black Consciousness* (New York: Oxford, 1977), p. 429-433.

6. Ralph Ellison, "Mister Toussan," *New Masses*, 4 November 1941, p. 140.

7. J. Saunders Redding, *They Came in Chains* (New York: Lippincott, 1973), pp. 46-47.

8. Langston Hughes and Arna Bontemps, *Book of Negro Folklore* (New York: Dodd, Mead, 1958), pp. 294-295.

9. *The Negro in New York: An Informal Social History*, ed. Roi Ottley and William J. Weatherby (New York: Public Library, 1967), p. 52.

10. Ralph Ellison, "That I Had the Wings," *Common Ground*, 1943, p. 30.

11. Richard Kostelanetz, "Novelist as Brown Skinned Aristocrat," *Shenandoah*, 1969, p. 61.

12. "Ralph Emerson," Center for Cassette Studies, no. 7508, ca. 1965.

13. Ralph Ellison, "In a Strange Country," *Tomorrow*, July 1944, p. 86.

14. Quoted by Levine, *Culture and Consciousness*, p. 236.

15. Walter Blair, *Native American Humor* (New York: Harper and Row, 1960), p. 7.

16. Ralph Ellison, "American Humor," appendix to Elwyn E. Breaux's dissertation, "Comic Elements in Selected Prose by James Baldwin, Ralph Ellison and Langston Hughes," May 1974, p. 147; on file at Fisk University and at the Library of Congress.

18. Richard M. Dorson, *American Negro Folktales* (Greenwich: Fawcett, 1956), pp. 178-180; note too that Wright also uses a fragment of this folktale in *Lawd, Today* (New York: Avon, 1963), p. 219.

19. Ralph Ellison, "Flying Home," *Cross Section*, 1944, p. 477.

20. Quoted by Levine, *Culture and Consciousness*, p. 321.

21. Ralph Ellison, "King of the Bingo Game," *Tomorrow*, November 1944, p. 29.

5. Invisible Man: Black and Blue

1. A good sampling of Ellison criticism may be found in *Twentieth Century Interpretations of Invisible Man*, ed. John M. Reilly (Englewood Cliffs: Prentice-Hall, 1970). See also *CLA* [College Language Association] *Journal*, 13 (3), and *Black World*, 20 (December 1970).

2. Leon Forrest, unpublished manuscript on folklore in *Invisible Man*; and Susan L. Blake, "Ritual and Rationalization: Black Folklore in the Works of Ralph Ellison," *PMLA*, 93 (January 1979), pp. 121-136.

3. See "Ralph Ellison's Modern Version of Brer Dog and Brer Rabbit in Invisible Man," by Floyd R. Horowitz, *Midcontinent American Studies Journal*, 4 (1963), pp. 21-27.

4. See Gene Bluestein, "The Blues as a Literary Theme," in his *The Voice of the Folk* (Amherst: University of Massachusetts Press, 1972). See also William J. Shafer's "Irony from Underground—Satiric Elements, in *Invisible Man*," *Satire Newsletter*, Fall 1969, pp. 22-28; *Mother Wit from the Laughing Barrel*, ed. Alan Dundes (Englewood Cliffs: Prentice-Hall, 1973), pp. 354-55.

5. See Roger D. Abrahams, *Deep Down in the Jungle* (Chicago: Aldine, 1963), pp. 39-60.

6. George W. Kent, *Blackness and the Adventure of American Culture* (Chicago: Third World Press, 1972), pp. 152-163, 184-201.

7. Ralph Ellison, *Shadow and Act* (New York: Random House, 1964), p. 173.

8. See Daryl Dance, *Shuckin' and Jivin'* (Bloomington: Indiana University Press, 1978), p. 77.

9. Ellison, *Shadow and Act*, p. 173.

10. See Phillis R. Klotman's "The Running Man as Metaphor in Ellison's Invisible Man," *CLA Journal,* 13 (1970), pp. 277-288.

11. "Run, Nigger, Run!" *The Black Poets,* ed. Dudley Randall (New York: Bantam, 1971), p. 5. See also Newman I. White, *American Negro Folk-Songs* (Cambridge: Harvard University Press, 1928), pp. 168-169.

12. Ralph Ellison, *Invisible Man* (New York: Random House, 1952), p. 497. See also Lawrence Levine, *Black Culture and Black Consciousness* (New York: Oxford, 1977), p. 262.

13. "Promises of Freedom," *The Black Poets,* pp. 5-6. See also Levine, *Culture and Consciousness,* pp. 192-193.

14. See Sterling A. Brown, "Negro Folk Expressionism," *Phylon,* 2 (1952), p. 323. See also Newbell Niles Puckett, *Folk Beliefs of the Southern Negro* (Chapel Hill: University of North Carolina Press, 1926), p. 35.

15. Reprinted in *Negro Caravan* from Zora Neal Hurston's *Mules and Men* (Philadelphia: J. B. Lippincott, 1935), p. 489.

16. See Ulf Hannertz, *Soulside* (New York: Columbia University Press, 1969), pp. 139-158.

17. Stanley Hyman, "The Folk Tradition," *Partisan Review,* 25 (1958): 197-222; Albert Murray, *The Omni-Americans* (New York: Outerbridge, 1970). See also John Wideman, "Stomping the Blues—Ritual in Black Music and Speech," *American Poetry Review,* July-August 1978, pp. 43-46.

18. Murray, p. 167.

19. Albert Murray, *The Hero and the Blues* (Columbia: University of Missouri Press, 1973), p. 107.

20. Ellison, *Invisible Man,* p. 11.

21. David L. Carson, "Ralph Ellison: Twenty Years After," *Studies in American Fiction,* Spring 1973, p. 13. See also Levine, *Culture and Consciousness,* p. 331.

22. "Black and Blue," Louis Armstrong, Columbia Record CL 854; Carson, "Ralph Ellison," p. 13; Levine, *Culture and Consciousness,* pp. 239ff.

23. In his unpublished paper on *Invisible Man,* Leon Forrest points out these contrasting pairs or "doubles" in the novel: Norton, Trueblood; Emerson, "Wheatstraw."

24. This phony-letter ruse comprises a greenhorn's initiation; see Robert H. Moore, "On Initiation Rites and Power: Ralph Ellison Speaks at West Point," *Contemporary Literature,* 15 (Spring 1974), pp. 165-186.

25. Note, "Boogie Woogie," Count Basie and Jimmy Rushing, Decca Record DXSB 7170.

26. This line echoes one from Ernest Hemingway's *For Whom the Bell Tolls* (New York: Scribner's 1940).

27. Ralph Ellison, "Out of the Hospital and Under the Bar," in "Author's Note," *Black Writing,* ed. Herbert Hill (New York: Knopf, 1963), pp. 243-244.

28. Lonnie Johnson, "She's My Mary," Bluebird Record B-8322; listed in

Negro Caravan, ed. Sterling Brown, Arthur P. Davis, and Ullysses Lee (New York: Arno Press, 1970), p. 477.

29. Ibid., Brown et al., p. 429.

30. "Back Water Blues," Bessie Smith, Columbia Record G31093; text printed in *The Blues Line,* ed. Eric Sackheim (New York: Grossman, 1969), p. 50.

31. See Richard Dorson, *American Folklore* (Chicago: University of Chicago Press, 1959), pp. 166-198.

32. See Levine, *Culture and Consciousness,* p. 230.

33. Ibid., pp. 278-279.

34. See Maria Leach, *Standard Dictionary of Folklore* (New York: Funk and Wagnalls, 1972), pp. 1123-1125.

35. Ellison, *Shadow and Act,* p. 181. See also Levine, *Culture and Consciousness,* pp. 107-118, and Dorson, *American Folklore* p. 259.

36. See Bruce Jackson, *Get Your Ass in the Water and Swim like Me!* (Cambridge: Harvard University Press, 1975), pp. 29-30; Constance Rourke, *American Humor* (New York: Harcourt, 1931), pp. 3-32.

37. "Jelly, Jelly," Count Basie and Billy Eckstine, Roulette Record R 52111. See also Sackheim, pp. 294-295.

38. Levine, *Culture and Consciousness,* p. 433. Note that Ellison also used a version of this song in an early story, "Afternoon" (1940); see Chapter 4.

39. Note a performance by the composer of this blues, Jelly Roll Morton, "Buddy Bolden Blues," Atlantic Record SD2-308; see also Albert Murray, *Stomping the Blues* (New York: McGraw-Hill, 1976), p. 182.

40. Levine, *Culture and Consciousness,* p. 24.

41. John Lovell, *Black Song: The Forge and the Flame* (New York: Macmillan, 1972), p. 284.

42. See Henry H. Mitchell, *Black Preaching* (Philadelphia: J. B. Lippincott, 1970).

43. Lord Raglan, *The Hero* (London: Watts, 1936).

44. See Lovell, pp. 443-444; and *The Negro and His Folklore,* ed. Bruce Jackson. (Austin: American Folklore Society, 1967), pp. 263-273.

45. Ellison, *Invisible Man,* p. 222; "Move On Up a Little Higher," Columbia Record CS 8804; Tony Heilbut, *The Gospel Sound* (Garden City; Anchor, 1975), pp. 64-65.

46. "Many Thousand Gone," transcribed in Brown et al., *Negro Caravan,* p. 441.

47. See Langston Hughes and Arna Bontemps, eds., *Book of Negro Folklore* (New York: Dodd, Mead, 1958); Zora Neale Hurston, *Mules and Men* (New York: Harper & Row, 1935); Brown et al., *Negro Caravan.*

48. This inability to dispose of a significant item is folkloric. See Richard M. Dorson, *American Folklore* (Chicago: University of Chicago Press, 1959), pp. 253-254.

6. Visions and Revisions: New Fiction

1. Ralph Ellison, "Sidelights on Invisibility," *Saturday Review,* 14 March 1953, p. 20.

2. Ralph Ellison, "Author's Note" to "Out of the Hospital and Under the Bar," *Soon, One Morning,* ed. Herbert Hill (New York: Knopf, 1963), p. 243.

3. Ibid.

4. Ralph Ellison, "Out of the Hospital and Under the Bar," *Soon, One Morning,* p. 247.

5. Introductory note to Ralph Ellison's "Did You Ever Dream Lucky?" *New World Writing,* April 1954, p. 134.

6. Ellison, "Did You Ever Dream Lucky?" pp. 136-137.

7. Quoted by Paul Oliver, *The Meaning of the Blues* (New York: Collier, 1963), p. 208; see also Count Basie and Jimmy Rushing, "Blues in the Dark," *The Best of Count Basie,* Decca Record DXSB-7170.

8. Such tales are discussed in many places, including Harold Courlander, ed., *A Treasury of Afro-American Folklore* (New York: Crown Publishers, 1976).

9. This is brought out in several tales in Richard Dorson's *American Negro Folktales* (Greenwich: Fawcett, 1956, 1967).

10. Ralph Ellison, "American Humor," appendix to "Comic Elements in Selected Prose of James Baldwin, Ralph Ellison and Langston Hughes," unpublished thesis by Elwyn E. Breaux, Fisk University, 1971, p. 148.

11. Ralph Ellison, "A Coupla Scalped Indians," *New World Writing,* 1956, p. 236.

12. See the discussion of circumcision in *The Interpreter's Dictionary of the Bible* (New York: Abingdon Press, 1962), pp. 629-631; and William G. Cole, *Sex in Christianity and Psychoanalysis* (New York: Oxford University Press, 1955), pp. 15ff.

13. See Richard M. Dorson, *America in Legend* (New York: Pantheon Books, 1973).

7. The Hickman Stories

1. Richard Kostelanetz, "Novelist as Brown Skinned Aristocrat," *Shenandoah,* 1969, p. 65.

2. Ralph Ellison and John Hersey, "Introduction: 'A Completion of Personality,'" in Hersey, ed., *Ralph Ellison* (Englewood Cliffs: Prentice-Hall, 1974), p. 6.

3. Ralph Ellison and James A. McPherson, interview, "Indivisible Man," *Atlantic Monthly,* December 1970, p. 57.

4. Ralph Ellison and Leon Forrest, "A Conversation with Ralph Ellison," *Muhammed Speaks,* 15 December 1972, p. 29.

5. Ralph Ellison, "And Hickman Arrives," *Noble Savage,* 1960; reprinted in

Black Writers in America, ed. Richard Barksdale (New York: Morrow, 1974), pp. 693-712.

6. Constance Rourke, *American Humor* (New York: Harcourt, 1931), pp. 134-35.

7. Ralph Ellison, "The Roof, the Steeple and the People," *Quarterly Review of Literature*, 3 November 1960, p. 128.

8. Ralph Ellison, "It Always Breaks Out," *Partisan Review*, 24 (Spring 1963), p. 17.

9. Ralph Ellison, "Works in Progress" (1965), a film available through the University of Nevada library system.

10. Derived from the Old Testament Book of Ezekiel, "Dry Bones" is also an Afro-American spiritual.

11. Langston Hughes and Arna Bontemps, eds., *Book of Negro Folklore* (New York: Dodd, Mead, 1958), pp. 253-254.

12. Ralph Ellison, "Juneteenth," *Quarterly Review of Literature*, 1965, p. 262.

13. Ralph Ellison's prefatory note to his "Night-Talk," *Quarterly Review of Literature*, 1969, p. 317.

14. Ellison, "Night-Talk," p. 318.

15. Ralph Ellison, "A Song of Innocence," *Iowa Review*, Spring 1970, pp. 30-40.

16. Bibliographical note to Ralph Ellison's "Cadillac Flambé," *American Review*, February 1973, p. 272.

17. Ellison, "Cadillac Flambé," p. 267.

18. Norm A. Mauler is a take-off on the name of Norman Mailer, who in *The White Negro* (San Francisco: City Lights, 1957) argues that the white American hipster models his behavior after that of "the Negro": "Knowing in the cells of his existence that life was war, nothing but war, the Negro (all exceptions admitted) could rarely afford the sophisticated inhibitions of civilization, so he kept for his survival the art of the primitive, he lived in the enormous present, he subsisted for his Saturday night kicks, relinquishing the pleasures of the mind for the more obligatory pleasures of the body, and in his music he gave voice to the character and quality of his existence, to his rage and the infinite variations of joy, lust, languor, growl, cramp, pinch, scream and despair of his orgasm. For jazz is orgasm" (p. 4).

19. Ralph Ellison, "Backwacking: A Plea to the Senator," *Massachusetts Review*, 18 (Autumn 1977), pp. 411-412.

20. Ralph Ellison, *Shadow and Act* (New York: Random House, 1964), p. 51.

8. Shadow Actor: Ellison's Aesthetics

1. Ralph Ellison, *Shadow and Act* (New York: Random House, 1964), p. xix.

2. To illustrate this point, Ellison tells of an incident in which a white man rushed toward him and another black man who were deep in the woods hunting.

That black writers may illustrate their works by using the Old Testament is underscored by Ellison's use of references to the story of Noah, Ham, Shem, and Japheth. Ellison is saying, subtly, that black writers can snatch symbols from anywhere—even from Howe's own progenitors.

3. Lecture by Jeannetta Coles, Harvard University, April 1972.

9. More Shadows, More Actors

1. Ralph Ellison, "Romare Bearden: Paintings and Projections," *Crisis,* March 1970, p. 82.

2. McPherson, *Hue and Cry* (Greenwich: Fawcett, 1969).

3. McPherson, *Elbow Room* (Boston: Little, Brown, 1977).

4. Foreword to Forrest, *There Is a Tree More Ancient than Eden* (New York: Random House, 1973), pp. i-ii.

5. *The Omni-Americans* (New York: Avon, 1970).

6. In more recent interviews, Ellison does seem familiar with the work of Ishmael Reed and Toni Morrison and some other black writers. See his interview with Michael Harper and Robert B. Stepto, "Study and Experience," *Massachusetts Review,* Autumn 1977, pp. 417-435; see also the interview with Ishmael Reed, Quincy Troupe, and Steve Cannon, "The Essential Ellison," *Y-Bird Reader,* 1977, pp. 126-159.

Index